Fightnomics

The Hidden Numbers and Science in Mixed Martial Arts
...and why there's no such thing as a fair fight

By Reed Kuhn

With New York Times Bestselling Author
Kelly Crigger

Fightnomics® is a registered trademark of Calvert Strategies LLC.

ISBN: 978-0-9912382-0-0

Graybeard® is a registered trademark of Graybeard Publishing LLC

Printed in the United States of America

Disclaimers:
Ultimate Fighting Championships (UFC), the Octagon, World Extreme Cagefighting (WEC), Strikeforce, Zuffa, PRIDE, and DREAM are all registered trademarks, and are referenced here as part of the public domain.

fight · nom · ics

fight: an attempt to overcome opposition, especially physically, through confrontation

-nomics: suffix meaning "law;" the laws defining the underlying properties of a given subject

This book is dedicated to the men and women "of the Arena."

Where to Find Stuff

Foreword

There really is no such thing as a fair fight. The first time this realization punched me in the gut was when Pete Williams knocked out Mark "The Hammer" Coleman at UFC 17. Williams was a 22-year old unknown in his UFC debut while Coleman was an Olympic silver medalist wrestler and former UFC heavyweight champion who had ground and pounded through more impressive opponents, with his only loss being a decision in a championship fight. He was virtually unstoppable, and in my mind Williams was taking a quick trip to the hospital with a healthy dose of trauma counseling afterward. It was like watching Friday the 13th when idiot teenagers get drunk in Jason's house. You watch, but only to see them get what's coming for making such a horrible decision.

Within seconds Coleman had taken Williams to the mat and was implementing his very violent will and I was heading to the fridge for another beer. I thought this fight was already in the record books, but after twelve minutes there was no winner and we were going into a three-minute overtime. Suddenly Williams knocked Coleman out with a brutal head kick that he'd set up with several low strikes. He rejoiced while the MMA world's smartest guys slumped along with Coleman's body. Using the basic fundamentals of mixed martial arts Williams negated Coleman's strength and exploited his weaknesses. I was dumbfounded, awestruck, and kerfuffled.

Williams displayed the three main tenets of battle that every soldier learns – know yourself, know your enemy, and know the ground on which you fight. Utilizing these principles is what separates good fighters from the ones who get Gatorade commercials, but what about the rest of the chaotic chaos? A variety of external and internal factors can affect a fight – heart, chance, jitters, ring rust, and newborn babies – so the big question is "how do we account for all those things?"

With data.

Watching fight tapes to know your enemy and the ground you fight on is great, but it's limited and only provides a fighter with a piece of the pugilistic puzzle. He still has to know himself and what he can and cannot do. Hard data is far more definitive and allows a fight camp to develop a sound strategy long before fight day.

Gathering and analyzing that information sounds like a simple concept, but in fact it's laborious and monotonous to mine numbers from fight videos. It's even harder to then find patterns and develop actionable intelligence that arms a fighter with all the knowledge he needs to win. It also takes a 200-pound brain wired for science. I never would have believed someone could develop analysis that could be used to more accurately predict future performance in MMA based just on numbers. This is the first time anyone has had the hard drive and moxie to attempt it.

I've always been skeptical of numbers because they can be skewed to reach whatever conclusion the writer desires. Numbers are the whores of bias that will lead you to whatever conclusion they want with just a little manipulation from the John. That's why I like Reed's approach. He doesn't let the data become cheap or easy. He treats it with respect like a beloved daughter and presents it in a fair, unbiased way until it's a bride at a white wedding and he's the proud papa giving it away. No one else has had the gumption to attempt anything like what Reed has accomplished, so he's a true trailblazer in MMA statistics and it was a no-brainer to get involved with this project. If he's Meriwether Lewis on a journey of discovery, then I'll happily be his William Clark.

While writing this book I learned exactly why Williams shocked everyone and defeated Coleman at UFC 17. While Coleman's takedown attempts and accuracy were high and his time in a dominant position was even higher, his cardio endurance and head-strike defense were low, which tells us that he gets gassed and drops his hands more as the fight wears on. He was also a heavyweight and that weight class is more prone to knockouts than any other. A bad combination. Conversely Williams's takedown defense was solid, his cardio was steady, and his knockdown power was a real threat. Plus, he had the Youth Advantage on his side. While the casual observer saw a lopsided contest and bet on Coleman, the numbers told a different story and accurately outlined the outcome.

The factors were all there, but had not been added up yet. It was still an invisible matrix of voodoo that no one saw. Fifteen years later, we can see the sport more clearly. For me the future is clear: I will never venture to pick the winner of a fight without consulting Fightnomics first. Thank God for text messaging.

Kelly Crigger
October, 2013

"The Man in the Arena"

It is not the critic who counts; not the man who points out how the strong man stumbles, or where the doer of deeds could have done them better.

The credit belongs to the man who is actually in the arena, whose face is marred by dust and sweat and blood; who strives valiantly; who errs, who comes short again and again, because there is no effort without error and shortcoming; but who does actually strive to do the deeds; who knows great enthusiasms, the great devotions; who spends himself in a worthy cause; who at the best knows in the end the triumph of high achievement, and who at the worst, if he fails, at least fails while daring greatly, so that his place shall never be with those cold and timid souls who neither know victory nor defeat.

Theodore Roosevelt
Excerpt from the speech "Citizenship in a Republic" delivered at the Sorbonne, in Paris, France
April 23, 1910

Prologue

Do you remember the moment you got hooked on MMA? I do. It was a Wednesday night in Nashville in 2009, but it started earlier than that. The mid-2000's were the heyday of the "Iceman" Chuck Liddell and the first rabid seasons of "The Ultimate Fighter" reality show. Professional mixed martial arts was penetrating the highly coveted 18-35 year old male demographic like a social virus. "Dude, did you see this Ultimate Fighting stuff on Spike?" was the hot button topic at gyms, bars, and golf courses alike. At first blush the spectacle was fresh and foreign, yet easily understood. It was a perfect combination of primal skill and strength disguised as an exotic underground circus dealing the athletic taboos of unabashed blood loss, occasional unconsciousness, and the general perception of legalized violence. To my own peaceful and risk-averse mind it was enthralling. I didn't feel the usual need to put a stop to the conflict. I just sat back and watched it happen like a guilty pleasure, and apparently much of America felt the same.

It was a resurgence of interest gone dark since I once ordered an early UFC pay-per-view event back in 1994 while I was still an awkward kid in high school, rife with the delusion of maturity. But the sport was no longer the mystery it had been during those murky experimental days. Not only did I now know what and whom I was watching, but friends who were also hooked on The Ultimate Fighter series knew how awesome it was that I had hopped a last second flight to attend a live UFC event in Tennessee. By khaki-wearing, suburban standards, I was living on the edge.

Wednesday, April 1, 2009

On a pleasant spring evening, I'm wearing jeans and a Ranger Up t-shirt, jazzing it up with a blazer to hide my tattoo-less arms made weak from decades spent living in front of a computer. The arena tonight is a lot farther away from my life as a Washington DC strategy consultant than simply the physical miles I have traveled to Nashville. It's a crowded and raucous place filled with rugged fans and edgy fashion. The in-house DJ has a party on his hands, and people are drinking like they can't possibly have an early client meeting tomorrow. Together we are all watching two fighters locked inside a cage engaged in hand-to-hand combat. And there in the second row, close enough to hear every collision of leather on skin and see every resultant cloud of sweat explode in the air, trickles of my own nervous sweat are leaking down my sides. The age-old gladiator contest is taking hold of me, and there's nothing left but to embrace it. I scream for more.

Inside the Octagon UFC veteran Jorge Rivera is locking horns in a grueling back and forth fight with World Extreme Cagefighting crossover Nissen Osterneck.

I have spent the last 24 hours with the Rivera camp. Total strangers a day ago, they welcomed me into their hotel room after weigh-ins thanks to my friendship with their sponsor. After witty banter and channel surfing, sushi and beers with the cornermen, and then more candid discussions about fighting and life, they have become friends. And one of them is being punched in the face right in front of me. Right now. Unlike when I watched fights on TV at home I am just feet away from the action, cheering for a fighter, not just a fight. With primal biases welling up inside me, adrenaline and cortisol rushing through my system, I am living and dying with each strike.

Having lost the first round, Jorge Rivera is already fighting with a heavy heart. It's his first fight since the death of his teenage daughter, and not only is he exhausted early, but he's hiding a broken hand. The 37-year old's shoulder is already scheduled for surgery as soon as he gets home and the fight isn't even half over yet. Suddenly towards the end of the second round, Rivera drops Osterneck with a short right hand and turns the tide of the fight to his favor. The scream that escapes me as I shoot out of my seat may have drawn stares and revulsion from nearby spectators, but I can't imagine I was alone in my elation. Not in this crowd. I don't even know or care really as I'm oblivious to the 10,000 fans surrounding the moment. It seems like it's all transpiring just for me. I am completely transfixed by the two fighters battling for position, striking and retaliating tit for tat, trying to out-duel one another in this sweaty and now bloody contest of human chess.

I care who wins. I care about every second of the contest. When Rivera finally learns of the split decision victory he grinded out so doggedly, he is immediately brought to tears while honoring the memory of his daughter. He had known defeat too personally, and he had to earn his own respect back by stepping into the cage and pushing himself far beyond the limits of the average man. It was a cruel cleansing. He did it through the oldest and truest struggle: a fight. It was brutal and gritty, yet skillful and strategically elegant. It was simple and straightforward, yet nuanced far beyond the comprehension of the observer. The fight game is the pinnacle of one-on-one competition, the ultimate test of any athlete, of any person. And before the pain of the damage they have caused each other overwhelms the endorphins summoned by the fight, the competitors stop to acknowledge their appreciation of the other's performance.

The rest of the night plays out to the mixed roars and occasional indifference of the fans. I end up seated with a number of victorious undercard fighters just out from the showers, who are beaten, swollen, and stitched but healthy enough to avoid a trip to the hospital. I see the raw gratitude and emotional support exchanged between family and friends, and I am left wondering where the losers went. Is the downside as down as the upside is up? Each fighter's personal story and struggle before he even enters the cage appears more clearly, and his performance inside it becomes that much more impressive. This sport is so vivid now that I have pressed my face against its window, seeing what victory and defeat mean to those who live to fight and excel at what few can even attempt.

MMA had me in a rear naked choke and I wasn't struggling to break free. Unlike my first interactions with a variety of other, often more popular sports, I'm aware that something strange is happening. I have bounced and sung among the diehard fans of a soccer team, and been absorbed into the rabid fanaticism of college basketball, and those experiences weren't even close to being emotionally invested in a fighter on fight night. The natural draw of watching fighting and the inevitability of humans to compete all make for a compelling attraction for fans of sport.

Now I want to understand how it all works. Recalling Roosevelt's "Man in the Arena" speech I am fully aware that my opinion from outside the cage carries little weight for those who fight inside it. But I've also found that the questions I have about MMA lack sufficient answers from the sports community and even the most expert insiders. Knowledge is a powerful drug, and I am an unapologetic addict. The first taste of MMA analysis fueled my increasing desire to go deeper, to learn more, and to answer the unanswered questions. I wanted to understand the most advanced evolution of combat sport in ways that no one else has before.

This analysis is overdue for the fans of, and participants in the sport of MMA, partially because its popularity has outpaced understanding. Modern MMA should be observed and appreciated with the benefit of quantitative reasoning just like any other mainstream sport. There is a game hidden within every fight, and it has rules and strategies just like any other. The framework of metrics for fighting hasn't existed for long, but we already have a large and robust dataset to analyze. This additional layer of understanding will become part of the sport's continuing evolution.

Sifting Signal from Noise

"What can some 'quant jock' possibly learn about sports by looking at numbers?" I've heard it before and so have many others, some of whom now run major league teams. I want to do for MMA what has already been done for every mainstream sport through analytics. The objective of this book is simple: to gain a better understanding of the sport of mixed martial arts through quantitative analysis. We're interested in identifying and quantifying the underlying drivers of the fight game. We want to know, not just believe that something is true. So we will attack the common ideas we have about combat sports, put them to the test, and see what passes and what fails. In the end we'll have a better understanding of the sport and a better appreciation for the athletes who compete in it. To accomplish this objective we need numbers and analysis to keep things on the level, because traps are everywhere and we're not as smart as we think we are.

I am fully aware that all the math in the world may not change the way a fighter competes, or allow us certainty in predicting the outcome of any given fight. But to ignore such a valuable angle of insight into a chaotic and still nascent sport like MMA would be to welcome ignorance and surrender to chance. Patterns are all around us, at least to the human brain. We see them easily when they emerge from the noise, but we also see them even when they aren't real. Our brains evolved to look for patterns as the fundamental unit of identifying candidates for cause and effect. Many living things have the same tendencies, but we take "patternicity"[6] to lofty and sophisticated heights. We used it to domesticate food supplies and cure disease. It is the very basis for our survival and success. Yet if we are left to simply infer meaning from what we witness we're also liable to believe that animal sacrifice makes it rain, or that lucky charms make us win roulette. We see things and immediately think we understand them. Patterns are real to us the second they stimulate our senses and fire our neurons a certain way, and then they become impossible to shake. Our initial, rough-cut assessments, our reliance on our "gut" also makes us overconfident in our opinions and leads us towards false conclusions. When trying to answer questions that haven't been answered before, we can't take the easy way out. We're great at being wrong and stopping our investigation too early. So we have to look deeper, be prepared to do the math, and be willing to reject commonly held notions about what we *think* we know.

That's where analysts come in. They document and quantify real world events, organize and aggregate this data into information, analyze it in a variety ways from the simplest counting to the most complex transformational models, then derive insight that would be impossible from interpreting through the naked eye alone. Whether confirming or debunking, these insights allow us to put a reality check on our brains that are so eager to leap to flimsy conclusions. It doesn't assure us of victory, but this simple algorithm of hypothesis testing is the surest way to discover truth. And as the astronomer Neil DeGrasse Tyson reminds us, "The good thing about science is that it's true whether or not you believe in it."

I am an armchair scientist; a jack of many trades, but a master of none. As a human I reserve the right to screw up the science part and tell bad jokes along the way. For that matter, I'll apologize now for using word "data" in the more popular singular usage and focusing mostly on men's MMA. I'll use lots of clarifying language and frequent qualifiers that may make me look timid in my conclusions, but such is the nature of this type of research. A scientist cannot speak in absolute truths, nor can he analyze away the possibility of anything real, however improbable. This book emphasizes data mining to determine interesting trends, not to test each hypothesis to the level of significance required for scientific publication. If I gloss over some details or use a rule of thumb to summarize, remember that eventually I must respect the finite patience of the reader. When I leave the door open for the future it's because there are no absolutes in human nature, and as we'll see this sport derives from our earliest human nature. Many of the ideas and questions explored here have never been answered with numbers and even then we can only ascertain trends from history, without perfect knowledge of the future. This is professional cagefighting. I use this term when I want to emphasize the volatility of it all. The unpredictable nature of the sport is part of the reason we watch and enjoy it, but that doesn't mean we can't make it a little less unpredictable with a little bit of science (and a whole lot of numbers).

This book is loaded with analysis, sprinkled with historical perspective and occasional expert quotes, and then summarized with statistics often graphed to visually clarify the main point. In every chapter there is something to learn, ammunition for the next debate, and takeaways that you can bring to the cage or barstool to understand the trends, drivers, and context of MMA on a deeper level than before. But as much analysis as I've managed to stuff into this one book, keep in mind that we've only just begun. Even more nascent than the sport itself, MMA statistics and analytics are just now entering a rapid maturation process that will blow one more gust into the sails propelling this ship towards creating a truly global and mainstream sport.

I'll break down MMA into its component parts. I'll test the common theories about how fights go down, and I'll uncover some truths that were waiting to be discovered. For the first time ever, the modern sport of fighting will be put under the microscope and analyzed from a variety of angles. This book will create a foundation for examining the sport from the outside in. It will document some of the obvious, while also exposing some hidden gems.

After UFC 101 I was in the back of a taxi with various industry insiders when I was confronted with the blunt stubbornness that "there's no way statistics could be useful in cage fighting." I accepted the challenge, and now ask you to accept my invitation to sit back and ride along while I prove it. But before we start deconstructing the fight game with science and numbers, we'll walk before we run. Let's briefly examine how humans ended up fighting in cages in the first place.

Food for Thought

If you take four street corners, and on one they are playing baseball, on another they are playing basketball and on the other, street hockey.
On the fourth corner, a fight breaks out. Where does the crowd go?
They all go to the fight.

Dana White
UFC president
April 2007, Las Vegas Sun News Interview

Introduction: The Evolution of Combat Sports

Where did combat sports come from?

Whatever you've heard is probably wrong. Most point to the early Greek Olympiads, which by everyday standards was a really long time ago. In fact, that definitely plants MMA's roots firmly in "ancient" history. At the earliest documented Olympic games in 786 BC, the first events involved various forms of foot races and lasted only a day, but over the next century the games grew in popularity and scope. By 708 BC, the Olympiads increased in duration to accommodate the addition of several combat sports to the program.[1] Whether or not local tunic-sewers and winemakers advertised on the signage for the events is a question lost to history, but in my mind the entrepreneurs were already using sports for the marketing purposes that helped build the infrastructure around the games.

Boxing, wrestling, and Pankration events pitted young athletes against each other in formalized combat sports. Boxers struck each other with and without various hand covers to protect the striker's hands instead of the target's head. Wrestlers attempted to pin each other to the ground, or force each other out of a specified boundary like Sumo wrestlers today. In Pankration, from the Greek root words meaning "all powers" or "all strengths," fighters used a combination of combat techniques roughly resembling mixed martial arts, except they were naked. They did all this without any singlets, fight shorts, or even a protective cup. Woven fabrics in ancient times were valuable items intended to last a long time, so there's no way you were going to shred your tunic just for a wrestling match. Plus, they didn't have the whole body image or obesity issues back then that we do today, so we shouldn't freak out over some nude wrestling. It's just a shame those athletes couldn't wear sponsor logos.

Going back a few millennia makes the Greeks the first ones to stage competitive fights, right? Nope. A tomb at the Beni Hassan cemetery site in Egypt dates back another thousand years before the early Olympiads, and is decorated with a series of images showing a variety of grappling positions. With some squinting you'll see the earliest known picture of a single leg takedown from sometime around 2000 BC, and yet we aren't even close to the first wrestling match yet. Not by a long shot.

Depictions of wrestling in Beni Hassan Tomb 15 in Egypt (single panel, separated). The image contains more than 400 wrestling pairs using techniques seen in modern freestyle wrestling. The images are approximately 4,000 years old. Image source: Wiki Commons

The Natural Evolution of Fighting

The earliest upright human males a few million years ago very likely grappled with each other to compete for meat, fish, berries, and hot cave women in their perpetual fight for survival, sex, and social status. The behavior is referred to as "agonistic" fighting. How can we know what prehistoric humans did without the visual proof? Just take a quick field trip to your local zoo, and if you're lucky enough to spot gorillas wrestling you'll recognize it immediately. What starts off as loud and wild posturing between apes sometimes leads to a direct face off. That's when things get spooky.

The mannerisms and gesticulations are uncannily similar to modern human wrestlers "hand fighting" at the initiation of a match. An ape will stand up on his legs, then lean forward, pawing at his opponent's head in an attempt to pull him off balance to the ground. They will try to circle around their opponents, darting back and forth to cut off each other's advances. Keep in mind that humans are a branch of the great apes making up the Hominidae family. This fighting behavior is typical among hominid species, and was probably also shared by our common ape-like ancestors many millions of years ago. Sorry Egypt and Greece, you get credited for innovating the fight game, but not inventing the fight itself.

Humans are smart and learned enough to make amazing things at will like iron, bronze, and bourbon, but for millions of years we were just a brainier version of our ape cousins. We like to think our superiority to other apes has everything to do with our brains. But there's another important difference between humans and other apes: humans can make fists. The amount of force that can be delivered with a hand strike approximately doubles when we curl our fingers. Other hominids could do this too, but only humans are able to then curl fingers further downward buttressing our fingers on the palm of our hand in the compact and sturdy form that we know as a fist. That simple maneuver doubles again the amount of force we can deliver with a hand strike over the simple curled fingers approach (that's now four times what a slap or knife-hand strike can do). Of all the evolutionary traits that were being selected as humans split off onto their own branch of the ape family tree, the ability throw a punch was one of them. When it comes to our ability to use our bodies forcefully, our weapon of choice in fighting was not teeth or claws, but our hands.

Aggression and fighting are ritual behaviors that evolved in a wide variety of species, so there must be a good reason for them. The answer is simple: killing is risky work. When two animals arrive to make a claim on the same precious resource, be it food or a potential mate, they need to figure out who wins without putting themselves at undue risk. It's a combat philosophy that holds true to this day: hit without being hit, but only until there's a winner. Fighting to the death over every meal would probably lead quickly to extinction, because you'd end up with a lone, very exhausted, and probably injured Alpha male to sustain the entire herd. A scorched earth policy is a path to extinction.

So instead, flies, walruses, and dexterous great apes all rely on an evolutionarily honed behavior of ritual aggression through fighting. Black mamba snakes will wrestle in an attempt to pin their opponent's head to the ground repeatedly before the loser submits, rather than ever bite the opponent. Piranhas arc equally loathe to use their sharp teeth when fighting each other, instead using their tails in what could only be described as an ass-backwards slap fight. A wild kangaroo once ended a videotaped kickboxing session with a rear naked choke that rendered the opponent temporarily unconscious, with the victor standing over the defeated like the iconic Ali over Sonny Liston. The animal kingdom never lacks for diverse and dramatic examples. After fights like these are over, the winners don't apply force any further. The point here is that fighting for dominance is an evolved process that protects both participants from deadly harm while maintaining the social value of conflict. Most "fighting," therefore, is a competition within accepted rules that involves aggression, but limited real violence.[2]

When predator-prey inter-species fighting is removed from consideration (e.g., carnivores hunting, or as in TV movies, sharks killing anything and everything), the reluctance of animals to actually engage in real violence is admirable in the wild. The choice of "fight or flight" is actually a false dichotomy when we examine one on one intra-species aggression. What is actually a spectrum between those two ends is both elaborate and advanced. Retreat, contrary to popular maxims, is always an option. Often it is the best option, but only after some intricate posturing maneuvers. Many confrontations, therefore, result in no physical interaction at all, and when direct fighting does occur it shows restraint.

Have you ever watched gorillas fight? If not, fire up YouTube immediately. You'll see them bear their ferocious teeth during a scramble, but look closely and you'll also see that the intent is primarily to simulate dominance, not enact it. They fight to gain the upper hand in position where they could do real harm to their opponent, without actually doing it. They're playing "King of the Mountain" and relying on posturing and simulated violence much like a theatrical "pro" wrestler. Their gaping jaws will cover the back of their opponent's neck without ever clenching. The sensation of this move is akin to how some animal parents will nuzzle or even carry their young from the skin folds of the back of their necks. The recipient feels submissive under this dominance and the fight ends. This is the true origin of submission wrestling, complete with the loser's recognition of defeat, submission, and withdrawal from the contest.

Some animal contests are literally a ritual assessment of "who's bigger?" An obscure species of fly will face each other and spread their elongated eyes apart in order to see who has the larger body. The puffing of chests, bristling of body hair, standing up on hind legs, and the spreading of arms seen in so many animals are all attempts to convince their counterparts that they are physically superior. The "bring it bitch!" posturing serves to decide the fight, without any fighting at all, saving both participants from unnecessary risk while preserving the natural pecking order. When fighting occurs (and even when it doesn't) the submission of the defeated will often take the form of symbolic exposure of sensitive anatomy like the neck or belly, followed by retreat. One species of lizard will actually stand on three legs and use the fourth to wave in a circular motion. Long before anyone ever tapped out in a cage or cried "uncle" on a playground, a reptile actually "waved" a submission to a superior and victorious opponent. Hopefully you're now looking forward to scrolling through the science channels on your cable guide.

As we would expect, the times when animals actually follow through with a violent and potentially deadly match are when there is a combination of highly valuable resources at stake and a close call on the "Tale of the Tape" of physical characteristics. There has to be a massive reward to justify deadly force. Aggressive interactions also increase when two individuals are similarly sized, meaning the combatants need to think that they stand a chance.

Sound familiar? Of course it does. Imagine this: a huge guy at the bar steps up and says "you mind if we dance with your dates?" The more you have to turn your head upwards to meet his eyes, the more likely you are to back away and wave your arm like that funky lizard. But if he's equally sized and your date is a keeper, you may just dust off your soup bones and step up to the challenge. The Latin root for aggression is "aggressio," meaning to attack. And that word in turn is the combination of ad and gradi, which literally mean "step at." Some dude steps at you? Well, by definition, that means aggression, and he didn't have to learn that behavior because it's hard-wired into his brain and it's also in his genes.

It's also in his jeans. Testosterone is the primary hormonal driver of aggressive behavior, and is produced (mostly) in a male's testicles. The more testosterone, the more aggressive a man tends to be. A simplification obviously, but now that Testosterone Replacement Therapy craze in fighting is making more sense. We still have free will to restrain ourselves of course, but let's recognize that we are strongly influenced by our hormones. Higher testosterone males are likely to be bigger and have more lean muscle mass and body hair. You can spot them easily, mostly because they intimidate other males and attract the attention of the fertile females nearby. Behaviorally, they're also more likely to initiate and engage in conflict and fight on behalf of their friends, family, or their bitchin' Camaro when it gets dinged.

But it's not all beefcakes and heroism. High testosterone also increases a man's likelihood of getting arrested for a violent crime and cheating on a spouse. Knights in shining armor and the thug bully lurking at the corner, ironically, are both likely to have higher-than-average testosterone, something they boast about over beers before diving into the singles scene. So let's just say that that the evidence supports the idea that testosterone is very closely associated with aggressive behavior overall, and also with physical success in executing aggression through fighting. Knowing what we now know about the innate drivers of agonistic behavior and fighting, it's plainly obvious that testosterone plays a key role in the system.

And women can play this game too. Females produce testosterone in the ovaries and adrenal glands, albeit in smaller quantities than in men. As with men, there is a wide spectrum of variance in testosterone level across the animal kingdom, as well is within each species. The most extreme case is the spotted hyena, renowned for females with very high testosterone levels. Female hyenas are larger and more aggressive than males and even have external genitals that visually resemble a male's. It's the females that dominate the social structure, feed first, and protect territory. And when they are pregnant, their fetuses gestate in a testosterone-rich marinade. The result? When hyenas give birth to twins (as is often the case) the cubs are born with fully functional teeth ready for combat. The twins will almost immediately begin fighting, often to the death; the stronger and more ferocious of the two normally wins.[3] An argument from the extreme, perhaps, but a little "T" clearly goes a long way towards explaining aggressive behavior in humans and elsewhere. It also means that if you're female fighter, the nickname "The Hyena" is actually a massive compliment that should scare the bejesus out of everyone.

For men, who more frequently have the higher testosterone levels in the animal kingdom, fighting is therefore hormonally hard-wired. Males in many species may never witness fighting before experiencing aggression from a potential foe, yet immediately and instinctively go through the physical displays of posturing, threatening, fighting, and submission appropriate to their species. While animals clearly seem to follow their own silently agreed upon "rules" to their fighting, it took the human ability to communicate to determine do's and don'ts with scoring criteria to create an environment where contests have more clear winners, as well as safer outcomes for the participants. We took fighting and converted it from survival into entertainment, separating ourselves from the animal kingdom, but only by a matter of slight degree. It turns out that every sports channel is actually a "nature" channel.

From Common Ancestor to the Melting Pot

Every day up and down the animal kingdom, males posture to impose dominance in the social order. Sometimes it goes one step further to actual fighting, and that's when things get interesting. When the fight begins there is no longer a guarantee that the more impressive physical specimen will win. In some cases the bluff of posturing tall gets called by an undersized, but still able competitor. There's a physical chess match that must then occur with the objective that the winning position may imply a deadly threat without necessarily delivering it. Both players innately agree to these rules, and as the contest begins fighting prowess, rather than impressive physique, becomes the prime attribute for success. Time to put your money where your mouth is. We see it in the cage all the time. A scrappy and skilled David faces a massively muscled Goliath, and yet seasoned MMA fans know never to judge by appearances alone (see Roy Nelson vs Cheick Kongo, UFC 159).

In apes the objective may simply be a scramble for dominant physical position, resulting in one fighter gaining tooth-to-neck access to initiate a submission response. Securing the ability to deal a deadly blow appears to end most fights without continued resistance, even in the absence of modern language. The fact that submission wrestling in humans so clearly mimics this behavior right down to the lack (or minimization) of serious injury should not be overlooked. We all want to play by the rules otherwise we may not be allowed to play at all, and the last thing we want is for someone to take his marbles and go home before we have a chance to defeat him and prove our superiority. It turns out that other animals invented the "no punching in the face" rule long before it ever was conceived on a playground after school, or between rival news teams in "Anchorman."[4]

But leave it to humans to take the fun to extreme new levels. As soon as wrestling became a contest outside of normal resource competition (or maybe much earlier) we started using our brains as our best weapon. The development of "martial arts" and fighting techniques exploded and spread around the globe like a virulent strain of kick-ass. The fighting-educated boldly walked into the gathering grounds of new villages, sized up the local strongman and asked, "wanna try me?" Just imagine a modern expert in jiu-jitsu traveling back in time 10,000 years to tap and snap his way through an entire army of dumbfounded, hammer-fisting mouth-breathers. New combat techniques must have been a valuable commodity during eras of frequent regional conflict and even more frequent localized lawlessness.

Throughout Asia martial arts styles evolved and specialized, but interestingly, many of these combat techniques migrated primarily towards use in sport, rather than real-world conflict. They were also very specific to the era and geography as evidenced by the use of contemporary weapons in ceremonial demonstrations. The idea of "forms" turned hand-to-hand combat techniques into an art where skills were assessed as much on beauty and athleticism as they were on practicality. As culture progressed and the need for the common man to engage in combat on an everyday basis slowly subsided, martial arts evolved into something else. Being pretty was more important than being effective, an unfortunate trend that has persisted.

From the original boxing of ancient Greece to Russian Sambo to the more recognizable styles of Karate, Muay Thai, and Tae Kwon Do from Japan, Thailand and Korea, martial arts fragmented from its common ancestor into a wide spectrum of specialized dialects. Over the following millennia the divergent styles would create the broad global variety of non-competing martial arts that we see today. Fighting styles gained acceptance as a hobby, a sport, and a pastime, often with nationalistic focus. They were likely not ever used in direct conflict against one another or else the diverse and rules-specific styles would not have survived. The unrelenting chaos of real battle would not have allowed for it, but it wasn't until the global marketplace got frustrated selecting from the long menu of self-defense styles that the natural and eventual question gained traction: which style of martial arts is best? Once asked, it could never be undone.

Modern MMA originates from the revolutionary televised experiment that was the first Ultimate Fighting Championship, a competitive process that was decidedly American. Before I get chastised for that statement, let me clarify. The famed Gracie family from Brazil sent forth Brazilian jiu-jitsu missionaries all issuing the "Gracie Challenge" after being taught the tradition by Mitsuyo Maeda. Whether or not the large sums of money they offered to defeat them were ever really at risk, the idea of the challenge went beast-mode in the insatiable American entertainment market hungry for combat entertainment. No holds barred fighting was known as Vale Tudo in Brazil, a common sideshow distraction at circuses in the early 20th century and the closest thing resembling the contest that would become known as Ultimate Fighting. The UFC, therefore, truly was a televised circus event that found a home among Americans who have always loved a good show.

How the Gladiator Got on TV

In 1993 there were no barriers to enter the American combat entertainment market. The demand was higher than the supply in all facets of human combatives be they boxing, wrestling, or whatever some new visionary might bring to the table. If a movie had the word "ninja" in it, it made millions. The famously capitalistic and competitive country embraced the idea of dropping all martial arts into the same cage to see which one would win. History may be rife with horror stories that start off "it seemed like a good idea," but this one truly was. Americans who didn't have time to appreciate and value each and every diverse style on its own wanted to cut to the chase. You want to talk smack about how awesome your dojo is? Prove it. It was the ultimate bluff call.

What spawned was part science experiment, part circus. The generation of viewers targeted by the 1993 launch of the UFC had grown up on movies spanning the martial arts spectrum from "Enter the Dragon" to "The Karate Kid." America sensationalized martial arts and part of the lure of the UFC was the stacked deck the Gracie family had dealt. Many fans were unprepared to see the lanky, slightly nerdy Royce Gracie enter the cage and confidently steamroll the larger and more fearsome fighters from around the world. The Brazilian plot twist was Hollywood-perfect, but just as soon as Americans learned to pronounce and respect the term "jiu-jitsu" they immediately started to look for the antidote. We love to win but hate a winner, and we jump for joy when the king of the hill topples down it. The Brazilian Jiu Jitsu (BJJ) practitioner went from miracle underdog to undisputed champion in no time at all, and thus became a target. The game was afoot.

The history of these early formative years of MMA is fascinating from cultural and business perspectives full of rich stories by insiders, fighters, and storytellers more qualified to tell them than I.[5] But we all know the end result. The UFC spiraled downward due to regulatory problems and opened the door for its sale by the original owner, SEG, to the Fertitta brothers with Dana White entering as president of the operation. Equal parts entrepreneurial visionary, charismatic promoter, meticulous businessman, and enthusiastic movie producer, White catalyzed the process of regulatory and operational improvements that would make MMA a more palatable television product. He then hit the jackpot by getting MMA on regular TV. He was the right man for the right job at the right time. "The Ultimate Fighter" reality series was his ten-million dollar Trojan Horse gamble that not only solidified the UFC's long-term viability as a sport and as a business, but also made the fledgling Spike TV network a basic cable contender. MMA could now be seen by practically anyone.

Today, the two-million dollar purchase of the UFC by Zuffa in 2001 remains one of the most lucrative business deals ever. Zuffa was backed financially by the Las Vegas-based Fertitta brothers, owners of the Station casinos, who created Zuffa (literally Italian for a "scrap" or brawl) as the media entity to own the UFC. The company's valuation surpassed the billion dollar mark within a decade, and the promotion is only now infiltrating very large and fight-friendly international markets where it will likely flourish. The human need for competition and our visceral, primal understanding of combat sports has never wavered. The only changes have been the global accessibility to many styles, and the lack of an incumbent American style bias that enabled the UFC tournaments to capture the attention of fans. As in any highly competitive and immature system, the sport has rapidly evolved, inviting many competitors who challenge the

UFC before being put out of business or acquired by the juggernaut of the sport.

The modern mixed martial artist is now athletically multi-lingual, fluent across diverse fighting dialects because he or she has no choice. The core principle of Adam Smith's "Invisible Hand" guiding the market has filtered out one-dimensional fighters relying on a single style. One-trick ponies have short lifespans under unforgiving evolutionary forces. Yet in some ways we have come full circle all the way back to ancient Greece, when wrestlers and boxers were allowed to mix their styles in the sport of Pankration. The rules have changed, the training has modernized, the techniques have advanced, and certainly the level of skill and athleticism has pushed the benchmark of competition to new heights. What we are left with is possibly the best and last hand-to-hand combat sport, and it only took us a few million years to get here. Now, as Bruce Buffer would say: "It's tiiiiiiiiiiiiiiime!"

Chapter Notes:

1. "Olympic Wrestling," By Barbara M. Linde. The Rosen Publishing Group, 2007.

2. "On Killing: The Psychological Cost of Learning to Kill in War and Society," by Lt. Col. Dave Grossman. Back Bay Books; Revised edition, 2009.

3. "Sex, Time, and Power: How Women's Sexuality Shaped Human Evolution," by Leonard Shlain. Penguin Books, 2004.

4. Technically, anchorman Ron Burgundy proposed: "Rule number 1: no touching of the hair or face! And that's it! Now let's do this!"

5. For more on the history and culture of the UFC, I recommend the books "Title Shot" by Kelly Crigger and "Blood in the Cage" by Jon Wertheim.

6. For an excellent discussion of "patternicity" and how the human brain detects, believes, and deceives, read Micheal Shermer's "The Believing Brain," Time Books, Henry Holt and Company, 2011.

7. For a thoughtful history of the rise of the UFC, see Jon Wertheim's "Blood in the Cage." Houghton Mifflin Harcourt, 2009.

Food for Thought

Knowing what to measure and how to measure it makes a complicated world much less so.

If you learn how to look at data in the right way, you can explain riddles that otherwise might have seemed impossible.

Because there is nothing like the sheer power of numbers to scrub away layers of confusion and contradiction.

Steven D. Levitt, Stephen J. Dubner
"Freakonomics," 2010

Numbers in the Cage: What Stats Can Tell Us About Sports & MMA

Somewhere between the third grade science garden and high school physics, I decided to be a "science guy." Since then, I've meandered through college and graduate schools looking at the world differently than most, and applying the intellectual integrity of the scientific method across a variety of unusual disciplines. With the addition of advanced statistical analysis skills, I eventually realized science could be applied anywhere, not just in laboratories or homework assignments. The real fun in wielding science lies in examining things you are closest to, your passions and hobbies. In this more casual setting of pastimes, however, people are often more skeptical of what formal scientific thinking might find. The irony is that most will accept scientific research on things they know nothing about, but will reject it when it addresses something with which they are casually familiar.

Introduction to Quantitative Sports Mythbusting

Sports analysis is an excellent example. Athletes and coaches generally ignore analytical insights, especially ones undermining their own perceptions of their beloved sport. But as analytical tools have blossomed from improving technology, more and more analysts like me are bringing the inquisitive and unflinching process of hypothesis testing to sports statistics. The results can be surprising. Smart sports managers are now adopting analytics that gain any advantage – no matter how slight – to maximize performance at the highest levels of competition. So let's consider a couple of common beliefs in sports that have now been challenged by statistical analysis.

Myth: Basketball players get "hot" or "cold."

Everyone knows a "hot" shooter should get the ball, especially with the game on the line. A "cold" player needs to be benched, find his lucky socks, and only then go back in. It seems obvious; the confidence won by consecutive successes fuels players to make more buckets (hot), while the frustration of consecutive misses sabotages a player's rhythm (cold). Unfortunately, our perception of this phenomenon is completely false. The patterns we perceive support popular notions but we have completely misjudged reality when we fall prey to the "myth of the hot hand." Sports analysis is an excellent example. Athletes and coaches generally ignore analytical insights, especially ones undermining their own perceptions of their beloved sport. But as analytical tools have blossomed from improving technology, more and more analysts like me are bringing the inquisitive and unflinching process of hypothesis testing to sports statistics. The results can be surprising. Smart sports managers are now adopting analytics that gain any advantage – no matter how slight – to maximize performance at the highest levels of competition. So let's consider a couple of common beliefs in sports that have now been challenged by statistical analysis.

Reality: Shooting streaks don't influence the next shot.

Research by Nobel Laureate Amos Tversky, a Stanford University researcher in the 1980s and '90s, plus a deluge of deeper analysis since, have thoroughly proven that shooting streaks are not predictors of future performance. Whether a player has made or missed three, four or even more consecutive shots, his chances of making the next shot are no different than his normal shooting percentage under comparable circumstances. The best coaching decision when players establish streaks of success or failure is therefore to ignore these streaks. After all, it's entirely possible a particular shooter feels "hot" because he has made a few consecutive shots, not the other way around. The streak, therefore, is just in our heads. Free throws are the closest thing basketball has to a natural, controlled experiment because they afford the opportunity for reproducible research. Free throws further support the fallibility of the hot versus cold myth. It's also true at the game level. Entire teams don't go hot or cold through a season, there are simply runs of consecutive wins and losses, much as we'd expect coin flipping to produce occasional runs of many heads or tails. Along with Daniel Kahneman, Tversky helped pioneer the field of behavioral economics, melding applied human psychology and cognitive science with economic decision-making. In essence, this field investigates human (mis)perceptions when encountering randomness. Unfortunately, sound analysis and hard evidence are no guarantee that people will listen. High-profile coaches of Tversky's day famously dismissed the findings as irrelevant, including the Boston Celtics' Red Auerbach and Bob Knight, then of Indiana University.

However, Bob Dylan was right, and times they are a changin.' Duke University icon Coach Mike Krzyzewski recently adopted statistics for the Blue Devils, deploying a platoon of sober, stat-taking student volunteers. Coach K understands streaky shooting, properly coaching his team to optimize performance without falling victim to misperceived hot or cold streaks. When the game is on the line historically good shooters still give the best chances of success, regardless of a prior cold spell. This means coaches should not abandon good players gone cold like in the movie "Hoosiers," and should maintain discipline during hot streaks to prevent overly aggressive, lower percentage shot selection. The NBA no longer dismisses the benefits of statistics as when Tversky first fired the data-fueled nerd missile that destroyed one of sports' most popular misconceptions. Individual NBA teams now employ full time analysts to more fully understand basketball by the numbers, and to make more optimal decisions on how it's played and managed.

Myth: Football teams should always punt or kick on fourth down.

The concept of "loss aversion" is core to behavioral economics. Through an evolutionary lens, it was much safer for our caveman predecessors to err on the cautious side when confronting patterns in nature than it was to ignore the patterns or brazenly expose themselves to potential risks. Experiments, again by Tversky, illustrate that modern humans still value losses more than numerically equivalent gains, driving our natural risk aversion in decision-making. In the sport of American football, there is nothing perceived as more risky than going for it on fourth down. Not converting this play means giving up favorable field position to your opponent. Losing the gamble also means drawing everlasting criticism from fans, players, and even the Catholic priest secretly betting on Notre Dame. But again, this is a myth the numbers don't support, except under extreme circumstances.

Reality: Going for it on fourth down maximizes performance.

Analysis by Berkeley economist David Romer determined that "going for it" on fourth down actually maximizes overall team performance. Analysis weighing expected point outcomes of fourth down decisions against the expected scoring potential of opponents based on field position reinforced the rationality of aggressive fourth down strategies. In layman's terms, you have a much better chance converting fourth downs than you think, and even if you don't the other team isn't guaranteed to gain from the field position you give up. But coaches are generally unwilling to risk the perception of poor decision-making due to our natural loss aversion, and instead ignore the evidence by actually employing suboptimal strategies. They don't want to look like idiots and simply avoid getting into situations where it might happen, even though it costs them in the long run.

All, except a few. Coach Kevin Kelley of Arkansas' Pulaski Academy has forsaken kicking altogether, never punting and only executing onside kicks for kickoffs. Analysis of Pulaski's performance confirmed this as the optimal strategy for his team. He has since led his undersized private school squad to an impressive record and several state championships following this by-the-numbers approach.

While no team utilizes rational play quite like the Pulaski Bruins, one NFL team goes for it on fourth down more than any other: the New England Patriots. Since assuming the reigns as head coach, Bill Belichick has built nothing less than a dynasty, winning three national titles and three Coach of the Year awards in his first five years. Success earned Belichick the flexibility to be a "riskier" coach, further reinforcing his aggressive strategic posture. The irony is that although perceived as risk-seeking, he's actually implementing a more rational and optimal strategy.[1]

The human brain's tendency to identify false patterns and rely on fallible emotional perceptions rather than rational objectivity drives belief in sports myths and astrology alike. We want to believe that going for it on fourth down is a bad idea just like we want to believe that horoscopes are accurate, and we'll ignore any evidence that contradicts our beliefs. Our species simply didn't evolve with the overwhelming amount of information we now confront daily. Mastering the mechanics of sound analysis enables discovery of new truths, but understanding how our minds deceive us helps us understand and believe what we've discovered. By stamping out cognitive and psychological biases and enabling intellectual integrity, science elucidates small and large, germs and gravitation, and everything in between. Even insights into sports we think we've already mastered can become clearer.

Debunking myths is all well and good, but sports statistics are applicable only in data-rich sports like baseball and basketball. What about in the confined cage of mixed martial arts where chaos reigns? Surely we can't expect real-time decisions to be based on statistical research. We certainly can't imagine a world where one of the three cornermen for a fighter is a statistical consultant screaming instructions to their fighter like, "his power head striking accuracy is low, press the attack!" But like Tversky and Romer before me, I am going to perform some research on MMA statistics regardless of naysayers. I'll draw defensible conclusions about the fight game, and then suggest strategic implications which could certainly be actionable for coaches and fighters alike. And yes, even in real-time situations.

MMA Stats 101: Winners, Losers, and Neithers

How do MMA fights go down? As in the Thunderdome, two men enter a cage, they fight, and one man leaves alive. Well not really, but the detractors of MMA would like you to believe this. In reality both are alive and one of them is victorious, but even that outcome is not certain. Must there really be a winner and loser? Let's start at the top and look at the highest level of how fights end.

At the most basic level of competition in the Octagon, fighters from opposing red and blue corners compete until the fight concludes in one of three ways: KO/TKO/stoppage, submission, or elapsed time. In the UFC fights last three five-minute rounds for most fights, or five five-minute rounds for title bouts and select non-championship main events at the discretion of the promotion. If you're thinking the expected win rate for any given fighter is 50/50, think again. In the game of roulette, you can't just bet on both black and red and keep your money in the long run. There's always a small chance of the green zero, or even more spectacularly, the green double-zero, that keeps the game from being truly 50/50 on color alone.

Such is the case in MMA fight outcomes. There's not always a blue or red corner winner; sometimes there's no winner at all. I've broken all historical UFC fights into three basic categories. For Win/Loss there was in fact a winner and a loser of the fight. Draws are when the fights ends and the result is a tie. And No Contests are when the fight ends too soon to declare a winner for reasons outside the fighters' control or the result is negated after the fact. We'll look at these special circumstances in more detail, but first let's just see how often they occur on an annual basis.

Annual UFC Fight Outcomes

UFC Year	Win/Loss	Draw	No Contest
1993	100%	0.0%	0.0%
1994	100%	0.0%	0.0%
1995	95.0%	5.0%	0.0%
1996	100%	0.0%	0.0%
1997	97.6%	0.0%	2.4%
1998	100%	0.0%	0.0%
1999	95.5%	4.5%	0.0%
2000	97.7%	2.3%	0.0%
2001	97.5%	0.0%	2.5%
2002	98.1%	0.0%	1.9%
2003	95.1%	4.9%	0.0%
2004	100%	0.0%	0.0%
2005	98.8%	0.0%	1.3%
2006	100%	0.0%	0.0%
2007	98.8%	0.6%	0.6%
2008	100%	0.0%	0.0%
2009	99.1%	0.5%	0.5%
2010	98.8%	1.2%	0.0%
2011	98.3%	0.7%	1.0%
2012	97.7%	0.6%	1.8%
2013	98.2%	0.0%	1.8%
Grand Total	98.5%	0.7%	0.8%

Going back through time to the rowdy and controversial "no holds barred" days2 of the UFC, and tracking forward to the multi-billion dollar mainstream combat sport that MMA has become, we see how rare it is that a fight doesn't have a winner. But Draws and No Contests can and do still happen. Since 2009 the number of fights with no winner has always been greater than 1% of the total, with the historical average at 1.5%. That's not a lot, but it's one of the simplest first looks at how data can quantify MMA. We now have a starting point metric that may be useful in later analysis. For example, if we analyze whether or not an advantage exists we now know that the average expected win rate of any fighter is really 49.3%, not 50%.

There are famous examples of fights with no winners in the UFC, but look no further than former lightweight title contender Gray Maynard to understand how fights can end in bizarre ways. In 2007 "The Bully" Maynard made his Octagon debut not with a bang, but with a confusing self-injury. In The Ultimate Fighter (TUF) 5 Finale show Maynard emerged as a highly touted semi-finalist. In his official debut in the Octagon he seemed to be in control of fellow TUF cast member Rob Emerson for over nine minutes.

Towards the end of the second round a vicious slam by Maynard injured Emerson into verbal submission, but simultaneously rocked Maynard into semi-consciousness. In the confusing final moments instant replay would demonstrate that while Emerson could not continue due to injury, Maynard was equally incapable of standing without assistance. The result was a No Contest. Neither fighter won, but neither fighter lost. It's MMA limbo, the lack of resolution and the denial of the purpose of the fight in the first place. It's the most unsatisfying outcome possible for fighters and fans alike.

Fast forward three and a half years and eight consecutive wins for Gray Maynard when he earned a title shot at UFC 125 against Frankie Edgar, a fighter he had already beaten years prior. In what would become a Fight of the Night bonus winning performance, and arguably the fight of the year for 2011, Maynard once again tasted the confusion of a fight with no winner. After dominating Edgar early on and winning one round 10-8, Edgar rallied to win a few of the later rounds. The judges were split. Two judges scored the fight 48-45, but for different winners. The tiebreaking judge scored the fight an even 47-47, resulting in a Split Draw. Because the fight was a championship bout the title remained with Edgar due to the fact that he was not technically defeated. UFC fans had to wait nine more months for a title rematch that eventually resulted in a definitive win for then champion Frankie Edgar. A recurring theme in MMA is that anything can happen inside the cage, but when we approach the sporting aspect of competition, it helps to know just how often these strange endings can occur. Now we know how often fights end by Draw or No Contest. But look a little more closely at the pattern of historical fight outcomes and we see something more interesting. Notice how the historical average of No Contests is just 0.7%, yet it has been 1.0%, 1.5% and 2.3% in the years since 2011. Isn't that unusual? A steady rise in the rate of No Contests could be part of the randomness of sports, but it could be tied to underlying forces at work in the same system. I theorize that two mechanisms are to blame for this rise in No Contests: eye pokes and drug testing.

No Contests declared on the spot usually occur when a fighter is accidentally injured from an illegal blow, such as an eye-poke. But there's another reason for No Contests: failed drug tests. If a fighter wins but later tests positive for a banned substance, the fight result is wiped from the records of both fighters and replaced with a "No Contest." If the fighter had lost and then failed the test, no action would be taken on the fight outcome because it would penalize the clean, victorious fighter. In either case, you can be sure the fighter who failed the test is going is going to be punished by the promotion, by the regulatory bodies, and probably most relentlessly by the fans.

Mixed Martial Arts, like any other professional sport, is a competitive place, and just like in baseball, bike racing, or the Olympics there are athletes who try to cheat the system by taking performance enhancing drugs. With the modernization of the UFC and the increasing controls put in place by athletic commissions to prevent fighters from cheating, fighters are more likely to get caught now than ever before. Despite some fighters "cycling" onto drugs during their offseason and then stopping far enough in advance of drug tests to be clean, fighters still get caught. The more fighters get caught and suspended for cheating, the less likely other fighters may be to try to beat the system. Or perhaps more insidiously, fighters popped for drugs will serve as a lesson to others on what not to do. Either way, the rash of suspensions and overturned fights since 2011 is not surprisingly coincident with the rise in popularity of the sport, but should also subside with time as the system stabilizes and regulatory policies mature enough to close potential loopholes.

These trends are consistent with the nature of a growing sport. As the stakes of the game (financial and otherwise) continuously rise into the lucrative range, the willingness of fighters to absorb an illegal strike and continue to compete may be falling, while the incentive to get a small pharmaceutical edge may be increasing. This makes sense from a scientific standpoint, consistent with what behavioral psychologists call "loss aversion." The greater the stakes, the more intimidating potential loss looms and the more we want to avoid it. Continuing to fight after an eye poke is a risky proposition that could cost a fighter a deserving win, or even a title shot. Under the current rules of MMA the fight cannot be stopped for long after an eye poke, meaning the fighter must either choose to continue while potentially impaired, or accept a No Contest decision and draw the ire of fans. Only when the fight is already beyond the halfway point of rounds (completed two of a three-round fight, or three of a five-round fight) will an injury stoppage result in a judges' decision where there can be a winner and loser. These "technical decisions" are rare, but notably several have occurred in recent history. In fact, at UFC 159 there were two technical decisions in the same night resulting from eye poke injuries in the final rounds of each fight. In both cases the fighter who received the injury ended up losing the decision. Many other times, however, fights were still in the first two rounds and so eye pokes led to No Contests.

Are fighters using illegal strikes more frequently, or are fights simply ending more often when they do? While it's a little early to judge, the data suggests that No Contest rates are on the rise, and there's reason to believe the pattern is real. Expect to see this phenomenon continue until the eye poke rule is amended to allow fighters time to recover before continuing, and the UFC implements more pervasive drug testing policies that more effectively prevent fighters from attempting to skirt the rules.

Now we're warmed up. We've seen that we can test the most basic underlying assumptions about the sport, and we've also seen that a little analysis can reveal interesting trends that warrant attention. Now let's move on to something more obvious and interesting: how do fights end?

How UFC Fights End (Take 1)

To observers new to MMA, and even for many avid fans, the question of how fights end often arises. According to our prior stats, between 98% and 99% of fights will have a winner and a loser. So the next level of detail should be determining how fights are won and lost. Fights can end by submission, by referee stoppage due to strikes (KO or TKO), by judges' decision, or by the aforementioned injury stoppage/ No Contest. At a glance we can give this nugget of truth: fights are more likely to end by decision than by any other method. Here is how all UFC fights have ended since its inception in 1993 through April of 2013, a data set containing over 2,000 fights in total.

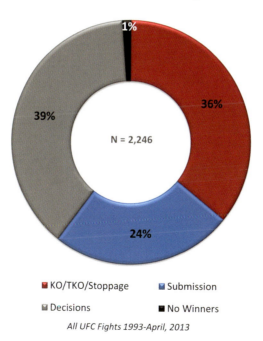

Fightnomics: How UFC Fights End

All UFC Fights 1993-April, 2013

At first blush we see that the gray section of the graph representing decisions has the largest number at 39%. But if we combine the methods of stoppage for KO/ TKO and submissions we get 60%, meaning that most fights UFC are "finished" by one victorious competitor rather than going to the judges' scorecards. This is why properly defining things is important even when we ask a seemingly simple question.

The data also shows that more often than not fights that are finished end by KO or TKO rather than submission. These are very basic metrics for understanding and appreciating MMA, but there's a wrinkle in this storyline. The history of UFC may not be long compared to most major league sports, but it's long enough that the game has evolved significantly from its earliest contests. It's no longer a bar brawl and is in fact a complicated sport no matter what anyone says. When UFC fights first aired in 1993 there were very few rules. Back then all fights had a winner and loser, every fight was "finished," and there were no judges or time limits. Fights were fought until someone won, and that usually didn't take long.

But as with any new and chaotic experiment, the results quickly led to changes in the rules. Time limits were introduced in the beginning of 1995, with judges added by the end of that same year. Instantly there were new possible outcomes to fights, but the evolution didn't stop there. In those early years of "Ultimate Fighting" most fights ended by submission. This was a testament to the efficacy of creating the competition in the first place, which was to showcase the Gracie school's Brazilian Jiu-Jitsu by testing it against all other styles. But to lump in the early days of the UFC with modern-day assessments of the evolved sport of mixed martial arts would be misleading.

Any aggregated statistic for all UFC fights would be skewed to represent more modern and recent fights. Keep in mind that before 2006 there were never more than 100 total UFC fights in a single calendar year. In 2012 there were 341! Each fight as a data point represented a larger share of the whole during the early years. But the number of UFC fights from 2010 through the end of 2013 will roughly equal all prior UFC fights in the sixteen years from its inception through 2009. That's how modern the database for the sport really is. Four years of data surpassing the volume of the preceding sixteen years is an astounding reflection of the rapid recent growth of the promotion. But despite that modern bias in the data, the UFC was a different enough battleground in its early years that the high level stats on finish rates can be deceptive. The first chart would lead us to believe that 60% of fights are finished. Is that still the case now? Let's take a more comprehensive approach to answering the question of how fights end.

How UFC Fights End (Take 2)

When we add time as a variable, the historical data isn't so one-dimensional and useful patterns take shape. Here's the same fight ending data, but now with the new variable of "year" added to the chart so we now have fight outcomes summarized annually.

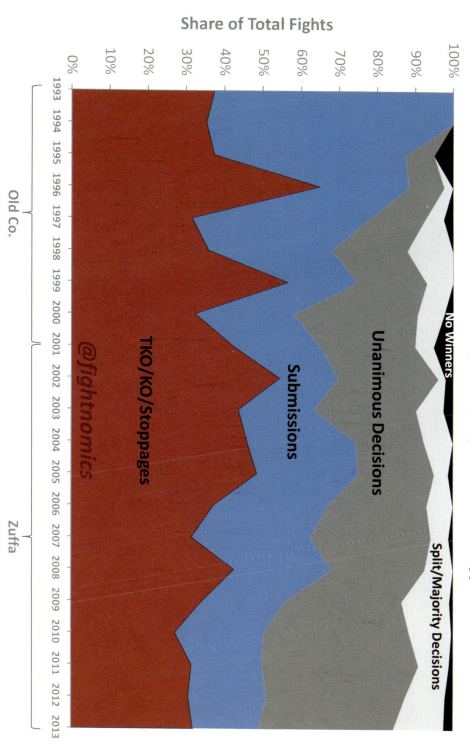

Annual UFC Fights by Fight Outcome Type

Share of Total Fights

TKO/KO/Stoppages

Submissions

Unanimous Decisions

No Winners

Split/Majority Decisions

@fightnomics

Old Co.

Zuffa

We can see patterns emerging, including recent trends that contradict analysis of all historical data taken in aggregate. First, you can easily see the introduction of rule changes to the sport. Draws are included in the black "No Winners" category and only started after time limits were first introduced in 1995. When time limits were implemented without the addition of judges, any fight lasting thirty minutes was declared a draw. By the end of the year judges were brought in to decide the winners after fights reached the time limit, although a very large majority of fights never reached that point. Nearly 90% of fights ended quickly, painfully, and most frequently by submission. MMA was still defining itself and submission grapplers reigned supreme while the rest of the world tried to catch up.

As the Gracie challenge spurred better training in submission defense and combat styles began to meld together in the melting pot of Mixed Martial Arts, the sport and the athletes within it quickly matured. Whether you prefer J. F. C. Fuller's "Constant Tactical Factor," Newton's Third Law of Motion, or simply the laws of efficient markets, the idea that advantages in any system will be met by a countering force is universal. The result of these forces at work in the UFC was that fights were more evenly matched stylistically, with fewer fighters being completely caught off guard by basic submission techniques. The era of one-dimensional fighters concluded, and the share of fights ending by submission plummeted from 63% in 1993 to just 25% in 1999. That submission rate then bounced between 20%-30% over the next decade, before another drop in the most recent years of competition. By neutralizing the submission imbalance, savvy fighters were able to work "ground and pound," use wrestling to control opponents, or more adeptly keep fights standing to use striking more effectively.

The striking game has also seen its ups and downs. What became the most common way to end a fight around the time that Zuffa took over the UFC probably fueled the rapid ascent of its popularity during the mid-2000's. These were the glory days of sluggers like "The Iceman" Chuck Liddell and "The Pit Bull" Andrei Arlovski, when every pay-per-view promised the sort of one-punch unconsciousness that most boxing fans had never seen before. At the modern day peak in 2005, finishes by KO or TKO represented 49% of all fights, which was also the time when Zuffa launched their "Ultimate Knockouts" series of highlight reel finishes. Since then, however, striking finishes like submissions before them have declined as fighter skill levels have reached greater parity. In recent years the share of finishes via strikes has plateaued at just under one third of all UFC fights.

Since 2005 the UFC has consistently increased the number of fights competed in the Octagon year over year, and in the most recent years we are finally seeing signs of stability in the system. Despite the introduction of smaller weight classes, the finish rate in the UFC has stabilized around 50%. So basically, half of all modern UFC fights end inside the distance, and half go to decision. Buried within those rough totals are the ~1% that result in a No Contest or overturned decision due to various rare circumstances or infractions.

So now you know that half of all fights on today's Octagon are finished early, but we're just getting started. There is still an ocean of numbers to navigate on our way to the new world of enlightenment. We'll return to the idea of finish rates and the patterns within them later in the book. Let's now turn our attention to the stats that allow us to look inside each fight in surprising detail, not just at the level of fight outcomes, but each and every action that occurs within each and every round.

The FightMetric System

In 2007 Rami Genauer watched a UFC event and then asked a simple question: where are the statistics for professional MMA? The writer from Washington DC initially scratched the itch of intellectual curiosity in an attempt to answer that question. He wanted statistics that could determine decisively who really won a fight when there was a controversial decision. Or at least, he wanted a way to objectively look back at fights to analyze how fighters performed. Numbers, he thought, could help tell the story of how a fight went down, and he launched FightMetric to fill that void in MMA.

Though FightMetric's success relies on a variety of technical solutions, it began simply as a whiteboard break down for everything that happens in a fight. Their mission was to measure every fighter's performance and effectiveness inside the cage, and to do this they needed a data architecture that every MMA fight could fit into. It needed to be simple, yet robust. It had to capture everything that could happen in a fight, but also be boiled down to simple metrics of fighter performance. It would be the first of its kind: a comprehensive sports data framework built from the top down, rather than built up and evolved slowly over time as in other major sports.

My own foray into the world of MMA analytics began with the FightMetric system. In 2009 the company had just finished quantifying every fight to date in UFC history, and then put out a call for Research Fellows to help crunch the numbers. As one of the first batch of analysts to gain access to the dataset for the purpose of general research, I knew that understanding its structure was a necessary first step before diving through to test ideas. As a professional management consultant I dealt with data analysis all the time, almost always trying to answer a question that hadn't been answered before. Getting to do the same thing for sports became my weekend hobby.

Organization of FightMetric Data

FightMetric data is organized in a hierarchical fashion, and I've created a graphical view (with their permission) in an attempt to capture that structure for reference. We'll start with striking. All strikes that have ever been thrown in the UFC – even the illegal ones – have been recorded. These strikes actually fall into 36 different categories within the FightMetric system depending on Position, Target, Strength and Success, with the position of the strike recorded based on the targeted fighter, not the striker. It's important to address each of these to avoid confusion as this data will become the playground for a variety of future experiments, in this book and beyond. Any serious MMA fan will benefit from understanding this data, and will no doubt be better equipped for the debates that rage on message boards throughout the MMA world.

We start with position because before a fighter can throw any strike, he must first have access to his opponent. But that access may come from a variety of positions. Unlike in boxing, MMA fighters can work from a clinch position, or even while on the ground, in addition to the standard boxing stance where fighters are standing and separated. According to the FightMetric system "Distance" means that two fighters are standing at a distance appropriate for striking, but not so close as to be holding onto each other as in the Clinch position. Once one of the fighters is on the ground, they are both technically in the Ground position. In most fights, fighters will assume each of these basic positions at some point, and every fight must start in the distance position initially.

To understand the analysis that will be presented in detail here we have to connect the dots between a strike thrown in the cage, and the data that shows up in the database. The hierarchy of data organization is the same for strikes in all positions, where the next level of classification beyond fighter position is the target. For simplicity all targets fall into the head, body or leg categories. It's not perfect, but it's good enough and keeps the system smaller than if we added every conceivable target on the body. Based just on position and target, we now have nine different groups of strikes, accounting for head, body and leg strikes from the distance, clinch and ground positions. But there are two more levels of classification that make a huge difference in understanding how fights are fought.

FightMetric Data

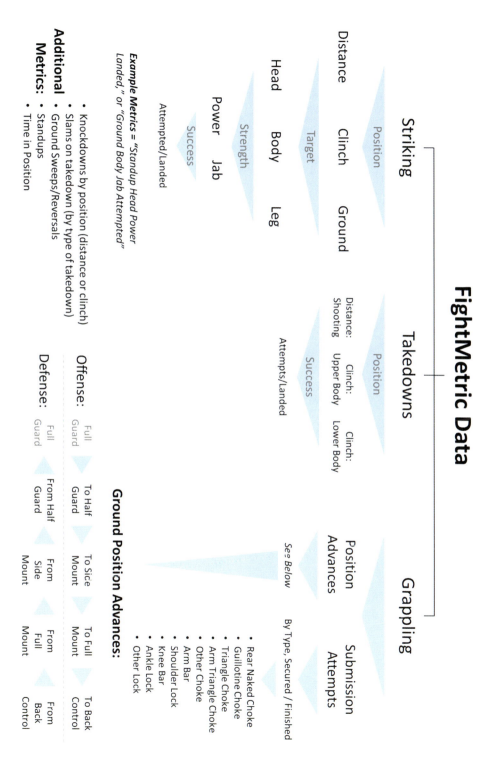

Striking

Position
- Distance
- Clinch
- Ground

Target
- Head
- Body
- Leg

Strength
- Power
- Jab

Success
- Attempted/Landed

Example Metrics = "Standup Head Power Landed," or "Ground Body Jab Attempted"

Takedowns

Position
- Distance: Shooting
- Clinch: Upper Body
- Clinch: Lower Body

Success
- Attempts/Landed

Grappling

Position Advances
- See Below

Submission Attempts
- By Type, Secured / Finished
  - Rear Naked Choke
  - Guillotine Choke
  - Triangle Choke
  - Arm Triangle Choke
  - Other Choke
  - Arm Bar
  - Shoulder Lock
  - Knee Bar
  - Ankle Lock
  - Other Lock

Ground Position Advances:

Offense:

| Full Guard | To Half Guard | To Side Mount | To Full Mount | To Back Control |

Defense:

| Full Guard | From Half Guard | From Side Mount | From Full Mount | From Back Control |

Additional Metrics:
- Knockdowns by position (distance or clinch)
- Slams on takedown (by type of takedown)
- Ground Sweeps/Reversals
- Standups
- Time in Position

41

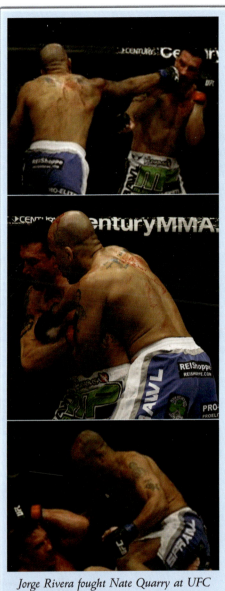

Jorge Rivera fought Nate Quarry at UFC Fight Night 21 in 2010 in Charlotte, NC. Rivera landed strikes from a distance, in the clinch, and on the ground on his way to a second round TKO. After the fight Quarry underwent surgical facial reconstruction and retired from MMA. Photos by Kelly Crigger.

Towards the bottom of vertical sequence of the data hierarchy describing striking is where things get tricky. When a striker is in a position and aiming at a target, FightMetric then assesses the amount of power being used in the strike. In this sense "jabs" are lighter strikes, while "power" strikes are obviously more powerful. This is a subjective interpretation, but one of very few in the system. When it comes to punching for example, jabs are not just strikes with the lead hand, and power strikes cover more than punches with the rear, usually dominant hand. A hook with a lead hand could be counted as a power strike, and some softer strikes with the dominant power hand could be counted as jabs if they aren't thrown with force. The gentle "pawing" motion that some fighters use as they measure distance to their opponent is not counted as a strike at all. Confusing? Of course it is. That's why we need people like FightMetric to keep it all straight and account for everything.

Note that strikes come in a variety of flavors, which technically are irrelevant in the FightMetric system. Whether it was an elbow, a knee, a fist, or a foot that smashes into the head of a target, it doesn't matter or get counted differently in the database. The system is focused on measuring the output of fighters and their effectiveness in a given fight, not on studying stylistic nuances. For the purposes of deeper analysis this is in some ways regrettable, but it is also understandable given the multiplier effect accounting for different types of strikes would have on the size of the database. Analysis has its limits, and so do I.

The last level of classification for striking is simply whether or not the strike landed on target. This too may seem fairly subjective considering that blocked strikes can still do damage (see Rich Franklin's arm in the Chuck Liddell fight), but again the team at FightMetric processes their data very carefully, and they watch all fights in slow motion to ensure data is recorded accurately. Each flurry of strikes during frenzied exchanges may seem like a blur to the fan (and unfortunately, also the judges), but slowed down these strikes come into much greater clarity. It's like watching a slow motion instant replay but for entire fights. One FightMetric legend is that it took 90 minutes to fully record data for the championship fight between Dominick Cruz and Demetrious Johnson because there was so much action during the 25-minute fight. Clearly, the data has a good deal of precision.

Striking is surely easier to grasp for most fight fans, but grappling is the glaring difference between MMA and boxing, and also probably the least understood aspect of the sport among the most casual observers. Again, we'll use the chart as a guide and walk down the levels of classification to understand how we get fight statistics from the ground game, and we'll begin by figuring out how fights end up on the ground in the first place.

Takedowns

Takedowns are easy to recognize as a technique of traditional wrestling, but in the MMA the cage itself can play a role in takedowns that is absent on open mats. According to our FightMetric data chart, takedowns are first differentiated by position. Shooting takedowns are all takedowns that occur from a distance (standing apart) position. But from a clinch position takedowns can either be Upper Body or Lower Body focused. The differentiating factor in clinch takedowns is how the offensive fighter creates the imbalance that causes the takedowns. If the takedown is executed by grabbing or tripping the legs, it's a lower body takedown, and if a fighter grasps above the waist of his opponent to drag or "suplex" him to the mat, then it's an upper body takedown. **So these are the three basic types of takedowns: Shooting, Clinch Lower Body, and Clinch Upper Body.**

All these takedowns are then recorded by success or failure for the offensive fighter. Dividing landed takedowns by the number of total attempts gives the takedown success rate, and although not recorded directly, takedown "defense" can be easily calculated by analyzing the attempts and success of a fighter's past opponents. The most basic insights that are gleaned from these metrics help quantify how frequently fighters attempt takedowns, how successful they are when they do, and how they deal with their opponents who attempt them as well. Greater insight is added by accounting for the different types of takedowns.

Down in the additional metrics I've also listed "Slams on Takedown," which are relevant to each of the three takedown categories. Whenever a takedown is completed, a separate assessment is made as to whether or not the offensive fighter slammed his opponent to the ground with force above and beyond a normal takedown. This is useful when looking back to understand how and why a takedown could have ended a fight, as with Gray Maynard and Rob Emerson in their unfortunate No Contest, or the welterweight title winning "power bomb" performed by Matt Hughes against Carlos Newton at UFC 34. Slams demonstrate greater control by the offensive fighter, do more damage on the recipient fighter, and may even impact the judges by creating the appearance of a more violently successful technique.

On the Ground

Whether it was a successful takedown that lands fighters on the mat, the rarer knockdown by strikes, or simply a fighter pulling guard by dropping to his butt, once they are grounded there are more variables that come into play. Again, we'll start with position and we'll follow a hypothetical fighter in top control working his way through various advances. The most common ground position is that of Full Guard. This occurs when the fighter in top position is between the legs of the fighter on the bottom. From a grappling and jiu-jitsu standpoint, we'll consider this the beginning of the offensive cycle of positions for the advancing fighter. From the full guard the offensive fighter (on top) has few options related to submissions, and is at risk for submission attempts from the fighter on his back. But striking is still possible and many fighters are able to use "ground and pound" to beat up their opponents at close range from guard.

Greg Jackson has a fighter in his guard. This is the "full guard" position.
Photo by Kelly Crigger, Victory Belt Publishing.

If the fighter is able to advance position past one leg of the defending fighter, he is said to be in Half Guard. Attacking from half guard opens up more potential submissions, and allows the controlling fighter great striking flexibility. It also negates some of the defensive capabilities of the fighter on his back. Working ground and pound from half guard is a common and relatively low risk game plan to cause damage, and win rounds.

Julie Kedzie is in Greg Jackson's "half guard."
Photo by Kelly Crigger, Victory Belt Publishing.

Advancing to Side Control requires freeing the last captured leg and putting the attacker's full weight on the torso of the grounded opponent. Side control offers additional submission and striking potential and is considered a dominant position, which is why it's also sometimes called "side mount." In some cases fighters use a free leg to trap the near arm of their opponent on the bottom, while using a hand to control the opponent's other arm. This results in the dreaded "crucifix" position that typically leads to the top fighter raining down elbows onto the head of the grounded opponent. Side control is also one potential launching point for submissions like the kimura, and also the increasingly popular arm triangle choke.

Greg Jackson demonstrates side control, or "side mount." Photo by Kelly Crigger, Victory Belt Publishing.

If a fighter straddles the torso if his opponent then he has achieved the "first and goal" of grappling positions, the Full Mount. It's inevitable at this time an announcer point out with increasing urgency that will that the bottom fighter is in a really bad spot. From the full mount, the top fighter has a great deal of power in controlling the fight. While maintaining the position throughout the inevitable bucking of the bottom fighter takes strength and skill, most high level fighters will do a lot of damage from a full mount. Strikes from this position have greater force due to the separation of the fighters (which allows the top fighter to generate higher velocity strikes) and clear access to the bottom fighter's head. The bottom fighter no longer has his legs to help defend or even attack. Fighters holding a full mount will typically attempt to pummel their opponents in a volley of punches until the referee stops the fight. Oftentimes grounded fighters panic to get away from the barrage and turn over, thus "giving up their back."

Greg Jackson demonstrates the full mount position. Photo by Kelly Crigger, Victory Belt Publishing.

The last ground position is back control. A fighter in mount who has his opponent turn underneath him can often keep his legs locked around the waist of the rotating opponent and use his arms to grasp the body. But fighters in a scramble can also attain the position, sometimes even while standing. Regardless of how it's achieved, back control means a lot of power for the controlling fighter. The main reason is the ease of access of securing a fight-ending rear naked choke. That submission (as we'll see later) has the highest success rate of any submission type, but to lock that choke the fighter first has to secure this hard-to-reach position. It's difficult to escape from, and even if the defending fighter avoids a rear naked choke attempt there will likely be another, and another, until it is successful. Many fighters locked in this position have to resign themselves to losing the round with no way to escape or mount an attack, focusing entirely on defending submission attempts and head punches until the round expires and they can survive for a fresh start in the next one.

Greg Jackson gets the back control position, also referred to a "taking the back." Photo by Kelly Crigger, Victory Belt Publishing.

In the FightMetric system each of these positions is accounted for separately. Any fighter achieving any ground position beyond full guard will have a data point credited to his round. Any fighter on the defense who escapes out of a position beyond full guard is also credited. In the data these variables are described as "advancing to" and "advancing from" a position.

For example, imagine if a fighter in full guard passes into half guard, then passes to side control, but the defending fighter then escapes to his feet. The two fighters scramble and have now returned to a "distance" standing position. The data will reflect that the top control fighter achieved two positions, "advance to half guard" and "advance to side control." The bottom fighter has tallied an "advance from side control" metric, as well as a "standup." "Sweeps" are recorded when any fighter who is in a non-dominant position reverses ground position on his opponent. These numbers are counted for each fighter per round, such that some fighters may achieve a certain position multiple times in a given round.

All this data helps us understand how fighters fight on the ground. Each offensive position advance counts as a "pass" in the FightMetric box score for any given fight shown on their website. While striking stats on the ground are included in aggregate with strikes thrown in other positions, ground passes demonstrate which fighters were more active and in control of the ground game.

In addition to strikes on the ground as we've already described, there's also arguably the most important aspect of ground fighting: submissions. In additions to stoppage by strikes, submissions are the other way to end a fight early. Whether a submission hold causes a fighter to tap (literally or just verbally) or a referee jumps in to save a trapped, injured or unconscious fighter, submissions really are what differentiates MMA from the better known combat sports, and they can end a fight just as spectacularly as a knockout. Such is the complexity of the crazy sport of human chess that is MMA.

While the total list of submission holds would be too long to describe here, FightMetric has a reasonable system for accounting for the most common types. Even the most casual MMA fans will immediately recognize the iconic arm bar or guillotine choke, but there's a lot more to the submission game than these industry standards. In FightMetric terms, all submission attempts must fall into one of the following categories (sorry, Calf Crusher, you're in "Other locks"):

- Rear Naked Choke
- Guillotine Choke
- Triangle Choke
- Arm Triangle Choke
- Other Choke

- Arm Bar
- Shoulder Lock
- Knee Bar
- Ankle Lock
- Other Lock

While this list may leave off some your favorites (like the spectacular Twister submission or the D'Arce choke) it accounts for the majority of submissions successfully completed in the UFC. Those not named explicitly fall into one of the "Other" categories depending on what particular body part the choke or lock targets. It doesn't matter what position a fighter is in when he attempts a submission, but any time a technique is fully administered, FightMetric accounts for the attempt in the fighter's round-by-round data. When a fight ends by submission, the method is also documented. For rare submissions, the name of the technique will be listed in special fight notes. Using all this data will allow us to explore which submission attempts are most commonly attempted, and the relative success rates of each kind.

On average there are one or two submission attempts per fight in the UFC, with an overall success rate of 20%. That means of all submissions attempted, one in five will end a fight. But not all submissions are created equal, and some of the most commonly attempted submissions are actually quite unsuccessful. For those patterns, and a few more that are even more intricate, check out Chapter 4.

This data can all be tied together. This is the FightMetric Box Score for the first fight between Carlos Condit and Martin Kampmann at UFC Fight Night 21. The result of the fight was a close split decision victory for Kampmann, but what else do the numbers tell us?

Fighter	Knock Downs	Significant Strikes	Sig. Str. %	Total Strikes	Take Downs	Take Down %	Submission Attempts	Ground Advances	Ground Reversals
Kampmann	0	26 of 61	43%	52 of 91	5 of 5	100%	6	3	2
Condit	0	35 of 86	41%	71 of 124	3 of 4	75%	3	4	0

At a glance, Condit was the more active striker, attempting and landing more total and "Significant Strikes." We'll explain Significant Strikes in more detail in the next chapter, but suffice to say those are the strikes that are capable of doing damage and affecting the outcome of a fight. Condit outworked Kampmann by more than 30%, and with similar accuracy as his opponent, landed a correspondingly greater number of strikes. Both fighters landed takedowns, and both were active in advancing position and attempting submissions on the ground. Given the overall close stat line, perhaps it is surprising then that the fighter who landed a lot more strikes and was more active overall ended up losing. Perhaps. But the picture becomes clearer when we consider position.

Don't Forget the TIP

A set of data not shared in the FightMetric box score is "Time in Position," or "TIP." TIP data only gets a passing mention on the data organization chart, but this metric equates to so much data that it already exceeds limits of processing using standard Microsoft Excel, despite only having been recorded for UFC events going back a few years. This data records each fighter's position down to the fraction of a second, differentiated by position and control everywhere in the Octagon. Fighters in a distance position require no other descriptors, but for fighters in the clinch, the fighter with outside control is designated as being in a "controlling" position. Fighters may also be "neutral" if neither has an advantage or if they are in transition or scrambling.

Similarly, fighters on top on the ground are considered controlling, and they can assume any of the positions on the chart from full guard, to half guard, to side control, to mount or back control, as well as neutral positions as in a scramble or when standing away from their grounded opponent. There is also a miscellaneous position for ground position in which the fighters are disengaged, as when one fighter is grounded and the other is still standing up. All this means we can look to see which fighters tend to be in top control more often, for example, or which fighters tend to fight from guard or are especially adept at maintaining side control. We'll break down how much time is spent in each position and other TIP patterns in the chapter "Assume the Position" later in this book.

Returning to the question of Condit versus Kampmann 1, let's add in the additional insight of TIP data to better understand what happened in that fight. The next chart shows the same FightMetric Box Score data with the addition of TIP, all in a graphical format.

What's now clear is that in a fight that spent two thirds of the time on the ground, Kampmann had control for the vast majority of that time. In an otherwise close fight, it seems this ground control was the difference. Kampmann landed five takedowns, but also swept for dominant position twice when Condit landed takedowns. So TIP data is a useful clue beyond the more discrete data metrics of strikes, takedowns and submission attempts. It's also interesting from a strategic perspective that in a rematch, Condit used improved takedown defense to keep the fight mostly standing, and superior striking combinations to eventually finish Kampmann by TKO, thus eliminating any doubt in their rivalry.

We've covered a lot of the basics here, and now we understand the variables used to analyze MMA in greater detail. The FightMetric system is intended to be mutually exclusive and selectively exhaustive ("MESE"). It captures everything that occurs during a fight and tries to categorize and prioritize what's most important. Even illegal strikes are tallied: an inside leg kick that strays too high to the groin would still be classified as a "landed distance leg jab," and an illegal elbow to the back of the head is still counted regardless of whether it drew a referee penalty. During the early years of head butts and hair pulls the job of the FightMetric analyst was far more confusing than today, but still the system was able to handle whatever the fighters threw at them (or, more accurately, at each other).

The dangers of subjectivity in the strength classifications (jab vs. power strike) is offset by the protocols FightMetric has put in place to quantify fights. Classifications are done consistently through all fights according to the same rules and thresholds they set in defining each category. This may fall into the bucket of "take their word

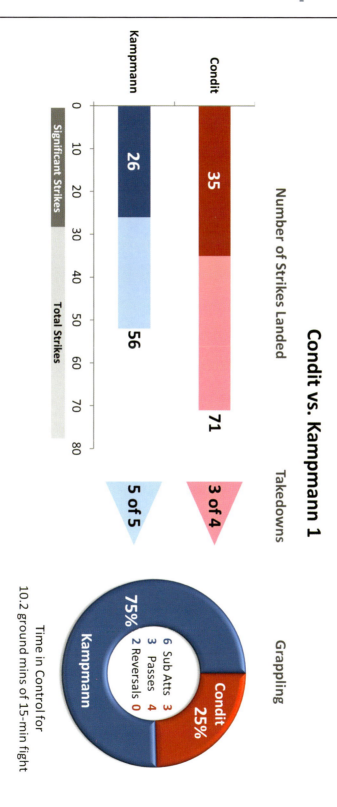

Condit vs. Kampmann 1

Number of Strikes Landed

Significant Strikes | Total Strikes

Condit — 35 — 71
Kampmann — 26 — 56

Takedowns

Condit 3 of 4
Kampmann 5 of 5

Grappling

Kampmann 75%
Condit 25%

6 Sub Atts 3
3 Passes 4
2 Reversals 0

Time in Control for
10.2 ground mins of 15-min fight

51

for it," but given the comprehensive structure of the data set, the robustness of their system, and the intelligence and experience that went into quantifying historical UFC fights in such excruciating detail (plus many other fights), we have to permit some faith that the data has been recorded accurately. Lastly, as someone who has worked with a lot of data and knows that small errors are inevitable in any large dataset, I also recognize that small errors will fall into the noise of most big picture analysis we'll run here and we'll avoid making drawing conclusions from small sample sizes.

Now that we have this detailed framework for accounting for MMA activity we can dive much deeper into striking data and see what we can learn about the standup game, as well as everywhere else strikes are thrown.

End Notes:

1. For an excellent read on statistics in mainstream sports, including the myth of the hot hand and 4th down risk aversion, check out "Scorecasting" by Tobias Moskowitz and John Wertheim, Three Rivers Press, 2011.

2. Technically, no biting or eye gouging was allowed, but otherwise it looked like no-holds-barred fighting. Groin strikes and even hair pulling was legal and was actually used during several UFC fights.

Food for Thought

Everyone has a plan until they've been hit.

Boxer Joe Louis

3 Advanced MMA Stats: The Standup Game

Now that we understand the variables that we have at our disposal in analyzing MMA fights, we can get a better understanding of how fights really go down by looking at what patterns these variables form. How do fighters tend to operate during a fight according to these variables? What's common, what's average, and what's rare? What's at the heart of these differences? Let's start – as all fights do – with standup striking.

Position-Target-Strength-Success

The "Distance" striking position is actually where fighters spend the majority of their time in the Octagon, and I will sometimes refer to it as "standup" here. When the fight begins, and for as long as it remains in a distance position, "position" itself is pretty straightforward. The statistics don't differentiate any further with a designation of control while fighters are in this position. Understanding the basic targets and success rates of various strikes from this position is then a good place to start our analysis of how striking really works. Strikes for any position are categorized by target, strength, and success, and in this chapter we're going to focus exclusively on distance striking.

Target

Let's start with target. Imagine two fighters squaring off, standing at a distance from one another. They briefly touch gloves and are now about to trade the first blows of the fight. The stance is their base that they always return to when not engaged and is an easily recognizable fighting position. The distance stance is generally facing forward, but with the hips rotated towards their (likely) dominant side. Like boxing, kickboxing, karate, or a number of other striking styles, fighters in the distance position must first decide on a target to attack. Where will they aim their strikes?

The easy answer is that all fighters are "Headhunters." About four of every five strikes thrown from a distance are aimed at the head. This includes jabs and power strikes, as well as all kinds of strikes regardless of the weapon of choice:

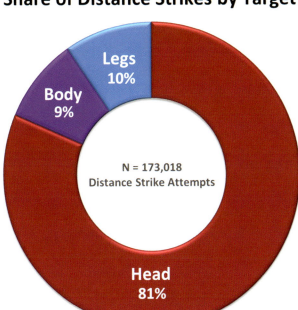

Share of Distance Strikes by Target

Legs 10%

Body 9%

N = 173,018
Distance Strike Attempts

Head 81%

All UFC Fights 2007-April, 2013

fist, foot, elbow, knee, or shin. The head really is the most important asset of the body, so it's no surprise that when fighters attack they prioritize this most precious target of opportunity. As the most valuable part of the body, the head is also the most passionately defended part. Not only is the head a valuable target, it's the smallest target compared to the torso or the legs, and the easiest to move suddenly. For these reasons, fighters train to move his head to avoid strikes aimed at it while counterstriking his opponent's head. It's the old boxing maxim: "hit without being hit." Otherwise, he likely wouldn't last long in this unforgiving sport.

Strength

The days of swinging for the fences like a bar brawler and hoping for a KO are over. Power shots have to be set up and the best way to do that is with a jab. The jab is a very versatile strike that can be used in both the offense and defense. By definition, a jab has less distance to travel to a target as it's normally thrown with a lead hand from the normal fighting stance. Because of this distance differential, jabs should be more accurate than power strikes simply due to defenders having less time to react to them. However, jabs are not power shots but instead are very effective at setting up the power hand, the classic "one-two" of a jab-cross combination. Fighters on defense may be more willing to absorb an initial jab strike, with the focus of their concentration on avoiding the secondary power strike.

A setup jab is usually thrown with the intent to set up a second, more powerful strike. In a sense, fighters may use a jab as a "spotting round" the same way artillery first drops a round to ensure proper range. Strategically, jabs may not be intended to do the real damage, but in this case would be used to ensure the opponent is within range or even to occupy the opponent's defenses while the more damaging strike is launched. For these reasons we might expect the accuracy of jabs to be lower rather than higher than power strikes. There's a lot of subtlety at work in striking that depends on the style and strategy of a certain fighter and his opponent that the aggregate stats don't capture. For example a fighter might throw a "pawing" jab that is just intended to disrupt his opponent's attack. These are counted as jabs, but they're not thrown with any intent to do damage or even strike an intended target. We'll look deeper into striking accuracy in a bit to try to answer some of these exact questions. What's important here is that jabs and power strikes are accounted for separately, and therefore can be analyzed separately as well.

The *landed distance power head strike* has a clunky name, but represents one of the single most important raw data metrics in the entire striking hierarchy. The numbers in this category represent the most devastating blows that are administered

Southpaw Diego Sanchez unloads a big left on Joe Stevenson. Photo by Martin McNeil.

inside the Octagon. The most common power head strike is undoubtedly the punch, though the data doesn't differentiate what's used to strike any given target. Traditional straights, crosses, and uppercuts, as well as head kicks and various spinning attacks can all be counted as a distance power head strike. When successful, these strikes are a big determinant in understanding who wins fights. When divided by distance power head attempts, the result tells us the accuracy of strikers with their most lethal weapon, and comparison among peers reveals who truly is a dangerous striker. When we examine how frequently knockdowns occur per landed power head strike, we'll be able to spot the punch-for-punch most powerful knockout artists. All this begins with capturing these individual metrics, blow-by-blow, and converting them to their proper data category: position-target-strength-success.

So just how many jabs are attempted compared to power strikes? That depends on the first variable, the target. While in a distance standing position, fighters can aim at three different general targets. They can then throw shorter, less powerful strikes or may choose to swing for the fences. Let's see if the use of power varies by the choice of target.

Using numbers in a practical way (especially when betting) is all about finding patterns and when we look at the data this way we start to see them. First, the ratio of head strikes shows a nearly even mix of power strikes to jabs. Again this reflects

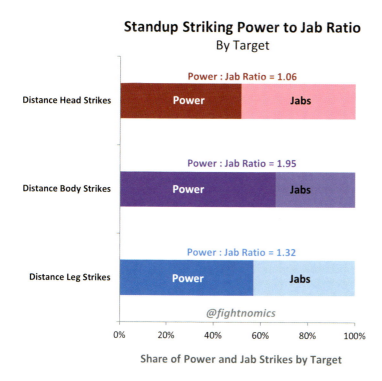

Standup Striking Power to Jab Ratio
By Target

Share of Power and Jab Strikes by Target

how easy head jabs are to throw, and how they may be used to gauge range, test an opponent's defensive strategy, or set up the entrance for a more powerful strike.

The even power ratio for head striking is the lowest of all targets and means jabs play a more important role in head striking than when attacking other targets. Jabs to the head are also low risk, since they don't expose the striker to takedowns the same way a kick to the body or legs might. Lastly, a straight jab to the head can still do damage, both physically and psychologically (like mosquitoes, jabs can be very annoying). Champion Georges St-Pierre punished Josh Koscheck with round after round of snappy jabs at UFC 124 that left the challenger with a broken orbital. Cuts and bruising due to a barrage of stiff jabs will certainly accumulate and demoralize an out-gunned or out-ranged fighter, but they will also influence the judges who are looking for which fighter is controlling the round. Plenty of rounds and even whole fights have been won thanks to an effective jab. For all of these reasons we should expect more jabs to be used when strikers are boxing their opponents out on the open mat.

The highest power strike ratio is for body strikes, which makes sense given that kicks to the body are rarely set up using lead leg "jabs" (unless you count Johnny from the Karate Kid who might sweep the leg first). Slow or weak body kicks in order to establish range would be easy to catch by the defender, and would offer little reward for a lot of risk. While punches can come in bunches, kicks are usually singular, or used along with other types of strikes as part of combinations. Body kicks whether they are classic "round house" style, the more exotic side kick, or even spinning back side kicks, are usually thrown spontaneously with the goal of landing squarely and doing damage. An example of a body jab would be a "push kick" or "teep" if you practice Muay Thai.

While body strikes occasionally comprise punches, this flavor of body shot is more commonly thrown at closer range in what is technically categorized as the clinch. For that reason we would expect the power ratio to be lower for body striking in the clinch, and indeed the data confirms that. While standing at a distance though, this high level look reveals that body kicks are thrown with bad intentions and lots of power about two thirds of the time.

Leg strikes sit in the middle of the power to jab ratio by target. Easier to employ than body strikes, and having lower risk and lower reward than head strikes, leg kicks have become a niche skill in MMA. Fighters routinely employ leg kicks, but typically in low volumes. They're the easiest way to draw first contact with your opponent, like the Field Goal of MMA. In the middle of the action landing one doesn't mean certain victory, but a lot of them can add up and make the difference in the end. In the case of Corey Hill a single leg kick caused him to tragically lose a fight via gruesome injury, but let's hope that's a unique circumstance.

Generally, fighters know that leg kicks will require power to be effective, but because leg kicks can come from either side of the attacker, and can target either leg of the opponent depending on whether it's an inside or outside leg kick, the variability means more kicks are simply thrown to maintain activity and gauge response. Kicks that fall into the jab category may also be used strategically to set up other, more dangerous kicks, but these strikes are infrequent. Many fighters have successfully landed a knockout head kick only after repeated leg kicks attacks that forced their opponents to lower their defensive focus. The stats reveal a middle of the road power to jab ratio for leg kicks. Multiplying the 10% volume of strikes thrown at the legs by the intermediary power ratio leaves us with only ~6% of total strikes that can do any real damage to the legs. This is lower than any other target, and makes legs the least likely target to end a fight, but we'll put that hypothesis to the test.

One last cut of the data from a historical perspective confirms the headhunting nature of the UFC fighter, but also gives us insight into what changes might be taking place inside the Octagon. Here are all standup striking attempts grouped by target selection over time.

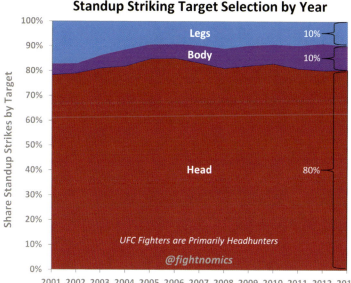

While the history of UFC striking has clearly focused on boxing tactics, there's an interesting slight downward trend in the share of strikes aimed at the head. Currently, there's an 80-10-10 percentage mix of head-body-leg strikes. Looking closer, this mix of shot selection has been changing slightly in recent years. What's interesting is that leg strikes were far more prominent in the very early days of the sport, accounting for nearly a fifth of all distance strikes. Body strikes back than were half as common as they are now.

Zooming in on the trend in the red area of head strikes reveals a negative slope. Slowly but surely since 2010, the share of strikes aimed at the head has been on the decline, and the tradeoff has been primarily with body strikes. From 2002-2007, the share of body strikes averaged only 6.1% of total strikes. Since 2008, that number has increased by about a half to 9.2%. In 2013 alone, body strikes account for 10% of all distance strikes, with some notable highlight reel finishes to help remind us. Think of Anthony "Showtime" Pettis's body kick finish of Donald Cerrone at UFC on Fox 2, or Chad Mendes's TKO of Cody McKenzie by punch to the body at UFC 148. The body shot may be on the rise, and fighters on the cutting edge of striking tactics like Pettis could be giving us sneak previews of what's to come as the UFC continues to evolve. This is yet another leading indicator in the data to keep an eye on, so the next time you see a body shot KO tell your buddy that it's the new "in" thing.

Accuracy

The definition of accuracy is simple – whether or not a strike landed on target. All strikes thrown at a given target on the body and at a certain strength count as "attempts," but only those that land on target increment the "landed" metric. Dividing landed strikes by attempted strikes gives us the accuracy. Finally. Like all other metrics, striking accuracy has its own set of patterns and benchmarks. Here's a simple graphic summarizing the average success rate for strikes from a distance based on their target and strength.

The clearest pattern in distance striking is that target, not power, is everything. For head and body strikes, jabs are slightly more accurate, while leg striking accuracy slightly favors more powerful kicks. More importantly, the accuracy of strikes is inversely correlated with the height of the target. Head strikes are least accurate, leg kicks are most accurate, and strikes to the body are in between, meaning **the higher you aim the less likely you are to land on target.**

However, the difference in success rates of striking (i.e., accuracy) is not much when comparing jabs to power strikes. This, of course, is

Average Distance (Standup) Striking Accuracy
By Target & Strength of Strike

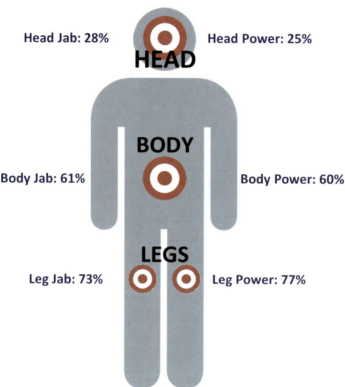

Head Jab: 28%   Head Power: 25%

HEAD

BODY

Body Jab: 61%   Body Power: 60%

LEGS

Leg Jab: 73%   Leg Power: 77%

consistent with how we described striking targets earlier and supports the overall finding that the head is harder to strike effectively for several reasons:

1. Fighters are most concerned about protecting their heads.
2. The head is also a smaller target than the rest of the body.
3. The head can be moved quickly out of the way of incoming strikes.
4. The head has more degrees of freedom in which to escape a strike.

It's not surprising that body and leg strikes are harder to avoid. When in a distance position most of these strikes are kicks. For leg kicks, the offensive fighter has the least amount of distance to cover to his target, and the recipient has the least amount of time to avoid the strike. The defending fighter is also reluctant to remove one of his support beams to avoid or "check" the attack to mitigate the damage done. The result is that most of the time leg kicks land with a "thwack" that can make an entire arena cringe. All of these factors together drive the huge difference in accuracy between head strikes and the rest of the body. They also suggest that the importance of position and target should not be overshadowed by the power of the strike. Therefore, we see that accuracy doesn't change much between jabs and power strikes for body and leg targeted strikes.

An interesting takeaway is that fighters could throw more power strikes to the head since they land with just almost as much success as their jabs. But that conclusion merits additional analysis into historical examples where fighters took that approach of just swinging for the fences.

Just to confirm the nature of the all-important "distance power head strike," we should examine how fighters perform in this metric as a group, and what that means for the metric itself. In analyzing fighters who competed in the UFC with at least 30 minutes of fight time, I've categorized them by their personal power head striking accuracy to date and then graphed the distribution of frequency for each accuracy score. The results tell us that distance head striking shows a roughly Normal distribution centered around a Mean of 25% and a Mode (most common score) of 24%.

The bell-like shape of the curve allows us to use this variable as a clear differentiator for assessing fighter skill in landing strikes. We have a true average (which doesn't

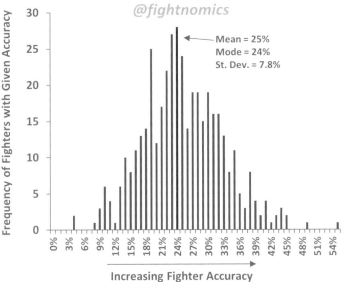

Distance Power Head Strike Accuracy
Frequency of UFC Fighters with Given Accuracy >30 mins. Fight Time

@fightnomics

Mean = 25%
Mode = 24%
St. Dev. = 7.8%

Frequency of Fighters with Given Accuracy

Increasing Fighter Accuracy

move if we change the duration filter, in case you're wondering), and we also have a standard deviation.

I won't go into the details of standard deviation and everything we can learn from this frequency distribution, but I will boil down a few key takeaways, and you'll have to trust my math. Think of a fighter's position on that chart with a certain accuracy score. Basically everyone to the left is "worse" and everyone to the right is "better" in terms of accuracy. If we want to know how good or bad relative to his peers a certain fighter is, we can use the standard deviation to help us. Given our Mean of 24% accuracy and the standard deviation of 7.8%, a little more than two-thirds of our UFC fighter population falls within +7.8% of the Mean.

If fighters have accuracy inside the range of roughly 16%-32%, then they are with the bulk majority of fighter skill sets. Moving outside that range is where we can really say that fighters are different from the others. Fighters with accuracy of less than 16% or more than 32% are in rare company. Each far side of the distribution beyond one standard deviation makes up about 16% of the population. That means strikers with 33% accuracy are better than 84% of all UFC fighters. Fighters with 15% accuracy are worse than 84% of all UFC strikers. If we go one more standard deviation out in each direction to fighters with accuracy of 9.6% or 40.6%, then we're truly getting the bottom of the barrel and the cream of the crop. Being two standard deviations away from the mean makes these fighters better or worse than a whopping 97% of the fighter population.

I'll use distance power head striking accuracy a lot as an indicator of a fighter's ability to connect with the most important strike of all 36 striking categories. Now at least we understand what's "normal," what's good, and what's bad. Looking back at the chart you'll see that the spread of bars to the right of the mean looks a little fuller than those to the left. That's a common characteristic when "zero" is close by, effectively creating a hard limit to scores on the left. The percentages aren't perfect, but as a rule of thumb they're still helpful. Contained inside the +1 standard deviation range is the majority of all UFC fighters, so whenever you see one who is outside that range, you can expect that there is something inherently different about his style, skill, or build (or perhaps several of these things) that sets him apart, for better or for worse.

We're not nearly finished though. Boxing is a critical skillset for MMA, and there's a lot of different ways to look at how head striking really plays out. We know that most strikes attempted while standing are to the head, and we've also seen that they land with a roughly one in four success rate, but what other patterns are there? Let's first consider who is throwing the strikes. For example, are bigger fighters slower and therefore less accurate? We can test that hypothesis by analyzing striking accuracy by weight class.

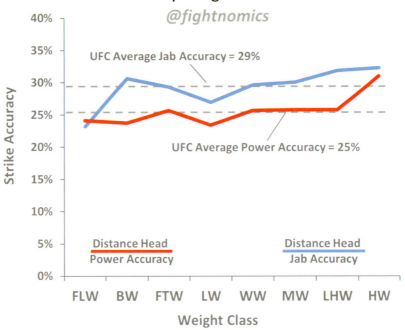

Distance Head Striking Accuracy
By Weight Class
@fightnomics

Interestingly, though larger fighters are probably slower and also have more distance to cover than small ones, it appears that for escalating sizes offense trumps defense. **Bigger fighters may be slower throwing a strike, but the defending fighter is even slower to react and evade the strike.** With all that body mass to move, heavyweights are like aircraft carriers that take 10 miles to turn. The numbers reveal that the big guys have the highest head striking accuracy of any weight class, regardless of whether they are throwing jabs or power strikes. There's a slight decrease in accuracy as the divisions get lighter, and presumably faster, and it's more pronounced with jabs.

Another pattern is also clear. Jabs are usually a little more accurate than power strikes. We already noted the proximity effect that could boost jab accuracy. It's quicker and easier to throw a jab without winding up or telegraphing the attempt. This gives the defensive fighter less time to react and avoid the strike, which leads to a higher overall success rate for jabs than power strikes. This pattern is not only true in aggregate, it holds true when isolated by individual weight classes. The only exception appears to be the smallest fighters, the Flyweights, who have nearly equal accuracy of jabs and power strikes, with jabs actually falling just short. Given that this weight class has the smallest sample size of the bunch, an interesting question is whether or not their metrics will normalize to be in line with the others, or remain differentiated even with a larger data set. The idea that smaller fighters might be more willing to "eat" a jab in order to focus on the next strike could also support this pattern. However, the notion that the jab may just be for effect and not intended to land doesn't seem to be the case.

Body Strikes

Fighters who attack the body or legs tend to land their strikes with much more success. The flipside is that these body and leg strikes generally require more repetitions to do damage. Perhaps the occasional devastating body kick can end a fight instantly, but these are rare (though spectacular) cases. Look up Cung Le's highlight reel for examples of fight-ending body kicks. Whether these strikes catch an opponent off-guard (and un-flexed) and knock the wind out of them, or whether they do real structural damage to the rib cage, body kicks that land can and do end fights. Bas Rutten popularized "the liver shot," which is just a normal punch (or knee or kick) to the body, but aimed at the right side of the defender's body. If you've ever been on the receiving end of a liver shot, you know that it hurts like crazy.

Though the mystique of Rutten's liver shot that ended numerous fights implies a magical reset button located on the right side of the body, the reality of this technique really lies in the anatomy of the human abdominal cavity. The peritoneum is a membrane encasing internal organs, including your liver. Flexible, but very sensitive, this membrane gets deformed during a body strike that penetrates the shield of muscles and bones protecting your core. As your largest internal organ, and also one that is not fully protected by the rib cage, the liver is indeed a likely source of pain during vicious body shots like the ones Rutten relentlessly dished out. As that sensitive membrane is suddenly impacted and temporarily deformed, your nervous system goes immediately into freak out mode. The effects of this shock to the system are instantaneous and potentially severe. The chain reaction of pain and an autonomic response leaves the victim feeling temporarily shut down, hunched in pain, unable to stand or even breathe. Bottom line, that's a bad day in the office if your office is a cage, so you don't want to experience this for yourself.

In recent history, Anthony Pettis TKO'd Donald Cerrone at UFC on FOX 6 in January of 2013 with a kick to the midsection (yes, specifically on Cerrone's right side). However, Russian-German fighter Denis Siver takes the cake for exotic body kick finishes. He has two TKO victories set up by spinning back kicks. This officially includes his Octagon debut at UFC 93 over Nate Mohr, but he unofficially did it again at UFC 105 against Paul Kelly (additional strikes were needed to seal the deal). Due to the rarity of a body blow finish, all three examples cited here won Knockout of the Night honors for their efforts, proving that the bonus award isn't just given to fighters who can alter the consciousness of their opponents with head strikes.

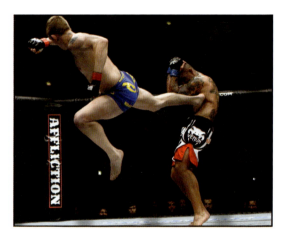

Alexander Gustafsson attacks the body of Thiago Silva in front of a Swedish crowd. Photo by Martin McNeil.

Leg Kicks

The last target area is the legs, which have yet another striking dynamic of their own. Leg kicks can be used to devastating effect. When it comes to the power ratio, we see that the share of power strikes falls somewhere in between the even mix for head strikes and the mostly powerful body strikes. When fighters employ leg kicks, they can throw them with either leg, and at different targets (inside versus outside, lead leg versus trail leg). Historically, the data shows that fighters throw powerful kicks in an approximate ratio of 4:3 compared to less powerful ones. Either way, leg kicks really must be used in high volume to make the difference in the fight.

Leg kicks alone can also win a fight by stoppage, but only do so in high volume. See the victories of Pat Barry over Dan Evensen and Matt Hughes over Renzo Gracie for classic examples. A TKO victory by leg strikes is an impressive and brutal feat, one that Pat Barry has actually accomplished three times in his professional MMA career. The most famous example of dangerous leg kicks is ironically not a fight that ended by stoppage. Feared Brazilian striker José Aldo landed a total of 27 kicks to the battered legs of Urijah Faber when they fought for the WEC Featherweight title at WEC 49 in 2010. Though they didn't end the fight, the kicks were the most memorable aspect of an otherwise competitive fight that ended in a unanimous decision victory for Aldo. The aftermath of the kicks were documented by Faber later on social media, revealing the extensive damage that explained why Faber was visibly limping for much of the fight. Go ahead, do an internet image search for "Urijah Faber Leg." I'll leave out the photos because this is a science book not a horror story.

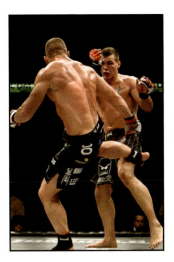

They may not look like much, but leg kicks will ruin your day.
Photo by Martin McNeil.

Leg kicks have more directly led to the stoppage of several fights in the UFC Octagon. Look no further than devastating UFC lightweight Edson Barboza, who has accomplished a TKO by leg kicks on three separate occasions in his career, with two of these wins inside the UFC Octagon. The first was at Barboza's UFC debut against Mile Lullo at UFC 123, then again versus Rafaello Oliveira at UFC 162. When used aggressively and in high volume, leg kicks can be terribly effective rendering the recipient unable to stand, and therefore "unable to intelligently defend himself" resulting in a merciful intervention and TKO stoppage from the referee.

Leg kicks may also be used strategically to set up kicks to other targets. A famous example was the repeated use of inside leg kicks by Georges St-Pierre against Matt Hughes at UFC 65. Throughout the first round St-Pierre peppered Hughes's legs, conditioning him to expect more low kicks. In round 2, GSP looked at Hughes's legs and started to throw a kick. This time Hughes prepared for another low kick, but it was a ruse. GSP's kick went straight into Hughes's head unblocked and put him on roller skates. The resulting knockdown led to a flurrying TKO finish by GSP that won him the UFC Welterweight title.

Now we can combine the metrics of target and strength to get a better sense of the standup game. In the next chart, all distance strike volumes have been bucketed by target and strength. We've kept the colors in this chart consistent with the prior framework. Given that the average UFC fighter today throws about 12 strikes per minute, we now know that five of them will be power head strikes. Here's how it all plays out.

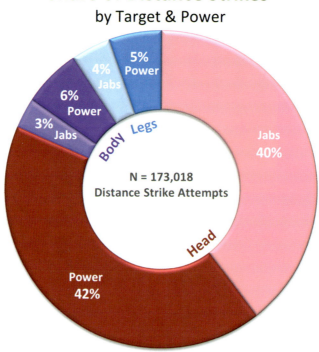

Share of Distance Strikes
by Target & Power

N = 173,018
Distance Strike Attempts

All UFC Fights 2007-April, 2013

That comes out to 25 attempted power head strikes per round that each fighter must deal with if the fights stays standing the entire time. Depending on the defensive capability of the fighter, and the strength of his "chin" to withstand these blows without succumbing to knockout (though it has more to do with necks than chins), we can establish a good benchmark for the amount of damage a fighter withstands during a round. In terms of the aforementioned landed power head strike, how many of these 25 attempts are likely to land? The short answer is one in four. About one quarter of all head strikes while standing will land on target. That accuracy metric is going to be the focus of a lot of additional analysis. When those head strikes land, there's always the chance of a knockout – and knockouts finish fights.

Strikes That Finish Fights

What finishes fights? The easy answer here is "punches," because punches are the most abundantly attempted strike. That includes the standard crosses and hooks, as well as uppercuts. For the sake of differentiation, however, we'll count spinning back fists separately. As always, we can dig a little deeper into the data. Let's consider just distance striking first, where a knockout occurs when the fighters are standing and trading – the most spectacular kind of knockout. When I said that FightMetric doesn't care what kind of strike (punch, kick, elbow, knee, etc.) is used I was only talking about round-by-round data. In fact, FightMetric does record the "finishing strike" for fights ending by KO/TKO, as well as the target of the finishing strike. When fighters get dropped by a specific strike, a body kick for example, then receive a few insignificant hammer fists on the ground before the ref can step in, the most important finishing strike is recorded (the body kick).

The granularity of the finishing strike means we can look at what kinds of strikes are knocking fighters off their feet, and eventually finishing fights elsewhere. We can answer a lot of questions with this data. What percentage of fights end with a KO/TKO from a distance standing position? About 16%. What strike most commonly ends a fight from a distance? A single punch. What are the chances of knocking someone out with some sort of crazy "spinning shit?" One in 357, but we'll get to all that in a minute.

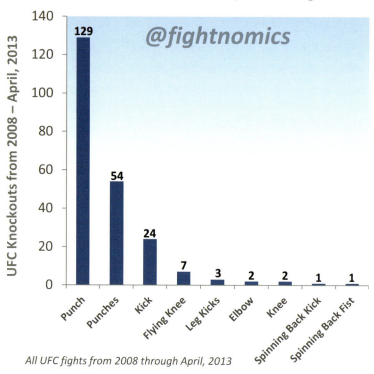

Distance Knockouts by Finishing Strike

@fightnomics

UFC Knockouts from 2008 – April, 2013

- Punch: 129
- Punches: 54
- Kick: 24
- Flying Knee: 7
- Leg Kicks: 3
- Elbow: 2
- Knee: 2
- Spinning Back Kick: 1
- Spinning Back Fist: 1

All UFC fights from 2008 through April, 2013

The graph here shows what caused the 223 standing knockouts in the UFC since 2008, regardless of target. Those knockouts account for 15.5% of all fights during that period, and so we know that we're only capturing about half of all KO/TKO finishes that happen inside the Octagon (the others occurring in the clinch or on the ground).

Overall, these finishes do include a good share of the highlight reels, since finishes from a distance are more brutally obvious than TKOs by numerous small strikes on the ground. Adding the single punch knockouts to knockouts from combinations of punches (the first two categories on the graph) we learn that 85% of distance finishes are due to punches. While head kick KO's probably make more highlight reels, fighters should first learn to defend punches as a fundamental defensive strategy. Furthermore, the basic kickboxing arsenal of punches and kicks are even more likely to end a fight than the more exotic attacks of Muay Thai. Flying knees, elbows, and leg kicks help make MMA an ass-kicking game of jack-in-the-box surprises, but a finish by these methods is also worthy of praise, bonuses, and a guaranteed spot in the highlight reels simply due to how rare they are.

That lone spinning back fist KO since 2008 came from John Makdessi, who dropped Kyle Watson at UFC 129 for a third round knockout. That particular move would not go on to win the Knockout of the Night award, only because later in the evening Lyoto Machida would drop (and retire) Randy Couture with a jumping crane kick he learned in the dojos of Steven Seagal no matter how badly we wished it had been on a beach with Mister Miyagi. The only other spinning back fist KO was from Shonie Carter over one-time welterweight champion Matt Serra at UFC 31, way back in 2001.

Fightnomics "Spinning Shit" Hall of Fame

John Makdessi
Spinning Back Fist
KO of Kyle Watson
UFC 129, 2011

Shonie Carter
Spinning Back Fist
KO of Matt Serra
UFC 31, 2001

Dennis Siver
Spinning Back Kick
TKO of Nate Mohr
UFC 93, 2009

David Loiseau
Spinning Back Kick
TKO of Charles McCarthy
UFC 53, 2005

As for the similarly rare spinning back kick finish, only two fighters have officially accomplished this feat in the history of the UFC: Dennis Siver at UFC 93 and David Loiseau at UFC 53. Renan Barao set up a nice title fight finish of Eddie Wineland at UFC 165 with a spinning back kick, but replay showed it didn't quite land flush and it was probably strikes on the ground that finished it. For some reason, the FightMetric system classifies spinning heel (or "wheel") kicks as simply head kicks, so buried in the third column of the graph are Vitor Belfort and Edson Barboza for their respective finishes of Luke Rockhold and Terry Etim. Giving credit to each of those close calls means that all in all, "spinning shit" (as Nick Diaz classifies it) only directly ended seven fights out of nearly 2,500. Even at the rapid current pace of UFC events, that's only once a year. While these finishes are a lot more fun to watch, they're really rare and so we'll focus our analysis on more common occurrences.

The Reality of Knockout Power: Size Matters

Somewhere between striking and finishing a fight there is an occurrence so intense and primal that it elicits an immediate visceral reaction from anyone witnessing it. When "knockdowns" occur in MMA due to a head strike, a human body of elite physical form can instantaneously collapse from an intimidating predatory weapon to a quivering heap of flesh in less than a second. It is the simplest reminder of the neuro-centric nature of our being. When the brain experiences a violent reset, the physical system goes lifeless for an instant, and sometimes longer. Many combat sports focused on mastering the skill of effecting knockdowns in opponents, and they do so in impressively diverse ways. The full spectrum of hand-to-hand combat disciplines will each make their case as to why their style is the most dangerous and effective, but let's take a step back from specific tactics. **There's another aspect of striking that heavily influences whether or not a certain strike will cause a knockdown and end a fight. It's not the type of strike thrown and it's not the target of aim. It's the size of the fighter that threw it.**

Knockdowns are a part of any striking combat sport, but thanks to the small gloves in MMA they resonate more loudly and vividly than in other sports like boxing. The connection of leather on chin is one of the more memorable sounds a fan hears at a live event, and when the crumpling of the target's body immediately follows (the rag doll impression), it generally draws the entire audience out of their seats in instantaneous gasps. "Knockdowns" that occur due to strikes are a great measure of damage done in a fight and of skilled striking by a fighter.

In order to score a knockdown, a fighter must first land a power strike. Since the vast majority of knockdowns are caused by head strikes, we'll use a simple estimation here to measure knockdown power that I call the "Knockdown Rate." It's calculated by dividing distance knockdowns by distance power head strikes landed. How many times a fighter falls down by how many licks he took to put him there. The resulting number as a percentage is essentially the likelihood of a fighter's power head strikes causing a knockdown whenever they land. As one of the key metrics in my "Uber Tale of the Tape," Knockdown Rate is a great indicator to a fighter's power and ability to drop opponents. It's a historical measurement, not a purely predictive one, but surely fighters that excel at scoring knockdowns generally continue to do so. In aggregate, it tells us even more about the sport of MMA.

The average UFC Knockdown Rate is 3.9%. That means for every 26 landed power head strikes while fighters are standing, there will be on average one knockdown. That's actually pretty frequent when you think about it. We already determined that if a fight stays standing for an entire round, each fighter will attempt about 25 power head strikes. Given that both fighters are striking, and assuming an average one in four strike success rate, that comes out to one knockdown for every 10 minutes of distance standing fight time. And let's not forget one true maxim in fighting and in life: size matters. That 3.9% knockdown rate benchmark varies by weight class, forming a clear pattern demonstrating that bigger fighters pack more power. Here's how Knockdown Rate varies by division.

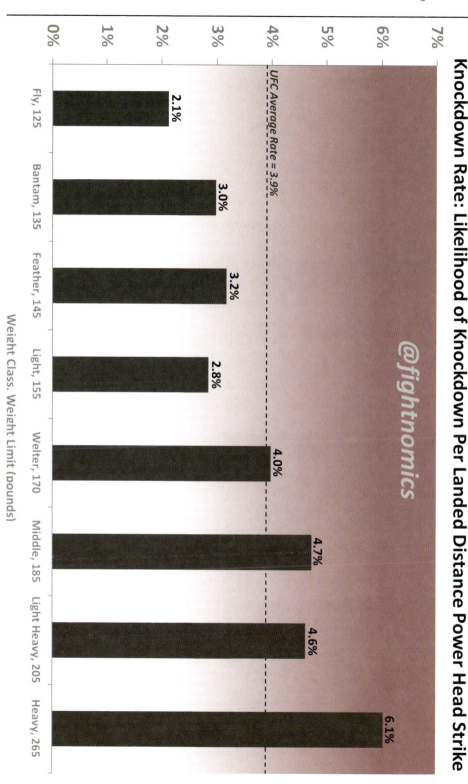

Knockdown Rate: Likelihood of Knockdown Per Landed Distance Power Head Strike

@fightnomics

UFC Average Rate = 3.9%

Weight Class, Weight Limit (pounds)	Rate
Fly, 125	2.1%
Bantam, 135	3.0%
Feather, 145	3.2%
Light, 155	2.8%
Welter, 170	4.0%
Middle, 185	4.7%
Light Heavy, 205	4.6%
Heavy, 265	6.1%

The analysis shows a strong correlation between fighter size and Knockdown Rate. Smaller fighters all come up short against the UFC overall average. The larger weight classes of fighters all have higher Knockdown Rates than the average. Right there in the middle, the welterweight division straddles the average benchmark as the pivot division between small and large fighters. That one knockdown per 25 power head strikes rule really equates to more strikes needed for a knockdown in the smaller divisions, and much fewer for the bigger guys. **That means larger fighters are capable of winning by strikes in less time, or simply more frequently overall, while smaller fighters are more likely to go the distance.**

Knockdown Rate and how it varies by weight class is a critical driver of how fights go down. When we rip apart the Tale of the Tape in Chapter 5, we'll see how size affects the outcomes of fights and leads to some of the clearest trends in MMA. Later we'll look at what happens when there's a knockdown but the fight continues. Is drawing first blood in the form of a knockdown a guarantee of victory? A number of gutsy and resilient fighters disagree, and have let their fists do the talking.

The Effect of Fatigue

The Knockdown Rate is a very helpful metric for determining the chances of seeing a knockout. In addition to varying greatly across divisions, and even among fighters within a division, the knockdown rate also is susceptible to change over the course of a fight. It turns out the knockout artists are most dangerous is the first round, with declining likelihood of scoring knockdowns in the second and third round. By re-running our knockdown rate by division analysis for knockdowns scored by round, a very interesting trend emerges: knockdown power fades. Here are division knockdown rate curves for rounds one through three.

"It's all over!" The moment Chris Weidman scored a knockdown that shook up the MMA world at UFC 162. Photo from my cell phone.

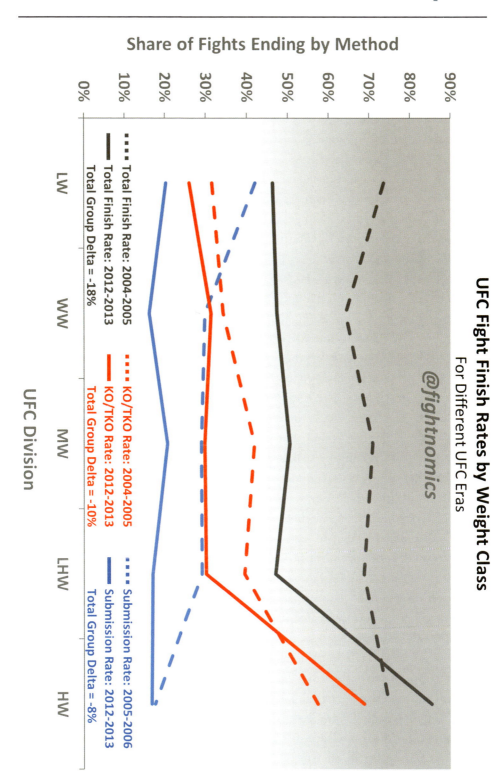

UFC Fight Finish Rates by Weight Class
For Different UFC Eras

Share of Fights Ending by Method

@fightnomics

UFC Division

Total Finish Rate: 2004-2005
Total Finish Rate: 2012-2013
Total Group Delta = -18%

KO/TKO Rate: 2004-2005
KO/TKO Rate: 2012-2013
Total Group Delta = -10%

Submission Rate: 2005-2006
Submission Rate: 2012-2013
Total Group Delta = -8%

The results show a clear change in knockdown power round-by-round. The pattern is pretty reliable for all divisions, with the hot hands of the first round cooling off for each additional round. Overall, the average knockdown rate for the entire UFC goes from 5.3% in the first round to 2.4% in the second, and finally just 1.5% in the third. If I expand my search to the championship rounds, it's notable that not a single knockdown has ever occurred in the fifth round of a UFC fight. Granted, we have a small sample size, but still that's some pretty damning evidence that knockdown rates fall continually once a fight starts.

Taking two extremes as examples, only 0.4% of landed distance power head strikes cause a knockdown in the bantamweight division once a fight entered the third round. That makes the chances of a KO finish at the end of a bantamweight fight very unlikely, especially when we remember the estimate that on average only six of these strikes will land during the course of any round. Since the bantamweight division came to the UFC, a third round striking finish has occurred only once when Johnny Bedford stopped Louis Gaudinot at the Ultimate Fighter 14 Finale by knees to the body on the ground two minutes into the third round. That fight didn't even include a knockdown at all.

On the opposite end of the spectrum heavyweights have nearly a 10% chance of scoring a knockdown for every landed distance power head strike in the first round of fights. That really boosts the odds of an early TKO/KO finish for heavyweights. Since 2007, one third of all heavyweight fights have ended by TKO/KO in the first round. For heavyweights surviving to see a third round, the likelihood of finishing by strikes drops to about one in five, still much higher than any other weight class, but lower due to knockdown rate that gets cut in half.

The most likely explanation for this trend is fatigue. The likelihood of landing a big shot later in the fight doesn't change much, but the likelihood of that strike causing a knockdown drops. Only two macro-mechanisms could be at work: the striker isn't hitting as hard, or the recipient of the strike is more able to withstand a blow that lands. Fatigue sapping some of the strength of strikes would explain why there's a drop in knockdown rate, and why the effect continues through multiple rounds. But there's also a more subtle effect that could be partially at work here known as "Survivorship Bias." The way this analysis works, fighters with "glass jaws" who are easily dropped by a big shot are more likely to go down early. That means our analysis of fighters who make it to rounds two or three of fights includes more fighters with strong "chins" who can take a shot and keep on fighting. It's impossible to filter out this effect without first categorizing fighters with strong versus weak chins, so I'll have to save that analysis for another time. I acknowledge that a little bias in the way the experiment is set up could be contributing to the effect we're seeing, but that doesn't change the reality of the situation that as fights continue, scoring a knockdown gets harder and harder.

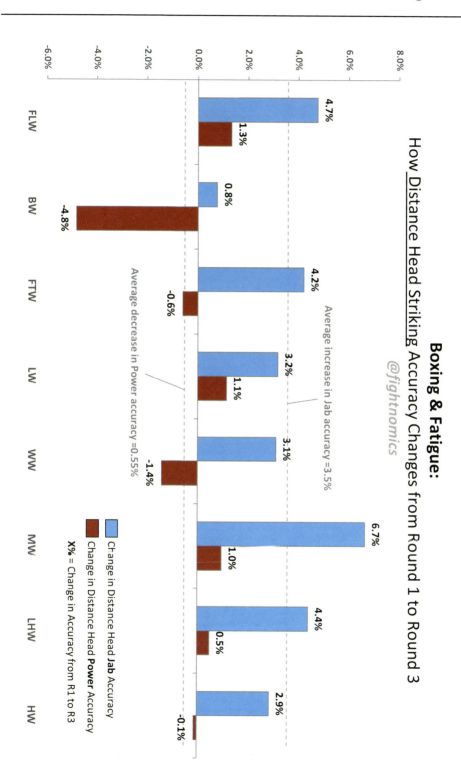

Boxing & Fatigue:
How Distance Head Striking Accuracy Changes from Round 1 to Round 3
@fightnomics

Legend:
- Change in Distance Head **Jab** Accuracy
- Change in Distance Head **Power** Accuracy
- X% = Change in Accuracy from R1 to R3

FLW: 4.7%, 1.3%
BW: 0.8%, -4.8%
FTW: 4.2%, -0.6%
LW: 3.2%, 1.1%
WW: 3.1%, -1.4%
MW: 6.7%, 1.0%
LHW: 4.4%, 0.5%
HW: 2.9%, -0.1%

Average increase in Jab accuracy = 3.5%
Average decrease in Power accuracy = 0.55%

Fortunately, the knockdown rate calculation already corrects for accuracy on the basis of landed strikes, not attempts. But it is reasonable to wonder how fatigue affects accuracy as rounds go on. Power certainly drops, but what about the ability to just land on target? Perhaps opposing trends could cancel each other out?

It turns that accuracy is indeed affected by fatigue, but in different ways. Jabs are more likely to land on target in later rounds, while power head strikes are less likely to land. It would seem that fighters on defense are consistently less able to avoid eating jabs when they're tired, but more able to avoid their similarly fatigued opponents when they wind up with a power shot. The drop off in power head accuracy is slight, but it exacerbates the already declining power of punches later in rounds, contributing to a lower overall likelihood of a knockdown late in fights.

 4   Beyond Standup: More MMA Striking Stats

No sport in the world allows striking from any and all areas of the fighting arena. Whether you're in a standing position, clinch, or on the ground, in MMA a strike can be thrown from anywhere at anytime and is the main reason for the referee's ominous pre-fight warning, "protect yourself at all times." Boxing allows hand strikes from a standing, distance position, while Kickboxing allows arm and leg strikes. Muay Thai kickboxing takes it a step further and encourages strikes within a clinch position, but none of them allows opponents a more diverse opportunity to strike while standing, and no sport allows for striking on the ground. MMA is a truly differentiated form of combat sport.

Clearly there's more to striking in MMA than just the traditional standup game, so analyzing the other categories of strikes after fighters have gotten up close and personal should show new and noteworthy patterns. This chapter will complete our analysis of striking by zooming in on Clinch and Ground strikes. We'll also define "Significant Strikes," and then look at how various striking metrics have evolved over time.

Clinch Striking

The clinch position accounts for less of the total time that fighters are on their feet than the distance position, but clinch work still adds up to a sizable 18% of total fight time in the Octagon. The Clinch occurs when the fighters are grabbing or just very close to each other while standing on the open mat, and also when one or both of the fighters are pressed up against the cage fence. Despite being a less common position for MMA fighters, clinch work has ended plenty of fights often spectacularly because of the devastating knee and elbow strikes that the clinch enables. Fighters in the clinch can employ both striking and takedowns, making it a strategically important position to master, though we'll save takedowns for the next chapter. When it comes to striking in the clinch, the first question is whether or not we see a different pattern of target selection than when strikers are at a distance.

Comparing this chart to a similar one in the last chapter, we immediately notice

Share of Clinch Strikes by Target

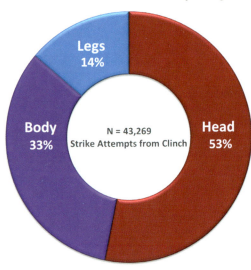

All UFC Fights 2007-April, 2013

that when fighters are in the clinch they are much more likely to attack the body than when they are standing at a distance. While over half of all strikes are still aimed at the head, this 53% is much lower than the 80% share of distance strikes to the head. The macro-trends for clinch striking are driven by the closer proximity of the fighters, which includes increased strike accuracy but also decreased power. Therefore, **the key tradeoff with all strikes in the clinch position is that while they may be easier to land, they do much less damage**. Here's how the striking accuracy map looks like for clinch striking.

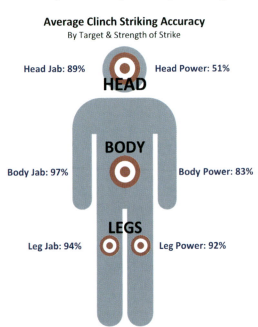

Average Clinch Striking Accuracy
By Target & Strength of Strike

Head Jab: 89%   Head Power: 51%
HEAD

BODY
Body Jab: 97%   Body Power: 83%

LEGS
Leg Jab: 94%   Leg Power: 92%

The map confirms a big takeaway: clinch striking at close range means far more strikes land on target. For all targets the accuracy of jabs is higher than power strikes, something we also saw for distance strikes. Upon closer inspection, these jabs aren't just more accurate, across the board they almost never miss. That's fine, because imagine two fighters locked in the clinch and one is "jabbing" the body of the other, and those strikes are unlikely to elicit fear. I refer to strikes like these as "activity strikes," and commenters will say a fighter is just "staying busy." They don't do damage and most recipients won't even attempt to defend or avoid them, yet some fighters when pinned against the fence will want to give the appearance of at least doing something. These micro-range strikes come out in high volume, but have little effect. According the numbers, they only miss 3% of the time.

The most important strike category in the clinch, like any other position, is the power head strike. Far and away this is the least accurate strike of the position with basically a 50/50 success rate, and the only strike metric with less than 80% accuracy. That's because these strikes are the most likely to do real damage, resulting in the most diligent defense by the intended recipient. However, the amount of power likely isn't the same as a strike thrown from a distance with a full wind up. Consider a clinch strike like a wrist shot in hockey, while a distance strike is more like a slap shot. More wind up means more power, and you put more of your body mass into the swing. **So while these strikes are so close that they land with high accuracy, we don't see them ending fights nearly as often.**

To test this idea we can isolate the knockdown rate just for the clinch, as we did before for distance strikes. Fortunately, FightMetric tracks clinch knockdowns separately from distance knockdowns, therefore we can calculate the same ratio of "knockdowns scored" to "landed power head strikes" from the clinch. If the hypothesis is true, then we should see much lower Knockdown Rates for clinch strikes.

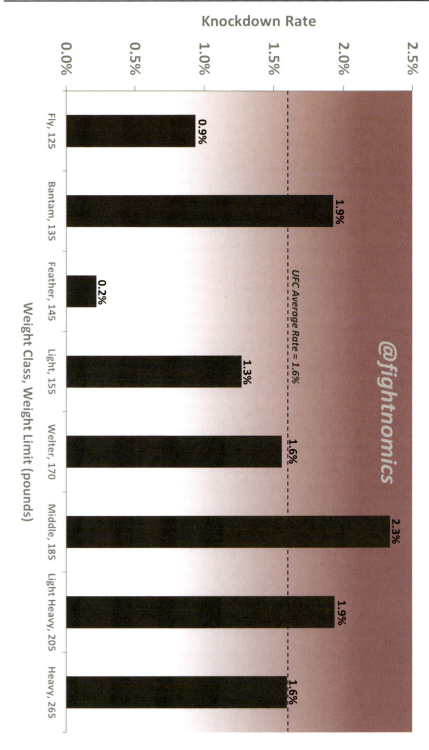

Clinch Knockdown Rate: Likelihood of Knockdown Per Landed Clinch Power Head Strike

Knockdown Rate

Weight Class, Weight Limit (pounds)

Weight Class	Knockdown Rate
Fly, 125	0.9%
Bantam, 135	1.9%
Feather, 145	0.2%
Light, 155	1.3%
Welter, 170	1.6%
Middle, 185	2.3%
Light Heavy, 205	1.9%
Heavy, 265	1.6%

UFC Average Rate = 1.6%

@fightnomics

As the chart demonstrates, while there is more variance in clinch knockdown rates (fewer overall clinch knockdowns means a smaller sample size), the overall likelihood of dropping someone with a clinch strike is less than half that of strikes thrown from a distance. The pattern that larger fighters have higher knockdowns rates is also true, though less consistent than with the larger sample size of distance knockdowns. During the period analyzed, there were fewer than one-fifth as many clinch knockdowns as distance knockdowns, which is a combined result of less time spent in the clinch, and the lower knockdown rate due to less power at close range. This convergence of factors makes using the clinch to win a fight a less likely scenario, but it certainly still happens. The clinch is where Muay Thai influences have the biggest impact in MMA. The UFC's highlight reels contain impressive displays of knockouts from a Thai clinch stance, but you would have to be very skilled (and somewhat lucky) to score a finish from this position.

Case in point is Anderson "the Spider" Silva. Before the expert Muay Thai striker set the UFC record for most title defenses (among many other records), he stormed into the UFC Octagon in 2006 with a violent destruction of the notoriously durable Chris Leben. A noteworthy takeaway from the Knockdown Rate chart is the spike at Middleweight. Anderson Silva's career clinch striking finishes in the UFC surely boosted this benchmark single-handedly (or single knee-edly?).

On his way to finishing opponents, Silva racked up a whopping 17 total knockdowns through 2013, seven of which were directly from the clinch. Remember, he did all that primarily engaged with title contenders. In fact, four clinch knockdowns came against a single opponent, Rich Franklin, during Silva's two TKO wins against the former champ. Even more ridiculous is that three knockdowns came in a single fight, their title rematch at UFC 77. Silva finally ended the fight 1:07 into the second frame after knocking Franklin down from the clinch for the second time that round. Among middleweight performances, Silva personally accounts for 20% of all clinch knockdowns recorded in that division since he joined the UFC. So in case I'm not being clear enough, DON'T clinch with Anderson Silva.

Silva is exceptional in many ways (ever see his Michael Jackson impression?), so we need to take a step back and see how fights get finished when they're in the clinch on a larger scale. The following chart summarizes the 64 clinch KO/TKOs in the UFC over the five-and-half year period analyzed.

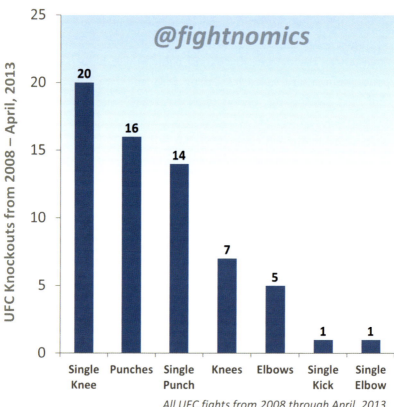

Clinch Knockouts by Finishing Strike

@fightnomics

All UFC fights from 2008 through April, 2013

Most clinch knockouts came from a single knee strike. Adding single strikes to multiple strikes has punches edging out knees 30 to 27, but overall there's a much more diverse mix of strikes causing clinch knockouts than those in a distance stance. Proximity limits the ability to throw clean punches, making knees and elbows much more likely to be employed at close range. Punching knockouts account for 47% of the knockouts in the period analyzed, much less than the 85% we saw in a distance position. Knees collectively account for another 42% of these knockouts, with elbows taking a 9% share. The lone "kick" finish from the data set came from Paul Taylor, who managed to kick Gabe Ruediger in the head while still technically in a clinch stance (Kelly had Ruediger hurt and up against the fence). Generally, kicks are hard to unleash at such close range, making knees the most effective leg strike and making Kelly's brutal head kick an exception to the rule.

Out of the 64 KO/TKO finishes in the clinch shown in the chart, only five of them were due to a body strike. When we imagine two fighters against the fence, one of them grasping his opponent behind the neck and pulling his head downward in the "Thai Plumb" position, it's hard to picture the stance without hearing the crowd yell "kneeeees!!" Most often those knees are aimed at the head when they end a fight. Knee strikes to the body accounted for three of the 20 total finishes from a single knee. Two more body strike finishes came via punches, making body strike finishes a rare method of victory even at close range. However, these body strike finishes made up 8% of the total knockouts from the clinch, which is twice the rate of body strike finishes at a distance. For fighters with sharp knees or a penchant for liver shots, the lesson is that the chances for a body strike finish are double when they close the distance and work the clinch. Yet overall, the head is still the best target if you want to finish the fight early.

Ground Striking

Do you get frustrated when a fight continually goes to the ground? Many do because the ground game is the most intricate, nuanced, and confusing aspect of a fight. In addition to the discrete acts of striking, arms and legs frequently and deceptively slither into joint-destroying and life-threatening arrangements that are easy to miss if you're not watching closely. Grappling represents a world of knowledge that even in isolation from other arts can take a lifetime to master.

Before we dive into what statistics can tell us about grappling, we should first close out our striking analysis of positions by examining how strikes are thrown when fighters are on the ground. Will the target of strikes be any different on the ground than on the feet?

Share of Ground Strikes by Target

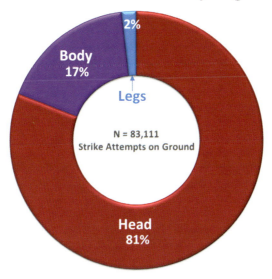

All UFC Fights 2007-April, 2013

Ground striking has a flavor all its own due to the close proximity of the fighters, but also the high likelihood that legs are being otherwise occupied in maintaining, advancing, or defending position. With the added constraint that legs cannot be used to attack the head of a grounded opponent, the result is that legs and knees are rarely used on the ground. The net result is that a target profile for ground strikes looks more like the one for distance striking than it does clinch striking. Four of every five strikes are aimed at the head, with most of the rest targeting the body. Occasionally a top control fighter may use his knees or elbows to attack the legs of his opponent when they have reached a stalemate position, but this is rare. Like 2% rare.

With fighters so close it must be impossible to miss with punches, right? As it turns out, because the defending fighter can so easily interfere with the limbs of his attacker, there is clear filtering of which strikes fighters focus on avoiding. The accuracy map tells the story that only one of these kids is not like the others.

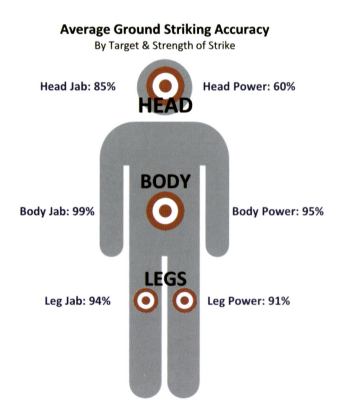

Average Ground Striking Accuracy
By Target & Strength of Strike

Head Jab: 85%   HEAD   Head Power: 60%

BODY

Body Jab: 99%   Body Power: 95%

LEGS

Leg Jab: 94%   Leg Power: 91%

As with other fighting positions, the power head strike remains the most critical element of striking, even on the ground. Based on historical UFC averages it seems that most fighters don't even try to avoid any other kinds of strikes on the ground, because they nearly all land on target. As with clinch striking, every strike type other than power head shots has greater than 80% accuracy. However, it's not just the threat of the power head strike that makes it the focal point of ground striking, it's also the position of the fighters.

A vital aspect of ground fighting is position dominance, which has a big effect on who can strike, where, and with how much violence. Top control fighters have more range of motion to drop strikes, and a big advantage in landing damaging blows. A fighter pressed to the mat, like a fighter pressed to the cage, is in the more difficult position because range of motion is limited. Bottom fighters literally cannot wind up with force to inflict a powerful blow. Go ahead; try throwing a punch without letting your elbow retract behind your body. Pretty weak, right? Makes you rethink that "Rock 'Em Sock 'Em Robots" game. Fighters on the bottom are left mainly with ineffective mini-punches that only use a sideways wind up. The lucky ones might catch an opponent in their guard and attempt short-range elbow strikes, but these are more likely to do superficial damage than knock someone out.

On rare occasions an upkick to the head can change the course of a fight, as it did when Benson Henderson first fought Frankie Edgar for the lightweight title at UFC 144 in Tokyo. A second round kick that Henderson launched while lying on his back wobbled Edgar, who was hovering above him. The upkick also caused damage and bleeding from Edgar the rest of the fight, and the visible damage may have helped sway rounds in Henderson's favor during an otherwise very close fight. That one kick was a rare case when a fighter on the bottom benefited from a strike, and not a submission attempt, though it required some space to pull it off. In retrospect, Edgar might have been better off fighting from guard at closer range, but then we'd have to consider the grappling threats. Such is the conundrum MMA fighters face even when they are in control of a fight.

From the top, regardless of ground position, dominant fighters normally have the ability to use larger wind ups and even a little assistance from gravity to rain down leather and elbows on their opponent. Filtering fights ending by KO/TKO for situations when the fight ended on the ground, we can check the weapon of choice for top control fighters. The finishing strike data is even more skewed on the ground than it is elsewhere in the cage. Part of that is the nature of the position and the Unified Rules of MMA that don't allow kicks or knees to the head of a grounded opponent.

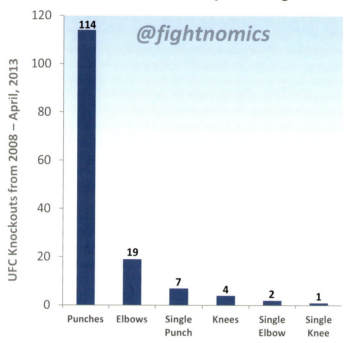

Ground Knockouts by Finishing Strike

All UFC fights from 2008 through April, 2013

That limits some dangerous close range weapons, especially when we remember how many strikes are focused on the head when fighters are grounded. Punches and elbows collectively account for 82% of finishes in this position. Elbows chalk up 14%, while knees (which can only be aimed at the body), round out the last 3% (percentages are rounded). So while elbows on the ground – or "hell-bows" – may look nasty, they are much less common than punches when it comes to finishing a fight. Again, we have to consider the range vs. power tradeoff. **Elbows are usually employed at a much closer proximity than punches that are thrown with more range of movement. The reduced length of wind up equates to less energy delivered on contact.** Close range elbows on the ground may do more to cut opponents, which is one reason they are banned in some MMA promotions or in certain rounds of tournaments. When it comes to knockout power though, it's hard to argue that elbows are as likely to finish a fight as punches that can come from far greater distances and connect with more force.

The five total knee stoppages in the chart were due to strikes to the body, and two of them actually happened on the same night at the TUF 14 Finale in 2011. That night both Johnny Bedford and Michael Bisping finished their opponents Louis Gaudinot and Jason Miller, respectively, with knees to the body. Bisping's finish came in the main event, after an exhausted Miller could no longer defend himself. Another more vivid use of a knee to the body came from Rashad Evans in the main event of UFC 133. I was there that night to witness his surging knee to the chest of Tito Ortiz, who was already sitting against the fence and proceeded to crumple as Evans added some punches for effect. While rare, the knee to the chest or abdomen can still have devastating effects.

Proximity Matters

We've now covered striking in each of the primary positions of the cage, and we've already seen that head striking has the most variance in accuracy by position, while other types of strikes are practically unstoppable at close range. By isolating head strike accuracy and varying the distance/position of the fighters, we might learn something about the basic property of range in a fight. The results are quite obvious: proximity matters.

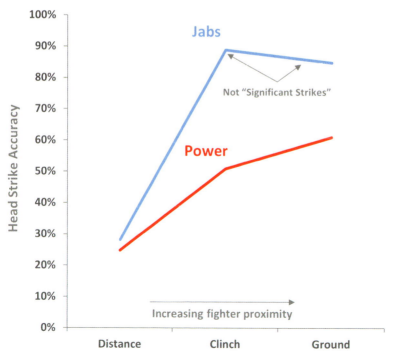

Head Strike Accuracy by Position & Strength

The closer two fighters are to one another, the higher their accuracy goes in terms of landing the most critical strikes of all, power head strikes. The accuracy of clinch jabs is likely inflated by fighters pinned against the cage who barely have room to wind up a strike, but nevertheless pat the side of their opponent's head for the appearance of staying busy. The more important metric, power head striking accuracy, shows a clear and steady pattern of increasing accuracy at closer range. Distance strikes land somewhat rarely, clinch strikes are a 50/50 proposition, and ground strikes land more often than not. Like darts, shuffleboard, and beer pong, the closer you are the more accurate you are.

There's a price to accuracy, however, and that's power. **The Knockdown Rate for distance strikes is nearly twice the average for clinch strikes**. If we were to look at TKO's on the ground only and divide by the number of power head strikes landed there, the likelihood of finishing a fight with a single close range blow would fall even further down.

The basic realities of position and body mechanics will affect trends in MMA, no matter how hard a fighter is trying to be accurate with strikes or how desperately his opponent is trying to avoid them. Along with the strong correlation between proximity and accuracy, there's also that tradeoff of power that is lost when fighters close the distance. So connecting with an opponent's head is a lot easier the closer you are, but the strike will have less impact. Depending on a given fighter's strategy to knock someone out or score points and win rounds, this seemingly obvious insight can have real-time implications.

Consider a fighter facing a known power slugger, closing the distance will mitigate the chances of a knockout blow. Conversely, if a fighter is down two rounds and in top control against a grappler, his best move may be to relinquish control and stand up. After all, if the best chance to win is by knockout, range will only help a fighter's odds of making each have the greatest impact.

On March 19th, 2011 in Newark, New Jersey, Brendan Schaub put this knowledge to devastating use. It was the third round of a much anticipated heavyweight matchup with feared striking legend Mirko "Cro Cop" Filipovic. Schaub had been getting the better of tentative standup exchanges, and had become the first UFC fighter to land a takedown on the Croatian, something he did multiple times this fight.

However, Schaub also had his nose smashed while clinching with Cro Cop against the cage. The blood might have swayed judges in Cro Cop's favor for these tight rounds, but it was a second round point deduction for an illegal strike to the back of the head that made the situation even worse for Schaub. Likely close on the judges' cards, the deduction meant a potential draw if the fight went the full three rounds, something the fans did not anticipate from two heavyweights with such clear knockout power. Towards the end of the final round, things got interesting. Schaub had landed more takedowns on Cro Cop, but working from top control was proving to be difficult with the Croatian tangling, stifling and dodging Schaub's strikes. Fearing an unjust decision from the judges, Schaub did something very unusual: he stood up.

At this point in the fight the final round was still up in the air, and sustaining top control with ground and pound was sure to win the round, but probably not result in a stoppage. The decision to stand reflected a conscious awareness by Schuab that he had a better chance to score a knockout on his feet, even with just a few minutes left in the fight. So up they stood. Seconds later, after blocking one of the famous head kicks from Cro Cop, Schaub stepped in with a heavy overhand right. Crop dropped the mat stunned, with Schaub landing one more tentative blow before Herb Dean confirmed the KO.

The decision by Schaub to stand was curious. He was succeeding with takedowns and fatigue was setting in for both fighters. Schaub could probably have won the round using a conservative approach of ground and pound, thus mitigating Cro Cop's most dangerous weapon. The point deduction for Schaub, however, meant more uncertainty than usual on the judges' cards. Very late in the game he abandoned the strategy of securing the final round and decided to focus on the knockout, requiring him to relinquish top control on the ground in favor of more neutral, but also more dangerous open ground. The gambit worked, and Schaub took home a Knockout of the Night bonus just one day after his birthday, which hopefully made up for some of the lasting pain of that brutal fight with a legend.

When and Where UFC Fighters Strike

Now that we know how to Paint the House, Paint the Fence, Sand the Floor, and Wax On, Wax Off, let's look at all strikes thrown in the UFC by position and target, and see how it all ties together. What's important is to know what strikes get thrown more often, and also how successful each type of strike is. I've summarized that all on one chart, like a striking fingerprint of all UFC fights.

The height of each bar indicates the relative frequency of a certain strike in terms of total attempts, while the relative height of the dark area within it indicates how many of those strikes actually landed. The calculated accuracy for that strike (e.g., Distance Head Power Landed divided by Distance Head Power Attempted) is shown atop each bar (in this case 25%). I've added a little bit of context for certain types of strikes as well, and here's how they all shake out. This is essentially the fingerprint of all striking in the UFC, and it ties together a lot of what we've covered so far.

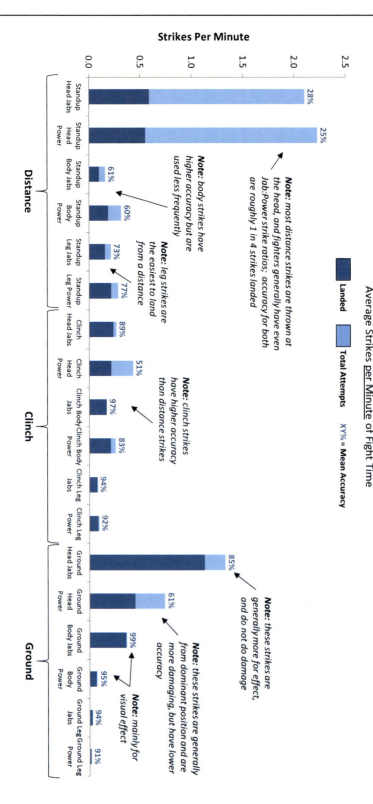

Rate & Accuracy of Strikes by Target and Position
Average Strikes per Minute of Fight Time

Strikes Per Minute

Legend: Landed ■ Total Attempts ■ XY% = Mean Accuracy

Note: most distance strikes are thrown at the head, and fighters generally have even Jab:Power strike ratios; accuracy for both are roughly 1 in 4 strikes landed

Note: body strikes have higher accuracy but are used less frequently

Note: leg strikes are the easiest to land from a distance

Note: clinch strikes have higher accuracy than distance strikes

Note: these strikes are generally more for effect, and do not do damage

Note: these strikes are generally from dominant position and are more damaging, but have lower accuracy

Note: mainly for visual effect

Distance
- Standup Head Jabs — 28%
- Standup Head Power — 25%
- Standup Body Jabs — 61%
- Standup Body Power — 60%
- Standup Leg Jabs — 73%
- Standup Leg Power — 77%

Clinch
- Clinch Head Jabs — 89%
- Clinch Head Power — 51%
- Clinch Body Jabs — 97%
- Clinch Body Power — 83%
- Clinch Leg Jabs — 94%
- Clinch Leg Power — 92%

Ground
- Ground Head Jabs — 85%
- Ground Head Power — 61%
- Ground Body Jabs — 99%
- Ground Body Power — 95%
- Ground Leg Jabs — 94%
- Ground Leg Power — 91%

A few things should strike you about the striking chart (see what I did there?), starting with the left-most bars. First, most distance strikes are thrown at the head. We knew that. Obviously, the best way to win a fight with a single blow is by hitting the head, and these strikes are the most commonly attempted in the Octagon by a long shot. Fighters spend much less time attacking the body or legs, despite the fact that fights can and do end by strikes to these targets. Head striking while standing is generally evenly split between jabs and power strikes, which reflects the even Power Ratio we examined earlier. It also reflects distance jabs and power strikes occurring with almost exactly the same frequency in aggregate. Finally, we see that distance head striking is the least accurate of all strikes (i.e., the share of dark area in each bar is the lowest). Fighters on offense know this is potentially the most damaging strike to land, which means they also know the exact same thing when they're playing defense. Fights are often won or lost based just on these strikes, which makes head striking a key battleground within the fight itself.

When fighters aren't headhunting from a distance, they're throwing high success strikes at the body and legs, with a stronger preference for more powerful strikes. As we move to the right of the chart, we see that clinch striking is the least frequent of all based on the limited time that fighters spend there, and also the increased threat of takedowns from that position. The second most dangerous strike on our chart is the power head strike from the clinch, which lands with twice the success as the more distant power head strikes, but as we know, results in half the knockdowns blow for blow.

On the ground there's another spike of activity for head strikes. The head jabs, however, are probably a fluke of positioning. Fighters on the bottom trying to strike the top fighter's head are probably using a lot of weak jabs due to their constrained position, often clutching their opponents to restrict movement. Fighters on top may be using more power strikes, but also some jabs as well. Expected trends hold true in that the most important strikes show the lowest success rate, while the rest of the strikes to the body and legs on the ground are likely trivial due to the fact that no one bothers to avoid them.

Tallying all these categories of strikes up comes to 9.3 total strikes per fighter per minute of fight time or 93 total strikes by both fighters in a five-minute round. Assuming each strike takes one second that means fighters are trading blows 31% of the time. Doesn't seem like a lot of action, but consider this: on average there are around 11 minutes of action during a 60-minute NFL football game, which is only 18% of total game time. UFC fighters are engaged in striking for over 30% of fight time, and that's just striking. We have yet to even consider takedowns, slams, or submissions. I love watching football too, but that's one statistics-based argument that says MMA is the more action-packed sport on a pound-for-pound, second-for-second basis.

How the Strike Became "Significant"

It's a testament to the rapid evolution of the sport of mixed martial arts that a common debate is over the definition of a manufactured metric. The "Significant Strike" is commonly referred to in UFC pre-fight shows, often specifically in terms the rate of strikes landed, the accuracy, or strikes absorbed (a defensive measurement). Even more common is the question among MMA fans as to what constitutes a "significant" strike. Our hierarchy of 36 separate striking metrics encapsulates "Total Strikes," but as we all know when watching a fight, not all strikes thrown can be expected to do damage. There are times when a fighter's strikes appear to just be for the effect of staying busy. We also saw evidence that a lot of strikes in the clinch an on the ground are almost worthless, with few fighters attempting to avoid them.

Fighters pressed up against the cage with an arm trapped via underhook may repeatedly pat away at their opponent's body. Or a fighter pinned to the ground under an opponent in side control may do the same. In either scenario recipients of these strikes are unlikely to be hurt, and rarely adjust their position to avoid the strikes. It's exactly these kinds of strikes that don't make the cut for "significance." Basically, close range strikes that lack power are not significant. They're counted in the total, but they don't hurt, or impact the eventual outcome of the fight.

This simple table summarizes the definition of Significant Strikes in the FightMetric system. All strikes thrown while fighters are standing at a distance are considered significant, and the only strikes that aren't significant are jabs thrown in the clinch or on the ground at any target. Got it?

What Strikes are "Significant?"

Strike Range	Power Strikes	Non-Power Strikes
Distance	Significant	Significant
Close Range (Clinch/Ground)	Significant	Not Significant

As FightMetric endeavored to create a performance measurement that could be summarized in a single number, the idea of the Significant Strike was born. It measures the total meaningful offensive output of a fighter's striking. The aggregated success rate of Significant Strikes reflects how accurately fighters can inflict damage on their opponents, while the relative rate at which these strikes land measures their efficiency. To ensure that they had properly selected the right strikes as significant, FightMetric ran the mother of all regression analysis on every category of striking to see which strikes correlated with success. In the end we're left with a metric that is simple, singular, logical, and helps filter out some of the deceptive shows of activity with no real meaning. Significant Strikes are the ones that matter.

If the summary table above isn't detailed enough for you, consider the chart on the next page where the 36 striking categories are laid out and coded for significance based on the original FightMetric data organization chart from Chapter 2.

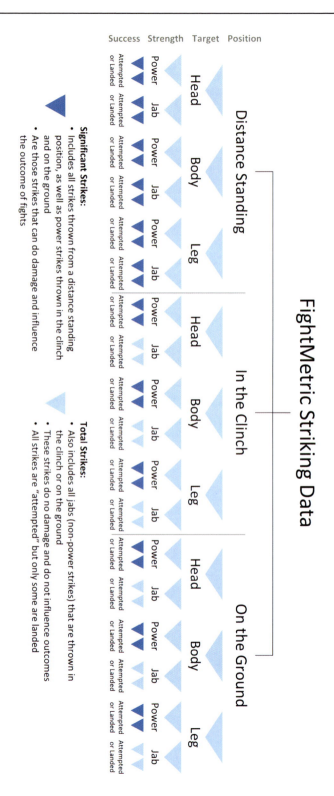

FightMetric Striking Data

Distance Standing

In the Clinch

On the Ground

Success	Strength	Target	Position
Attempted or Landed	Power	Head	
Attempted or Landed	Jab		
Attempted or Landed	Power	Body	
Attempted or Landed	Jab		
Attempted or Landed	Power	Leg	
Attempted or Landed	Jab		

Significant Strikes:

- Includes all strikes thrown from a distance standing position, as well as power strikes thrown in the clinch and on the ground
- Are those strikes that can do damage and influence the outcome of fights

Total Strikes:

- Also includes all jabs (non-power strikes) that are thrown in the clinch or on the ground
- These strikes do no damage and do not influence outcomes
- All strikes are "attempted" but only some are landed

When we analyzed all the types of strikes and how fights are finished, distance striking was clearly dangerous in many ways, while clinch and ground striking were really only threatening with power head strikes, usually for the fighter in control of the position. The Significant Strike metric captures these nuances. While technically some obscure categories like "clinch power leg strikes," or "ground power body strikes" are included, the strike frequency charts show that these make up a very small share of the total striking output of fighters on average. True, a fighter who employs a lot of leg kicks that typically produce high success rates can inflate his Significant Strike Accuracy. However, the metric still tells us how often meaningful strikes will land on target when thrown, so accounting for those strikes is important. Just ask any fighter who has limped away from the cage after of a barrage of leg kicks.

The Significant Strike metric is a rolled-up combination of more dangerous but less accurate strikes, plus less dangerous but more accurate ones as well (I know – it takes a minute to fully grasp it). Given the detail that I've provided in this chapter on position and target benchmarks, we now have some context in which to understand significant striking in the UFC. Don't forget the basic kickboxing metrics of power head striking as critical clues to any given fighter's ability in the cage. Anyone who follows my "Uber Tale of the Tape" for key UFC matchups will see these head striking metrics specifically called out for comparison (see Chapter 16), as they are often indicative of who will be the sharper striker on fight night.

Have you got a full understanding of all the categories of strikes within MMA? Good. Now we can start getting creative with how we analyze them from a historical perspective

The Evolution of MMA Striking

General George S. Patton famously warned that "fatigue makes cowards of us all." This insight is powerful and timeless, and it remains as absolutely relevant in sports today as it does in warfare. Imposing your will on someone else migrates from difficult to impossible when you're exhausted. Perhaps more importantly, preventing others from imposing their will on you is even more impossible under exhaustion. Given the rapid evolution of MMA in the last two decades, it's reasonable to expect a similar evolution in the caliber of athlete who competes in it. A closer look at conditioning in the UFC will tell us how competition has changed over the years, and confirm the response of athletes to the increased stakes of the sport.

Stories of fighters like Tank Abbot walking straight from the bar stool to the Octagon are the legends of yesteryear. The modern mixed martial artist is most likely a full-time fighter, on a strict diet, and generally a much better athlete than the cage fighters of the 1990's. The data suggests that this new school of fighters has picked up the pace of action in the Octagon both significantly and consistently as the sport has grown and matured. To analyze the fitness and productivity of fighters, we need a proxy metric, and now that we understand what data is available to us within the FightMetric system, striking makes as good a starting point as any. How has the average pace of striking changed year-over-year in the UFC?

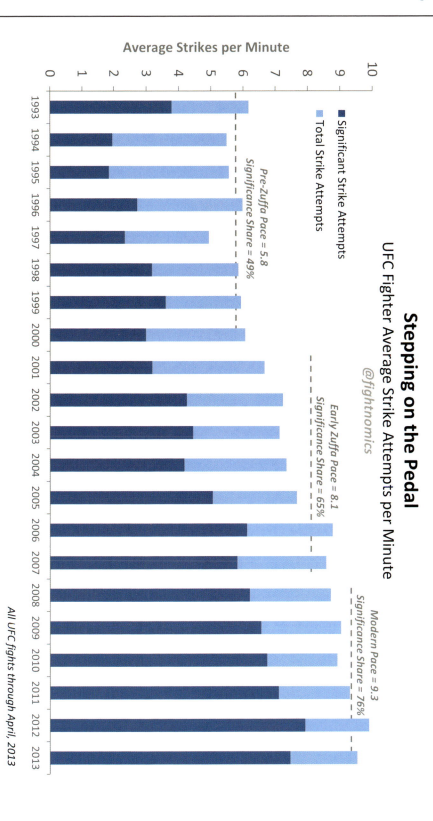

Stepping on the Pedal

UFC Fighter Average Strike Attempts per Minute

@fightnomics

Average Strikes per Minute

Legend:
- Significant Strike Attempts
- Total Strike Attempts

Pre-Zuffa Pace = 5.8
Significance Share = 49%

Early Zuffa Pace = 8.1
Significance Share = 65%

Modern Pace = 9.3
Significance Share = 76%

All UFC fights through April, 2013

The graph shows a clear and increasing trend of striking pace that has seen fighters accelerate from 5.8 total strikes per minute on average in the early years of the UFC, to 9.3 total strikes per minute since 2008. This increase in pace is big, and given the upward trend it looks like it will eventually result in a doubling of the original UFC pace within this decade. The year-on-year growth is impressive, and so is the immediate effect of new ownership beginning in 2001. Zuffa management added a variety of rules and regulations to help commercialize MMA, but one additional effect was the increase in the speed of fighting inside the Octagon as overall talent levels blossomed. Fitter fighters stepped on the pedal and never looked back. What fans observe today is a faster pace of action with more frequent engagement by fighters in the cage.

Looking closer, there's also a separate trend of Significant Strikes increasing as a share of total strikes. In the early days of the UFC only half of all strikes could be classified as significant, while modern fighters employ 76% of their strikes in these categories. That's a huge difference. This increase in the amount of "significance" of strikes could come from two macro-trends: an increase in power striking (and less use of jabs), and/or the position of the fighters where more distance striking equates to a higher share of Significant Strikes.

We already know that total striking includes some ineffective activity (meaning worthless "staying busy" strikes), so we can rerun the annual strike rate analysis, this time focusing just on Significant Strikes. Significant Strikes do damage, score knockdowns, set up submissions, or cause referees to jump in for the save. Analyzing this metric over time will also help us understand some of the numbers we hear quoted before big fights, since we'll have some context for individual fighter performance.

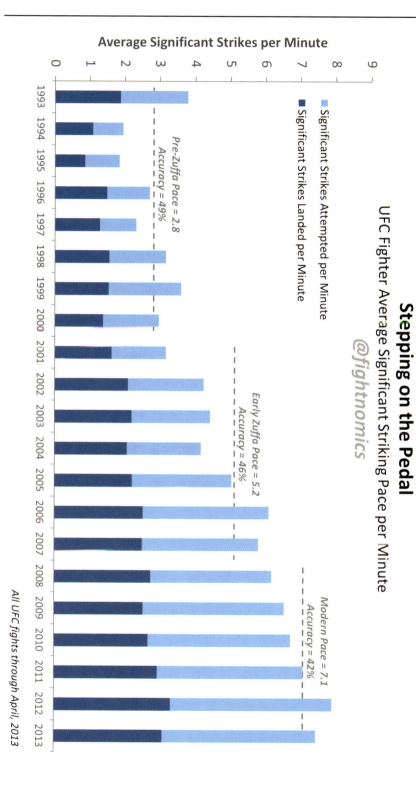

Stepping on the Pedal
UFC Fighter Average Significant Striking Pace per Minute

@fightnomics

Average Significant Strikes per Minute

- Significant Strikes Attempted per Minute
- Significant Strikes Landed per Minute

Pre-Zuffa Pace = 2.8
Accuracy = 49%

Early Zuffa Pace = 5.2
Accuracy = 46%

Modern Pace = 7.1
Accuracy = 42%

All UFC fights through April, 2013

Since 2008, UFC fighters have averaged 7.1 Significant Strike attempts per minute (SSApM) of fight time. Again, this is not just while standing, but also from dominant clinch and ground positions. Significant Strikes generally define the action in a fight, and as the analysis shows, fighter output by this metric has changed drastically since the early years of the UFC. Through the 1990's, UFC fighters attempted an average of only 2.8 Significant Strikes per minute. Averages for UFC fighters then more than doubled to 7.1 SSApM after the sport matured under Zuffa ownership.

Calculating accuracy as strikes landed divided by strikes attempted, about 42% of these Significant Strikes land on target today. This rate has not changed much in recent years as fighters improved simultaneously on both offense and defense, and there is greater consistency in fighter training and quality. Earlier in UFC history, accuracy was a little higher, then dropped during the maturation period of the mid-2000's, and has hovered around this 42% mark since 2005. Competition is a strong force, and as the sport has grown and evolved, MMA athletes have stepped up their game and their overall level of fitness and skill to bring a better conditioned product into the Octagon. Does that mean the best is yet to come? The numbers suggest so and how awesome is it to think that ten years from now UFC fighters could be drastically superior than they are now?

What about our question of contributing factors to the rising Significant Strike share? We can see plainly that Significant Strikes are rising in both frequency of attempts, as well as in terms of share of total strikes. Diving deeper into the question of accuracy might give us another clue as to how striking has evolved.

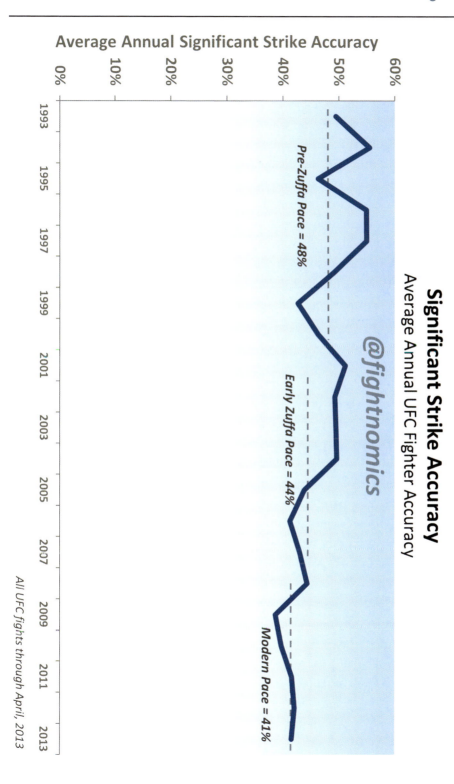

Significant Strike Accuracy
Average Annual UFC Fighter Accuracy

Average Annual Significant Strike Accuracy

@fightnomics

Pre-Zuffa Pace = 48%

Early Zuffa Pace = 44%

Modern Pace = 41%

All UFC fights through April, 2013

103

For Significant Strike accuracy shows a downward trend, but also one that indicates a plateau in the most recent years. Those same years also give us the biggest sample sizes, so it appears that we're in a period of relative stability, with about 42% of Significant Strikes consistently landing on target since 2011. The rise in the rate of Significant Strikes combined with the fall in accuracy demonstrates the underlying trend that we'll see in closer detail later in this book: **fights are staying standing longer.** Because all strikes while standing are significant, but also have lower accuracy, an increase in distance striking relative to other positions explains both trends. If there's one thing we should expect from MMA, however, it is evolution. Perhaps the rise of body kicks will change how standing exchanges take place, or perhaps more exotic attacks will decrease target accuracy, but increase the damage done. Whatever happens, expect the unexpected. There will be no shortage of new highlights in the years to come, and fighters are staying plenty busy in the meantime.

As for the Power Ratio of strikes changing over time, that's true too, but not in a way that would boost the overall share of Significant Strikes. In distance striking, for example, the ratio of power strikes to jabs has been on a decline from a peak in the early-2000's. A viable hypothesis is that striking back then was simply less technical, with more guys brawling and swinging for the fences with every strike. It's also possible that with fights staying standing longer, fighters have to be more disciplined in their striking mix in order to maintain pace and not tire too quickly. Either way, the rise in strike significance is not due to more power being used.

There's one more way to explore striker pace to confirm these trends. The working hypothesis is that the pace of activity has increased, which may be due to better conditioning and more aggressive expectations by fans, referees, and judges. Fighters feel the urgency to finish a fight now more than ever before. But because the rate of strikes thrown in each position may vary, the mix of positions can muddy our measure of true pace. We can isolate the position that fighters are in while throwing strikes to get a better apples-to-apples comparison. By focusing on strikes thrown in each position and dividing by the duration actually spent in each corresponding position, we can see how striking activity has really changed over time. This will allow us to answer the question of whether fighters have actually stepped up the action in the UFC, or whether macro trends like position are causing the change.

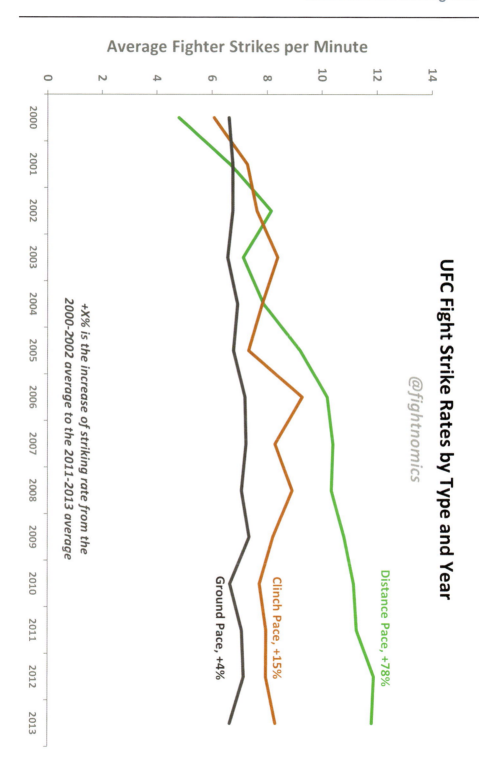

UFC Fight Strike Rates by Type and Year

@fightnomics

Average Fighter Strikes per Minute

Distance Pace, +78%

Clinch Pace, +15%

Ground Pace, +4%

+X% is the increase of striking rate from the 2000-2002 average to the 2011-2013 average

105

The results show that the pace of activity has indeed gone up overall, but mostly in distance striking. Like, a lot. As we'll confirm later, the portion of fights that stay standing is on the rise, so this double-whammy of effects has been behind that acceleration of MMA pace throughout history. The definition of Significant Strikes relative to position is at the heart of the trends we've seen, but this position-specific analysis eliminates any doubt about evolving fighter pace.

While ground striking activity has barely grown over the last decade, clinch striking has seen a more appreciable increase in pace. Distance striking, however, has totally changed. Imagine the modern MMA fighter attacking the fighter of yesteryear with 12 strike attempts per minute compared to just five or six. One word: overwhelming.

While the jury is still out on 2013, the trend could plateau. Or it could continue to rise as fighters realize the importance of maintaining a high pace for the benefit of management and the fans, while also trying to control the cage and win the judges' scorecards. Either way, the final analysis reveals that fighters are indeed fighting at a higher overall pace than ever before, employing a higher pace of Significant Strikes, and generally stepping up the action across all positions. Modern MMA, therefore, comes in extra-bold, in your face five-shots of knee locking Colombian sludge coffee as compared to the earlier, formative years when all we had were packets of instant, freeze-dried Earl Grey tea. And for that we should all be appreciative.

The Pace Advantage

The importance of pace should be obvious to fighters, fans, and judges alike. Pressing the action means launching more weapons, each one offering some small probability of being the one that counts. Even in fights that go the distance, a high pace of output means fighters doing all they can to control the action, impose their will, and win the round. To confirm the fundamental importance of pace in MMA, we can classify fighters by their average significant striking output and then examine wins and losses to see if being in a low- or high-pace group has any effect on outcomes. I did that math so you don't have to, and these results should be no surprise.

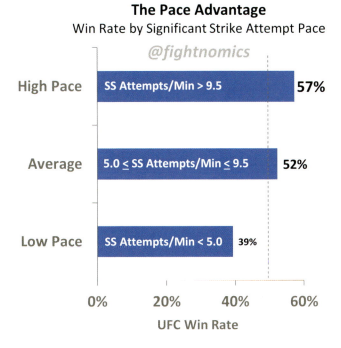

The Pace Advantage
Win Rate by Significant Strike Attempt Pace

@fightnomics

High Pace — SS Attempts/Min > 9.5 — **57%**

Average — 5.0 ≤ SS Attempts/Min ≤ 9.5 — **52%**

Low Pace — SS Attempts/Min < 5.0 — 39%

0%   20%   40%   60%

UFC Win Rate

For all UFC fights since 2008, fighters were grouped by their average Significant Strike pace, measured in attempts per minute where the average was around 7.2. I then created a threshold for "Low-" and "High-" pace fighters (as shown on the show), and reran fight outcome analysis using these groups, ignoring all other factors. The baseline win rate for this period of time was slightly less than 50% (remember there's always a few draws). The results show what we would expect, that low-pace fighters lose more often than not, while being a high-pace fighter carries an advantage. Separating fights that ended by stoppage versus decision did not change the numbers substantially, which suggests that a high pace is equally good for fighters who finish, as well as for those who win on the cards.

There's also a more subtle takeaway that while high pace is good, more importantly low pace is terrible. The degrees of those differences are not equal. The difference between the groups is more pronounced for the low-pace group of fighters in that they see nearly an 11% drop from the baseline win rate compared to a 7% boost enjoyed by high-pace fighters. "Average" fighters who didn't meet either differentiating threshold still fared a little better than our universal benchmark for win rates, meaning you don't have to work at a high pace to compete and survive in the UFC, as long you don't lag behind.

The "Pace Advantage" may be new to the MMA vocabulary, but this is the first of many "advantages" that I will test in this book. What's so simple and elegant about this metric is that it does not reflect skill or strength per se, but merely fighters who pull the trigger and push the pace. In terms of Significant Strike accuracy, however, there was actually an inverse correlation with pace, resulting in low-pace fighters having the highest accuracy, high-pace fighters having the lowest accuracy, and average fighters falling in between on both metrics. So Significant Strike accuracy doesn't seem to be a strong predictor of outcomes. We're also seeing the first hint that the rate of Significant Strikes landed may not be the key differentiator either compared to the rate of attempts. Apparently it's not always the damage done when it comes to winning fights, it's the thought that counts.

Gracies for Thought

Men are made in different shapes and sizes with different athletic ability, Jiu Jitsu makes us all equal.

Helio Gracie

A boxer is like a lion, the greatest predator on land. But you throw him in the shark tank and he's just another meal.

Renzo Gracie

 5 Advanced MMA Stats: The Ground Game

It's not an MMA fight if there's no threat of grappling. A fighter may have the best standup striking skills in the world, but they will be useless if he's planted on his back. Many strikers go into all-out panic mode in this environment. Just look at Anderson Silva, who landed just four power head strikes on Chael Sonnen in their first fight that lasted over 23 minutes at UFC 117. Fortunately for Silva, he also had the skills of a black belt in Brazilian Jiu Jitsu to save him in the final moments of that fight and secure his legacy in the "never ever give up" hall of fame.

In fact, grappling was really the whole point of the first ever UFC. When the Gracie family wanted to prove to the world that their system of fighting was superior to all others, they invited practitioners of other fighting styles and dropped them in a cage with a jiu jitsu master. Jiu jitsu grapplers were quickly proven the more effective fighters, much to the confusion of the spectators who still believed in the mysticism of the five-finger death punch or the clean choreographed combinations of the kung fu star.

When a chessmaster merely glances at chess pieces arranged on a board in the middle of a game, fluency garnered from deep experience provides him with instant and precise comprehension of how each piece is positioned relative to its opponents, and how and why each one got there. He perceives every pawn, rook, and bishop; his casual glance immediately tells him which player has the superior position and what moves each player is likely to make next. Just 32 game pieces spread over 64 possible spaces can lead to a mind-boggling – seemingly infinite – number of possible different games of chess. What the chessmaster sees is a single image with a precise meaning, a specific past, and a finite array of likely futures, while untrained bystanders can be so easily confused by any given detail that they miss the larger picture.

Such is the case with the game of human chess we call jiu jitsu. Experienced grapplers can instantly absorb the entirety of a complicated tangle of human limbs, and quickly grasp not only the "now," but also the "what next." The BJJ expert, like the chessmaster, can comprehend the timeline of each complicated human arrangement and know immediately where the best course of attack and/or defense lies.

The UFC has heavily influenced the public's education on the intricacies of grappling. The first ever UFC was Neolithic in comparison to today's high caliber MMA. UFC 1 was a time when a simple mount could cause a panicked boxer like Art Jimmerson to tap out. Most spectators (and even fighters) could not recognize a devastating limb lock before serious damage was done. Fast forward to the modern age of MMA, when UFC events pervade primetime network TV with arm bars and triangle chokes that punctuate the fight scenes of summer blockbuster movies. Grappling has evolved, modernized, and forced spectators through a crash course in how to understand fights that end up on the ground.

We touched on ground striking in the last chapter, but we have yet to address how fighters end up there or what fighters are doing on the ground other than striking. It's time to move on to the most complex aspect of MMA, the ground game.

How Takedowns Work in the UFC

Before we get to the deceptively dangerous art of submission, we first need to figure out how fighters get their opponents off their feet and to the mat. It's not all brute strength and bear hugs, there is in fact some science to it. According to the FightMetric system of data organization, takedowns can come in three different flavors:

1. Shooting takedowns
2. Lower body clinch takedowns
3. Upper body clinch takedowns

In the first scenario, two fighters are standing at a distance from one another and one "shoots" for a takedown, crossing open ground to grab the leg or legs of his opponent. Shooting takedowns will be familiar to anyone who's watched a wrestling match. Given the strong representation of former wrestlers in the UFC, it's no surprise to see strong shots across the Octagon on a regular basis.

The second and third types of takedowns are thanks to the cage fencing that surrounds the Octagon. This fencing is a huge differentiator from the open wrestling mats with no physical barrier on the outer perimeter because it prevents fighters from backing up indefinitely and gives the attacking fighter more opportunities to get hold of his opponent.

Once two fighters have grabbed hold of one another, either on an open mat or against the cage, there are two more takedown types that can then occur: upper body clinch and lower body clinch. The differentiating factor at this point is the location

A fighter at BAMMA shoots for a takedown.
Photo by Martin McNeil.

of imbalance for the takedown attempt, basically whether you're forcing the upper or lower body of the target fighter to be out of balance with the rest of the body.

A lower body clinch attempt is most common while leaning against the cage. Fighters frequently press their opponents against the fence. The offensive fighter grabs the legs of his opponent and presses his shoulder into their opponent's midsection. The target in this case is the lower body.

Using the fence to your advantage helps when attempting a lower body clinch takedown.
Photo by Martin McNeil.

Upper body clinch takedowns can be attempted from any position where the offensive fighter is holding the waist or torso of his opponent, either throwing his opponent as in a suplex, or dragging him down like a football (American style) tackle. Instances where a fighter may be grabbing the upper body of his opponent while tripping the legs to cause a takedown are counted as lower body takedowns due to the imbalance occurring at the legs.

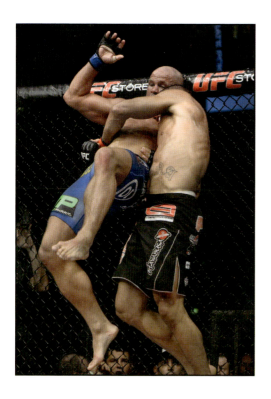

James Te-Huna uses an upper body clinch takedown of Ryan Jimmo. Photo by Martin McNeil.

So we have these three takedown types, which can each be analyzed separately: shooting, lower body clinch, and upper body clinch. The two most important metrics to understand when it comes to takedowns are the rate at which they occur and the success rate (or "accuracy") of the attempts. That allows us to assess how likely a given fighter is to attempt takedowns, and then how likely he is to land them when attempted. These metrics are the benchmarks for each takedown type.

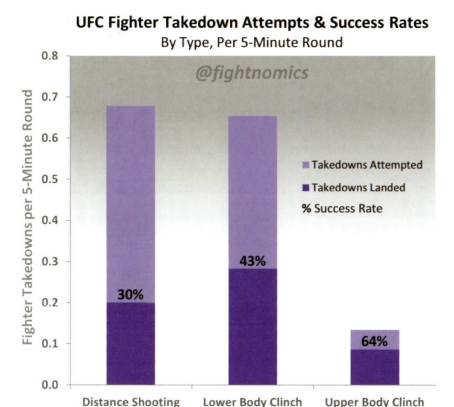

UFC Fighter Takedown Attempts & Success Rates
By Type, Per 5-Minute Round

Includes more than 8000 takedown attempts from all UFC fights 2008 – April, 2013

Fighters in the UFC average 1.5 takedown attempts per five-minute round with an overall success rate of 39%, based on data since 2008. The majority of these attempts are either distance shooting or lower body clinch takedowns, with upper body clinch attempts making up the smallest share of the total. As with striking, accuracy improves with proximity, meaning clinch takedowns are more successful overall than shooting attempts, and among clinch takedowns, those attacking the upper body are more successful than lower body attempts.

With such a diversity of fighters in the UFC, there's also wide variety of takedown preferences, both in how often they're attempted, and the particular approach fighters favor. Currently, the career UFC takedown leaders include some familiar names. These are the top ten UFC fighters in terms of takedowns landed as of October 1, 2013.

Top UFC Takedown Artists

Fighter	UFC Career Takedowns	Takedown Success Rate
Georges St-Pierre	84	75%
Gleison Tibau	71	57%
Jon Fitch	58	51%
Karo Parisyan	53	60%
Clay Guida	51	39%
Sean Sherk	50	47%
Rashad Evans	49	48%
Randy Couture	46	47%
Frankie Edgar	46	35%
Nik Lentz	45	38%

As of July, 2013

Career record lists usually comprise athletes who have simply been in the game a long time, but the names on this list combine longevity with high performance. Out of the top ten names, seven of them have takedown success rates that are well above the UFC average. Georges St-Pierre actually tops both lists for most landed takedowns as well as highest overall success rate. In this case, empirical evidence supports the claim that GSP is one of the best wrestlers in all of MMA.

When it comes to benchmarking a fighter's takedown prowess, however, it's better to look at a combination of success rate, and actual Octagon takedowns to determine how good they really are at getting opponents to the ground. The above list is a good place to start, but newcomers with fewer fights and could still show great potential to set a future UFC record. Considering 50% as a lofty goal for takedown success, any fighter above 60% is approaching the elite of the UFC. If a fighter is able to maintain such a high success rate through several fights, it's safe to say his wrestling ability is a strength. That includes fighters like Chris Weidman, Anthony Pettis, Michael McDonald, and Rustam Khabilov who have all shown very high takedown success rates to date, above 70%, but haven't logged enough attempts to show up in the record books. Given time, some of these young fighters will challenge Georges St-Pierre's position at the top of the takedown list.

The difference in frequency of attempts and the success rates of different takedown styles lead to some interesting trends when we zoom out from individual fighters and look at the UFC as a whole. From a historical perspective, testing our current benchmarks for takedown attempts and success rates might tell us more about the evolving nature of MMA. Here's the average number of takedown attempts per minute and the overall success rate on the same chart since 2005.

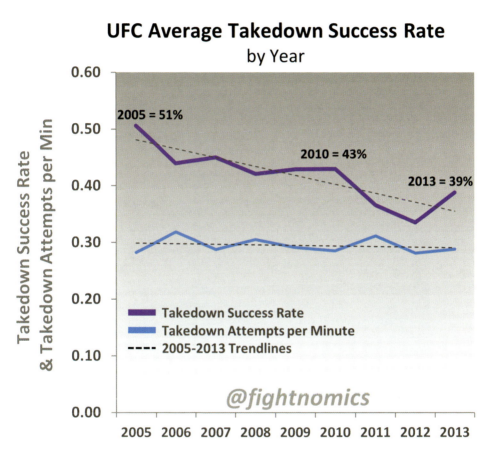

The analysis suggests that although fighters are attempting takedowns at a very stable rate, the success of these takedowns is falling over time. What's the explanation? Is this another instance where competitive forces combined with improved training has led to better overall takedown defense, and therefore declining success rates? Well, first we need to control for other potential trends. We already know that some takedowns are more successful than others, so perhaps the mix of takedowns has changed, leading to a shift in the overall average. Here's the annual share of takedowns evaluated by takedown type.

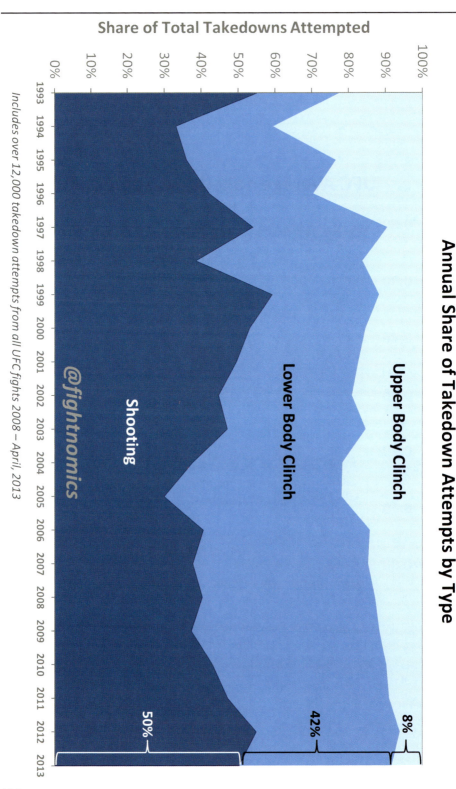

Annual Share of Takedown Attempts by Type

Share of Total Takedowns Attempted

Upper Body Clinch

Lower Body Clinch

Shooting

@fightnomics

8%

42%

50%

Includes over 12,000 takedown attempts from all UFC fights 2008 – April, 2013

We have a winner! Well, maybe. A potential explanation lies in what kinds of takedowns are being attempted rather than an improvement in takedown defense. Since 2005 three things have happened.

1. Shooting takedowns are increasing as a share of the total, and now comprise half of all takedown attempts.
2. The share of takedowns from the clinch where success rates are higher has been declining.
3. The highest success rate takedowns of all, upper body clinch attempts, now represent less than a tenth of overall attempts.

These trends have driven the total average success rate down and down despite a very consistent pace of overall attempts.

Is that all there is to this riddle of declining takedown success rates? Do polar bears live in Las Vegas? The question remains: why are fighters attempting shooting takedowns more often when that type of takedown has the lowest success rate? One would think that fighter camps would be wise to the differences in success rates, and when trying to get the fight to the mat would alter their game plans to maximize the likelihood of success. Yet here we are with more and more fighters shooting for single or double leg takedowns, knowing full well there's less than a one-in-three chance of success. Is there another unseen force at work?

Consider the possibility that fighters of different sizes have differing takedown metrics. Size may affect the success rates of various takedown techniques, and also the preferences in tactics that fighters employ. We'll start with success rates by weight class and takedown type.

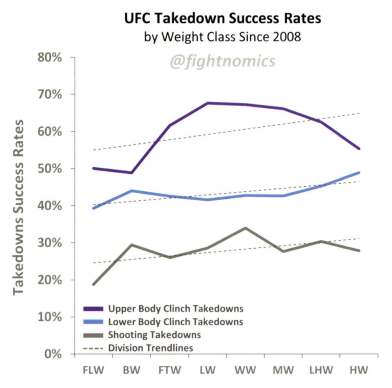

UFC Takedown Success Rates
by Weight Class Since 2008

There's an overall upward trend in takedown success rates by division size that also holds true for all types of takedowns. The pattern isn't perfect, but in general larger fighters are more likely to land each attempt than smaller fighters for all types. The trend that looks the most unusual is upper body clinch takedowns. It appears that the rule of thumb that success rate increase with size hits a limit for the largest weight classes. Perhaps this is understandable given that heavier fighters are harder to throw around. Or it could mean that recently added smaller divisions have more experienced wrestlers in their ranks, which translates into better overall takedown defense. These trends could partially explain why takedown success is falling in the UFC; the addition of smaller weight classes in recent years has shifted the mix of fights to the left of the graph in terms of weight classes. With more frequent fights competed in small weight classes, the macro trend that smaller fighters are harder to take down could be pushing the overall average in the same direction.

Just when you thought I was done, we have one more place to look before we can call it. If we analyze the mix of takedown attempts by weight class we can see if there are any differences in the type of takedowns fighters prefer. Here's each UFC weight class by the share of their takedown attempts by type.

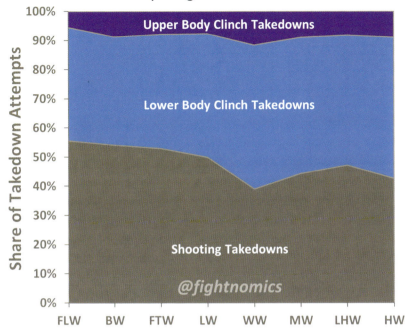

UFC Takedown Share by Type
by Weight Class Since 2008

Once again, we see a difference in trends based on the size of the fighter. It seems smaller fighters prefer to shoot for takedowns rather than clinch first, while larger and heavier fighters don't like shooting across the mat to snatch a leg. Perhaps this trend reflects a higher representation of former high-level wrestlers in the smaller divisions where undersized yet exceptional athletes migrated towards the size-controlled sport of wrestling rather than team sports full of giants. Regardless, there's a secondary driver of declining takedown success at work here due to the selection of takedown tactics and weight classes. The shifting center of mass of UFC fighters has dropped since the addition of the smaller WEC weight classes. Moreover, the newer flyweight division has had added to the effect on the overall amount of takedowns that occur in the UFC. Fans of standup fighting should be happy then that the little guys are keeping fights standing longer.

The final results here also leave us with one more takeaway: the decline in takedown success should be bottoming out with the recent stability in weight classes. Only time will tell if that prediction is true, but in the meantime we now know that the addition of lighter fighters in the UFC will mean fewer takedowns landed, and more time on the feet – that is, unless word gets out about the ineffectiveness of shooting takedowns compared to those from the clinch. But you won't tell anyone right?

Slam Science: With a Bang Not a Whimper

Not all takedowns are created equal, but it's also true that not all takedowns are finished equally either. Some are drag out wars of attrition that end with a whimper, while others begin with a take-up resulting in gloriously explosive feats of athleticism that end with a rib-cracking bang. "Slams" on takedown are recorded and categorized by which of the three types of takedowns was utilized (shooting, upper body, or lower body). Slams have their own subtle patterns, and in practice and extreme circumstances can even end fights. Although the most famous practitioner of the Power Bomb, Quinton "Rampage" Jackson, never actually used the maneuver to win a UFC fight, slams have resulted in TKO or KO finishes on eight different occasions in UFC history through 2013.

The first UFC slam knockout occurred at UFC 16: Battle of the Bayou on March 13, 1998. Then just 25 years old, Frank Shamrock retained the UFC Light Heavyweight (old division system) title against Russian-born Igor Zinoviev by slamming him into unconsciousness just 22 seconds into the fight. The slam also broke Zinoviev's collarbone, and he never competed professionally again. This brutal debut of the slam ended a fight, ended a career, and won a championship belt all in less time than it takes to drop a feather to the ground.

But wait; there's more. On November 2, 2001 at UFC 34, Matt Hughes took the UFC Welterweight title from Carlos Newton with a cage fence slam that is controversial to this day. Having already landed some slam takedowns in round one, round two saw Hughes get locked in a tight triangle choke that threatened to end the fight. Hughes used his infamous farm-boy strength to lift Newton up against the top of the cage and slam him down in a "power bomb" maneuver that knocked Newton out cold on impact. While referee Big John McCarthy tended to Newton in confirming the finish, he missed the fact that Hughes was essentially out himself as a result of the choke. Hughes quickly snapped back to reality, comprehended the situation and was declared the winner. Those final moments of the fight (and the resulting victory celebration) remain among his greatest highlights.

Out of the eight times a slam ended a fight, three were title fights. Tito Ortiz also accomplished this feat at UFC 30 with his 30-second slam KO of Evan Tanner in defending the Light Heavyweight title. So what's with these slams? Don't think they can hurt all that much? Let's run a very simple thought experiment.

Consider a slam where a body is hoisted into the air, then falls almost five feet to the mat. In many cases, fighters will carry opponents over their shoulders in a "fireman's carry" before leaping and diving into a slam. In this sense, a slam usually falls at least from the shoulder height of a fighter. We can now use two basic physics equations for "falling bodies" (in this case the formal name is quite appropriate) to determine the speed of impact on the ground: $t = square\ root\ (2d/g)$ and $v = gt$. Knowing the distance of the fall (estimated at five feet, or 1.5 meters) and the acceleration due to gravity (9.8 meters per second squared) tells us a free fall would last about a half second (t = 0.55). This tells us the velocity after the period of acceleration is roughly 5.4 meters per second.

In this rough estimate, the falling bodies would have been travelling at 12 miles per hour when they hit the ground from barely half a second of gravitational acceleration. That's over 1300 joules of energy on impact if you're into that sort of thing. Except that they aren't just falling with the aid of gravity. The offensive fighter's muscles are likely working to accelerate the recipient even faster towards the mat, so they could travel even faster. And the body of one is falling on top of the other, magnifying the crunch of the slammed fighter. We're already at the speed at which a normal person can sprint (roughly 12-15 mph on average). So now imagine sprinting full speed into a wall, back first. Sound like it might knock the wind out of you? You bet. That running speed of impact could easily knock someone out, as wide receivers in the NFL frequently learn when they come face-to-face with a sprinting Safety after stopping on a buttonhook route. Bottom line: being slammed is no fun, even if it doesn't result in such a brain-bouncing jolt as to render the recipient unconscious.

As with takedowns, some slams are easier to come by than others. Because FightMetric differentiates three flavors of takedown and slams, we can see which types of takedowns are most likely to end with a bang. It turns out, there is a difference.

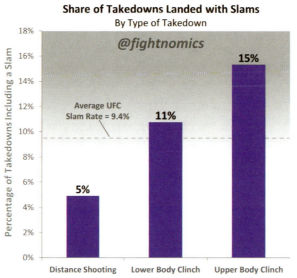

Share of Takedowns Landed with Slams
By Type of Takedown

@fightnomics

Average UFC Slam Rate = 9.4%

Includes more than 8000 takedown attempts from all UFC fights 2008 – April, 2013

Not quite one in ten takedowns will have a slam, but given how often takedowns occur that's still an appreciable amount of slamming going on. The chart clearly shows a difference in the slam rates for each takedown type relative the overall UFC average of 9.4%. Shooting takedowns rarely see slams, while clinch takedowns have double or triple the slam rate of shots. We already know that clinch takedowns are more effective than shooting from a distance in terms of success, and now we see the added benefit of increased ease of using slams from the clinch.

One of the biggest takeaways of wrestling analysis is that shooting takedowns are not the best strategy to get an opponent to the ground, but the prevalence of high level wrestlers in the UFC means this old habit may be hard to break. If fighters believed in the effectiveness of slams, you would think they would be utilized more often. Or perhaps, competitive forces had taught fighters to use better defense to stifle and prevent slams. To see which way slams are trending, we can look at the overall slam rate on an annual basis.

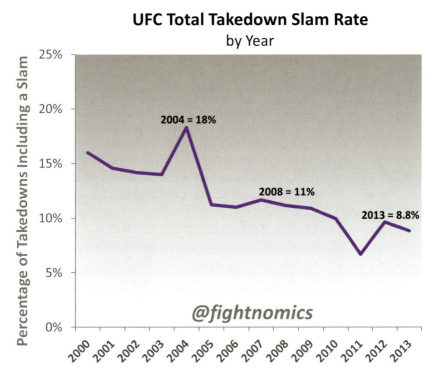

The chart demonstrates another clear trend that slams are occurring less and less frequently. Why? Are fighters attempting fewer high success takedowns (i.e., shooting more often?) or is the decline in slams consistent across all takedown types (i.e., slams are getting more difficult across the board)? We've been down this path before, so we can cut to the chase and test both those hypotheses in one graph.

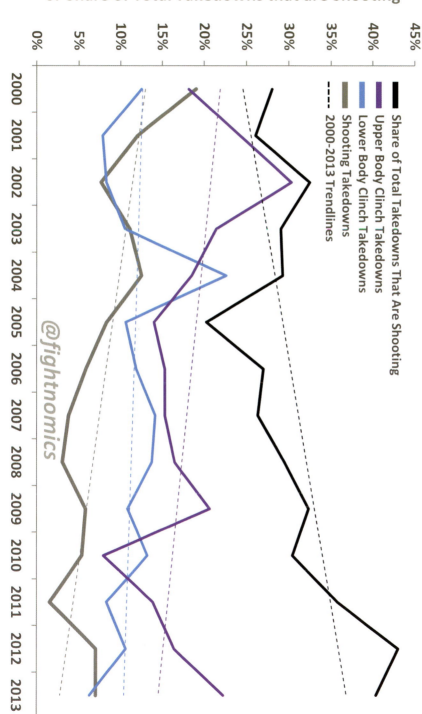

Percentage of Takedowns Including a Slam or Share of Total Takedowns that are Shooting

UFC Takedown Slam Rate
by Takedown Type & Year

- Share of Total Takedowns That Are Shooting
- Upper Body Clinch Takedowns
- Lower Body Clinch Takedowns
- Shooting Takedowns
- 2000-2013 Trendlines

@fightnomics

The answer to our questions seems to be "both." Shooting takedowns have risen in popularity from historically less than 30% of all takedowns landed, to more than 40% in recent years. Simultaneously the slam rate for every type of takedown, shooting or otherwise, has declined in the long run. There's a great deal of volatility year-to-year in these metrics, but the long run trends confirm the overall hypothesis that slams will be used less often than previously.

Strategically, slams emphasize cage control, put the exclamation mark on takedowns and generally scare the bejesus out of the entire crew of the slammed fighter. They could also be affecting a judge's perception of who is winning a round. The loud crash, the "ohhs" of the crowd, and the temporary stunning of the opponent that could lead to a quick position gain by the advancing fighter all mean that slams should not be overlooked as an influencing factor in the takedown game. Finally, it's important to note that some fighters are clearly better at this than others.

Here's a short list of some of the UFC's most prolific slam artists. I've ranked them by total slams, but you can see that some fighters have a higher rate of slams per takedown, indicating more aggression in their takedown game.

Top UFC Slammers

Fighter	UFC Career Slams	Slam Rate
Karo Parisyan	15	28%
Rashad Evans	11	22%
Matt Hughes	11	26%
Sean Sherk	10	20%
Mike Pierce	10	33%
Aaron Simpson	10	31%
Tyson Griffin	8	40%
Gleison Tibau	8	12%
Jon Fitch	8	14%
Josh Burkman	8	31%
Tito Ortiz	7	12%
Gray Maynard	7	23%
Georges St-Pierre	7	8%
Clay Guida	7	14%

As of July, 2013

The most prolific slammers have had enough appearances in the Octagon to rack up career stats, but within that list some guys have outperformed others on a per takedown basis. Notably, Tyson Griffin added a slam to 40% of his landed takedowns, and Mike Pierce, Aaron Simpson and Josh Burkman all surpassed a slam rate of at least 30%. While many of these career leaderboard fighters are no longer with the UFC, there's enough slamtastic talent floating around to ensure that the violent artistry of the slam will not die anytime soon.

UFC lightweight Rustam Khabilov, in particular, is the future star of the slam. His suplexes earned him a slam TKO victory over Vinc Pichel in his UFC debut at The Ultimate Fighter Finale 16 in December 2012. Beginning his UFC career 2-0 with two finishes, Khabilov also used takedowns to injure his second Octagon opponent, Yancy Madeiros. Despite not having enough career slams to show up on the career leaderboard, his slam rate is an impressive 50%. So just two fights into his career, Khabilov's takedowns and slams appear to be as dangerous a weapon as any inside the Octagon, and likely also highlight-reel fodder for a future remix of "Slam" by Onyx. Let the boys be boys.

One last consideration on the subject of slams: are some fighters more likely to get slammed than others? If so, then we should keep an eye on these frequent "slamees" who all tend to get planted at twice the UFC average slam rate or more.

Several names on the top Slamee list are guys who have fought in larger weight classes than where they are most competitive, which made them targets for slams. Diaz, Lentz, Edgar and Sanchez have all moved down a division to avoid being tossed around by larger opponents.

Top UFC Slam Recipients

Fighter Being Slammed	UFC Career Slams	Slam Rate
Nate Diaz	9	20%
Stephan Bonnar	8	36%
Nik Lentz	8	32%
Cheick Kongo	8	29%
Josh Neer	7	19%
Frankie Edgar	7	32%
Diego Sanchez	7	33%

As of July, 2013

How Submissions Work in the UFC

Getting to the ground is phase one. Submitting your opponent is phase two. Now that you know every which way fighters might end up on the mat it's time to analyze what happens next: the submission. As with takedowns and slams, not all submissions are created equal. Some are easier to attempt and some are easier to finish. But which ones are which?

In the average 15-minute UFC fight there will be 1-2 submission attempts, with an overall success rate of about 20%. Within these averages, however, there is a great deal of variety in submission technique success rates. To really understand how submissions go down in the UFC, we should look at the frequency with which they occur, as well as the success rate for each type. That will help us determine the correct answer for the perpetual question: what is the most popular submission in the UFC? For a submission attempt to be counted for statistical posterity, the technique must be "fully employed." That means an arm bar can't just be grabbing an arm; the recipient's arm must be extended to tally a real attempt. With all submission attempts logged on a round-by-round basis, we can then categorize and divide them by the confirmed finishes over the same time period, in this case five years of recent UFC fights. I've gone ahead and done the math, and here's what the numbers tell us.

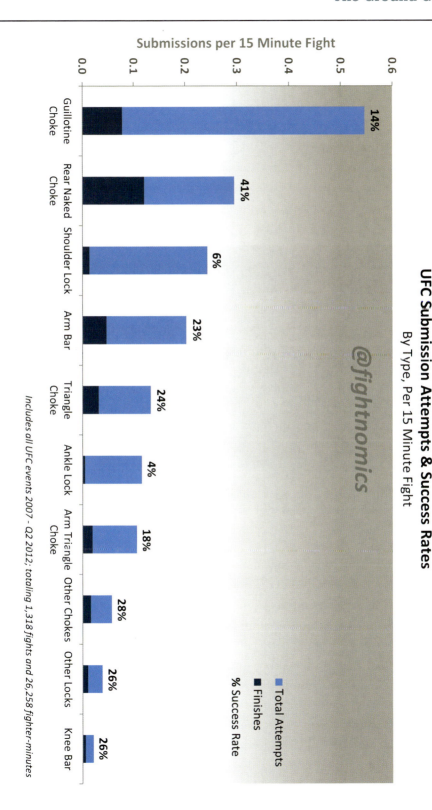

UFC Submission Attempts & Success Rates
By Type, Per 15 Minute Fight

Submissions per 15 Minute Fight

@fightnomics

- Total Attempts
- Finishes
- % Success Rate

Submission Type	% Success Rate
Guillotine Choke	14%
Rear Naked Choke	41%
Shoulder Lock	6%
Arm Bar	23%
Triangle Choke	24%
Ankle Lock	4%
Arm Triangle Choke	18%
Other Chokes	28%
Other Locks	26%
Knee Bar	26%

Includes all UFC events 2007 - Q2 2012; totaling 1,318 fights and 26,258 fighter-minutes

127

The conclusion: examining both the attempt and success rates for each submission type in the UFC reveals that some of the most common submissions attempted are actually the hardest to finish. Notably, Guillotine Chokes and Shoulder Locks (like Masahiko Kimura's favorite) have very low success rates despite being attempted fairly frequently. And really, who taps to Ankle Locks these days? No one still holding a UFC roster spot, that's who. Meanwhile, no submission is nearly as successful as the somniferous Rear Naked Choke, which ends a fight more than 40% of the time. The differences are indeed real, and some fighters may appreciate that

Though common, successfully utilizing the Guillotine choke is more difficult than it seems, although Terry Etim managed to make this one work. Photo by Martin McNeil.

When it comes to which submission ultimately translates into the most "W's" in the win column, the answer lies in the product of attempts and success rates together. Guillotine chokes are extremely common, probably because they are one of the easiest submission techniques to attempt due to the frequency of shooting takedowns placing the offensive fighter's neck into harm's way. But being a fundamental technique that is taught early to every former wrestler does not necessarily translate into success. The low success rate might be enough to knock the guillotine out of contention for the top submission spot. Meanwhile, some other techniques have less popularity, but better overall success rates. By taking a step back, we can just look at which submissions ended UFC fights by tap, nap or snap over the last five years.

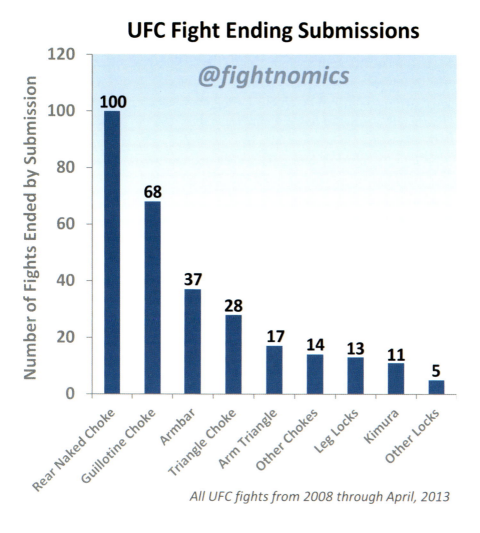

UFC Fight Ending Submissions

@fightnomics

All UFC fights from 2008 through April, 2013

Of the 293 submissions that occurred during the period of analysis, the Rear Naked Choke was the undisputed king of UFC submissions. On top of having the highest success rate, the high frequency of attempts pushes this submission to the top of the heap despite there being nearly twice as many guillotine attempts in the long run. Other popular techniques like the arm bar and triangle choke have finished a large chunk of fights, and secured their spots in the vernacular of the common MMA observer. These four submission types account for 80% of all fight-ending holds.

The Slickest Subs of All

As with striking, the more rare and exotic techniques can't be left out of this discussion because of their highlight reel appeal. The UFC rewards fighters employing an impressive submission finish with a Submission of the Night (SOTN) bonus, so an interesting question is how various techniques stack up just within the pool of SOTN winners. Instead of lumping rare techniques into the "Other" categories, I'll parse out as many as are available, but showing the SOTN award winning submissions in a frequency graph would actually be somewhat misleading. In fact, the graph would have an almost identical distribution and ordering of submission types as the analysis of fight ending submissions already shown. This is due to the larger trend that certain submission types are much more common than others. Combined with the fact that submissions are the least likely way to end a fight overall in the UFC, that means that some nights there are few options from which to choose an SOTN winner and the award goes to a fairly bread and butter technique.

A deeper analysis, however, can correct for how often a submission is used versus how often it wins an SOTN bonus. That will tell us the choke-for-choke, hold-for-hold winner of submission bonuses, and reprioritize the techniques based on some appraisal of their "impressiveness." What is the slickest sub of them all?

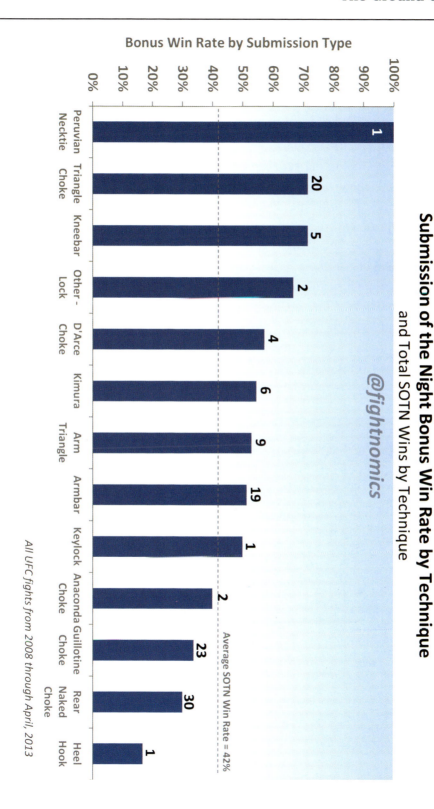

Submission of the Night Bonus Win Rate by Technique
and Total SOTN Wins by Technique

Bonus Win Rate by Submission Type

@fightnomics

Average SOTN Win Rate = 42%

Technique	Wins
Peruvian Necktie	1
Triangle Choke	20
Kneebar	5
Other - Lock	2
D'Arce Choke	4
Kimura	6
Arm Triangle	9
Armbar	19
Keylock	1
Anaconda Choke	2
Guillotine Choke	23
Rear Naked Choke	30
Heel Hook	1

All UFC fights from 2008 through April, 2013

131

And the winner is…the "Peruvian Necktie!" Sort of. The one time a Peruvian necktie was successfully administered in recent Octagon action was when CB Dolloway used the modified front headlock choke to tap Jesse Taylor at UFC Fight Night 14 in 2008. The fight lasted three minutes and 58 seconds, ending in a spectacular finish that stands out in UFC history even at a statistical level. Unfortunately for Taylor, the Peruvian Necktie wasn't just an epic, bonus-winning submission by Dolloway, it was the beginning and end to Taylor's UFC career.

Maybe we can't call the Peruvian Necktie the king of bonus worthy submissions just yet, especially since any fans not watching on that summer night five years ago would never have seen one. The current bonus win rate of 100% is a little skewed by the sample size of just one.

There is a more frequent submission type that still earns a very high bonus win rate: the triangle choke. As one of the only submission techniques that can be employed on an opponent in guard, and also one of the few that can be secured entirely with the legs, **the triangle choke combines a favorable mix of efficiency, resiliency, and flash. When these chokes are successful they earn a SOTN bonus 71% of the time**, giving fighters even more incentive to learn how to fight off their backs.

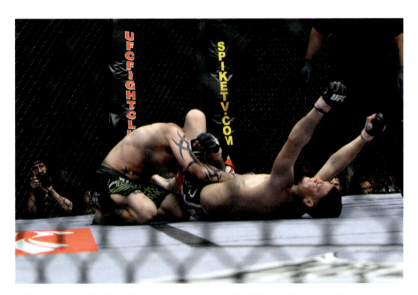

Look, no hands! Nate Diaz locks in a triangle choke and begins celebrating the inevitable tap of Kurt Pellegrino at UFC Fight Night 13. The photo was fortuitously snapped just before Diaz extended two middle fingers for the cameras. Photo by Paul Thatcher.

It's not surprising that the more vanilla guillotine and rear naked chokes end up on the bottom of the SOTN bonus win rate list, as these techniques are utilized most often and lack the flash of more exotic maneuvers. The heel hook in last place on the bonus win rate list is a head scratcher though, having only earned one bonus in six taps. It took Rousimar Palhares three fight-ending heel hooks (not including one knee bar) before he earned his first SOTN bonus. Leg locks of any kind remain an exceptional way to win a fight, but apparently aren't as impressive as they are rare. **Overall the trend in the SOTN chart shows rare submissions having higher SOTN win rates, with the most common submissions earning the least.** As irony would have it, Pahares was fired in 2013 for holding onto a leg lock too long (and didn't even get a bonus, despite having the only submission of the card).

Understanding the relative success rate of each technique and applying it to strategic decisions regarding ground position advancement is like a chess player thinking several moves ahead. During a fight, a grappler may wonder, "should I risk losing top position in order to pass guard to side control? What submissions are available there, or how does this position improve my expected success rates?" If you don't believe that fighters are thinking through some of these decisions during a fight, you are vastly underestimating the expertise of these athletes.

Remember, fighting may come from primal evolutionary roots, but the human brain has skillfully crafted a complex algorithm for competing in this game of human chess.

Some fighters understand more than others the power of submissions inside the Octagon. Here's a few that not only have won a lot of fights in the UFC by submission, but have done so with a good conversion rate on their submission attempts. For perspective, the overall average success rate for submissions in the UFC is 20%.

Top UFC Submission Artists

Fighter	UFC Career Submissions	Submission Success Rate
Royce Gracie	10	71%
Frank Mir	8	40%
Nate Diaz	7	30%
Kenny Florian	7	54%
Joe Lauzon	7	29%
Chris Lytle	6	19%
Demian Maia	6	35%
Cole Miller	6	29%
Rousimar Palhares	6	36%
Matt Hughes	5	31%
Jon Jones	5	63%
Martin Kampmann	5	24%
Dan Severn	5	83%
Ken Shamrock	5	45%
Oleg Taktarov	5	45%

As of July, 2013

It's fitting that Royce Gracie tops the all-time list of submissions in the UFC, but also no surprise when you look at his 71% submission success rate. With Gracie now retired, Frank Mir is just two taps away from tying Gracie, but Mir's submission success rate of 40% per attempt means it make take a few more fights. The preponderance of retired fighters here reflects how it takes a full career to end up on a list like this one, and the overall drop in submissions through the years makes it even harder for younger fighters to accumulate them fast enough. On the other hand check out Jon Jones, currently in the mix with five submissions and a dangerously high submission rate of 63%, the highest among any active fighter in the top 15. Given the long career that likely lies ahead of him, Jones is on pace to break a few more records in his already impressive career.

On the up-and-comers list, there are a few UFC fighters still working their way up the grappler's ladder having chalked up few wins, but having done so very efficiently. Renan Barao, Donald Cerrone, and Diego Brandao have all converted a perfect 100% of their submission attempts in the UFC into submission wins. Notably, each of these fighters is already fairly well known, and one is already a champion, showing once again that a little data can easily identify high performers.

The Grappler's Ticking Clock

It's true that the level of athleticism and conditioning has improved significantly during the rapid evolution of mixed martial arts, but let's not all high-five the conditioning coaches just yet. There are still limits to stamina and performance in the Octagon, even when it comes to grappling and submissions.

One key factor that declines with fatigue is a fighter's ability to secure and hold a lock. With only one exception, the success rate of submissions drops substantially in the third round. Accounting for the fact that submission attempts occur at a reduced rate in later rounds, it's still true that the success rate of these attempts is much lower than in earlier rounds. It's not a small effect, as third round attempts have barely half the overall success rate of submission attempts in the first two rounds. Grapplers be warned: don't waste any time going for the submission, because the clock is ticking, and as the fight wears on you're only getting more tired while your opponent is getting more sweaty. The numbers on this question don't lie.

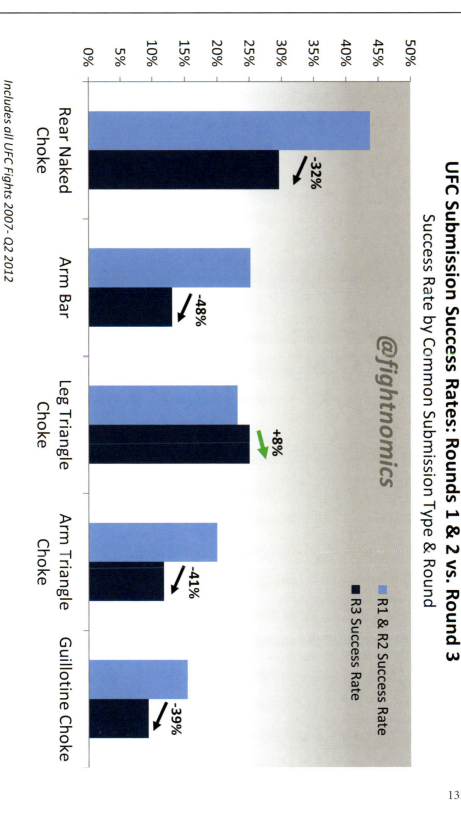

UFC Submission Success Rates: Rounds 1 & 2 vs. Round 3
Success Rate by Common Submission Type & Round

@fightnomics

- R1 & R2 Success Rate
- R3 Success Rate

Includes all UFC Fights 2007 - Q2 2012

Rear Naked Choke: -32%
Arm Bar: -48%
Leg Triangle Choke: +8%
Arm Triangle Choke: -41%
Guillotine Choke: -39%

135

Of the most common UFC submission types, almost all have been much harder to secure in the third round. The most obvious reasons are fatigue and sweat, both of which make holding an opponent tightly much more difficult. The lone exception is the Leg Triangle Choke, which notably, does not require arm muscles to sustain the lock. Legs have greater strength and endurance than arms thanks to their constant struggle under gravity and your generous diet, so this pattern isn't surprising. In this case, fatigue may have a greater effect on a fighter's ability to defend the triangle choke than on the fighter locking his legs in attack. **The lessons are: when you're gassed, use your legs, and whatever you do, don't sacrifice position in the third round for a shoulder or leg lock.**

Certainly, fighters who lather up like eels as the fight goes on make shoulder and leg locks more difficult. Many of these submissions have success rates that drop to 0% in rounds three and beyond. There are exceptions of course, often involving the best in the business (see Jon Jones' fourth-round Americana submission of Vitor Belfort). But the overall trend is quite clear, and it likely has a lot to do with muscle fatigue. Even pure position holds, like the RNC, are harder to keep locked for the duration necessary to elicit the tap, with early success rates of 44% dropping to just 30% in the third round. So fatigue is very likely a root cause of the drop in success rates by round. As with knockdown rates there's also a small window for "Survivorship Bias" to be leaking into the data here, as only better grapplers survive early submission attempts only to succumb later, but at a lower rate. It's possible that's a factor here, but it wouldn't explain the huge changes we're seeing round-to-round.

What's not in question is that flexing muscles for long holds gets harder with fatigue, and knowing this fact could change a fighter's strategy mid-fight. Even an exhausted fighter can still throw a haymaker that downs his opponent. Though knockdown rates decline through rounds, they still occur frequently enough to conclude that fighters remain dangerous in their striking while fatigued, still able to summon their fast twitch muscles for sporadic bursts. The slow twitch muscles required to squeeze and hold long enough to elicit the panic response from a defending fighter cannot perform nearly as well when exhausted.

The conclusion is that grappling specialists are most likely to secure submissions in the first two rounds of fights, and only remain dangerous with their legs or via back control in later rounds. Armed with this information, fighters may change their offensive tactics in later rounds. For example, knowing that the chance of locking up a guillotine choke is less than 10%, or that top game submissions will become nearly impossible, perhaps it's better to stand and trade in the third, or improve position to back control if you're down on the cards.

Conversely, **a fighter clearly ahead on the cards may be at less risk by going to the mat than by keeping the fight standing at the end of a fight**. Fighters can rely on their opponents' fatigue to mitigate the risk of submissions, potentially opening up their striking attack without worrying about takedown defense. How these findings are acted upon is up to fighters and coaches, but at least now we've confirmed a key hypothesis about mixed martial arts once and for all.

6

Hacking the Tale of the Tape: How Size Matters, and How It Doesn't

This Chapter in 30 Seconds:

- Size matters; bigger fighters pack more power but aren't as fast

- Competition has driven fighters down in weight class due to the UFC Arms Race

- The reach advantage is real, with longer reach differentials leading to more wins

- The reach advantage is accentuated for fights that stay standing longer, nullified on the ground

- Height is not an advantage if it doesn't also come with reach

Anyone who's watched a single boxing match knows what the "Tale of the Tape" is. Innovated by boxing, it was inherited by the UFC in the early years of the sport and has become just as integral a part of the pre-fight buildup as the voice of Bruce Buffer. As with any combat sport, the amount of information relevant to the viewer that can be translated through statistics is limited, but universally includes basic "anthropometrics," or physical human measurements like weight, height and reach. The traditional Tale of the Tape from boxing remains in use by the UFC today as the sole bit of hard data fans get before each match in the cage, and hasn't really changed in the decades that fighting has been on television. This Tale of the Tape certainly wasn't created for, or optimized to the sport MMA, but we're left with it nonetheless.

So we might as well hack this thing, and figure out what it's really saying. The basic measurements of fighter size may actually tell us some secrets, and with the help of some detailed historical analysis we'll definitely learn to read the Tale of the Tape from a new and enlightened perspective.

Weight Class Matters

We're often told that "size doesn't matter." At least that is what is said before you fail to make the high school football team because your bearded classmates already outweigh you by 50 pounds at the age of 15. There's always theater, they say, or chess, but let's just hope you've never endured this same platitude from a sexual partner. No comment? The point is that size is not supposed to matter in the grand scheme of things, but we all know it does. The reality is that inadequate size severely limits your likelihood of playing NBA hoops, following Ron Jeremy's career path, or even becoming president. Conversely, no Sumo wrestlers will ever be competitive divers, horse jockeys or fighter pilots because basic anthropometrics will follow us everywhere and influence our lives in subtle but significant ways no matter how much we wish they didn't. Much of our potential is genetic; the surrounding world exerts a gentle but constant push on our life trajectories towards pursuits that favor our genetic disposition.

In MMA, divisions are defined by weight limits. **While that means that the day before a fight any two competitors facing each other weigh roughly the same amount, it certainly does not mean they are the same size**. A side-effect of MMA rules that focus on weight limits distracts from all other anthropometric aspects of the fighter. The term "anthropometry" literally means the "measure of man," a term I picked up from the professional statisticians in the NBA. It describes basic measurements like height, weight, reach, age, or even hand dominance. As was explained by a head team analyst, drafting a guard with an extra 2" of wingspan should generate X more steals per minute played, and therefore a point differential of +Y points per game, where "X" and "Y" are some proprietary insight to a riddle that every team endeavors to solve. Basketball scouts aren't alone. For each sport, there is a specialized set of physical characteristics that gives athletes an advantage in competition. Many take a "bigger is better" approach, like in basketball, volleyball, or football. Smaller frames have advantages in sports like gymnastics or weight lifting, while others may require unusually imbalanced physical arrangements to be ideal, like swimmers with long arms but short legs. Coaches, trainers and athletes alike in many sports use anthropometrics to evaluate players or place them in the context of their position. We'll use these same data points to hack into the Tale of the Tape for MMA.

Although weigh-ins occur just 24 hours before fight time, most fighters recoup a substantial amount of water weight before the actual competition. We don't know how much fighters weigh when they finally step into the cage so we're left only with their division's weight limits when it comes to how heavy they are. Fortunately there are other more firm variables like height, reach, and age that populate the Tale of the Tape that are worth considering.

Take the fighter's "size" for example. Despite equal weigh-in values there are a variety of body shapes and sizes that carry those pounds to the scale. Then there are items that change each fight for the same fighter, like age, experience, and fight history. We'll stick with the basics of body size first and as you'll see, there's plenty we can learn from these simple numbers. You might never view the Tale of the Tape the same way again, but like any good classic tale your wisdom will allow you to appreciate it more fully.

With weigh-in values set in stone for all practical purposes, we need to first figure out how that translates into "frame size" for the human bodies that step on the scale. I took a snapshot of the UFC roster during the summer of 2013 and then created averages (means) for height and reach (wingspan) within each division. Here's how the fighters measure up. I'll apologize in advance that this book does not employ the metric system (I should have my science club card revoked), but I'm fully aware that most readers will be more familiar with the Imperial System of units.

Fightnomics: UFC Division Mean Height & Reach (Inches)

Wondering if you're "big" or just "average?" Just how big is average for a UFC fighter? Well that depends on the weight class obviously. Here's the current UFC roster of fighters put into divisions with average (mean) height and reach. Next time someone says a fighter looks big for their weight class, check the facts first.

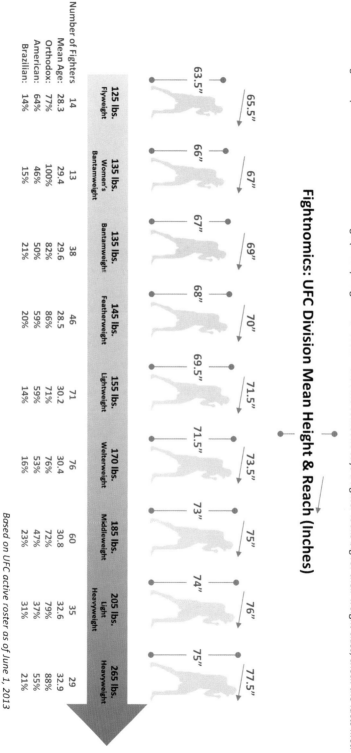

	125 lbs. Flyweight	135 lbs. Women's Bantamweight	135 lbs. Bantamweight	145 lbs. Featherweight	155 lbs. Lightweight	170 lbs. Welterweight	185 lbs. Middleweight	205 lbs. Light Heavyweight	265 lbs. Heavyweight
Reach	65.5"	67"	69"	70"	71.5"	73.5"	75"	76"	77.5"
Height	63.5"	66"	67"	68"	69.5"	71.5"	73"	74"	75"
Number of Fighters	14	13	38	46	71	76	60	35	29
Mean Age:	28.3	29.4	29.6	28.5	30.2	30.4	30.8	32.6	32.9
Orthodox:	77%	100%	82%	86%	71%	76%	72%	79%	88%
American:	64%	46%	50%	59%	59%	53%	47%	37%	55%
Brazilian:	14%	15%	21%	20%	14%	16%	23%	31%	21%

Based on UFC active roster as of June 1, 2013

141

The range of UFC divisions currently spans 140 pounds from Flyweight (125 pounds maximum) to Heavyweight (265 pounds maximum), which on average translates into nearly one foot of additional height and reach from the Flyweights to the Heavyweights, as well as an extra 12 inches of wingspan. It's important to remember that there is plenty of variability that occurs within each weight class. Some bodies are tall and lean while others are short and stocky, but the larger the division, the wider the range of maximums and minimums. Just think of heavyweights Stephan Struve and Pat Barry facing off with over a one-foot height differential in the same weight class. Conversely, it's unusual to see a large size discrepancy at bantamweight.

And just look at the new women's division. At Bantamweight there's a discernible size difference between male and female fighters weighing in at the exact same weight limit. The men's division has been around a lot longer and has greater competition from a larger pool of contenders, many of whom are experienced pros at cutting weight thanks to backgrounds in wrestling. The larger frames of the men manage to pack more muscle and bone onto the scale on weigh-in day resulting in an additional two inches of height and one additional inch of reach. Competition always pushes the limits of human anthropometrics, and the UFC is as competitive as ever.

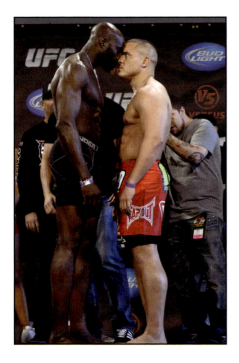

Heavyweight Cheick Kongo stares down Pat Barry before UFC Live: Kongo vs. Barry. Kongo had a 7.5" reach advantage and won in the first round despite being knocked down twice. It was one of only eight times in UFC history where a fighter who scored two knockdowns went on to lose. Barry did it twice, once against Mirko Cro Cop and a year later versus Kongo. Photo by Martin McNeil.

According to the US Centers for Disease Control the average American male stands just over 5' 9" and walks around at 195 pounds. That means the average American has the height of a lightweight, but is 40 pounds too heavy for their division. Just keep in mind that the UFC averages are based on weigh-in weights, and that the vast majority of fighters walk around approximately 20 pounds heavier than at weigh-ins. So when comparing yourself to these divisions find your height first, then add at least 10 pounds for the small divisions, 20 pounds or more for the middle divisions, and 30 pounds or more for the largest ones. That ought to give you a more realistic view of the natural size of these athletes. Also remember that these are professional cagefighters, and in no way does that mean what's "good" for them is what anyone else should aspire to. The most extreme edges of competition also breed a few unhealthy habits.

Living Large, Finishing Big

Studies have correlated a variety of trends with height – from income levels to leadership prowess – all with meaningful and statistically significant results. So size matters much more than just whether or not you can ride a roller coaster (sorry Mighty Mouse Johnson, come back next year), it can influence how different people perform, succeed, or fail at a variety of physical or social tasks. But what does it mean for MMA? Specifically, how much can we know about MMA fights based solely on weight class? Does size really matter in terms of fight outcomes.

Starting with a fundamental hypothesis, that bigger guys finish fights differently, I've arranged the vast database of UFC fights by how each fight ended separated by weight class. We know that weight classes are a fairly good measure of overall size despite the variations within them, so by using the proxy of weight class we can see how size generally affects how fights go down. For simplicity, I filtered out fights that were disqualifications or later overturned, as well as catch weight and women's fights, which were all small in number. I also isolated only fights occurring in the UFC spanning the over a six-year period of recent events for consistency of matchmaking in the "modern age of MMA." The results in the graph demonstrate one of the clearest patterns in fighting: Size Matters.

The trends in MMA consistently show that larger fighters end more fights by KO/TKO than smaller fighters, and lighter weight classes have a larger share of submission finishes that decline with increasing size. Overall, the share of fights ending by decisions decreases with increasing fighter size, implying that the increase in the knockout rate is steeper than the decline in submission finishes. Just knowing the weight class of two fighters stepping into the cage will give you some good hints as to the overall likelihood of a finish, and also the likely type of finish should the fight end inside the distance.

Fightnomics: How All UFC Fights End

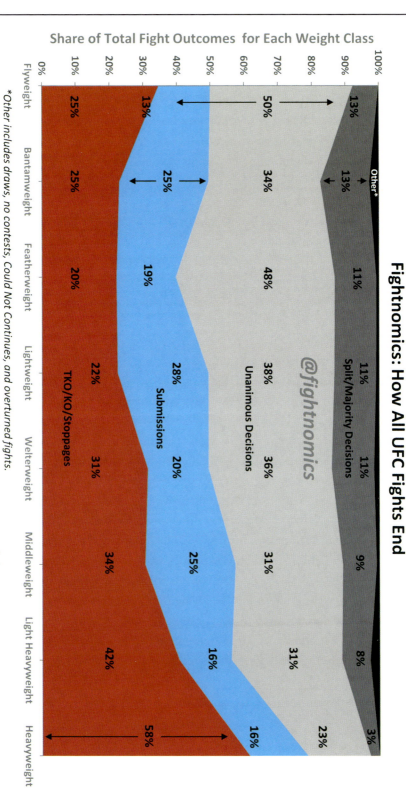

Share of Total Fight Outcomes for Each Weight Class

Weight Class	TKO/KO/Stoppages	Submissions	Unanimous Decisions	Split/Majority Decisions	Other*
Flyweight	25%	13%	50%	13%	
Bantamweight	25%	25%	34%	11%	13%
Featherweight	20%	19%	48%	11%	
Lightweight	22%	28%	38%	11%	
Welterweight	31%	20%	36%	9%	
Middleweight	34%	25%	31%		
Light Heavyweight	42%	16%	31%	8%	
Heavyweight	58%	16%	23%	3%	

@fightnomics

*Other includes draws, no contests, Could Not Continues, and overturned fights.
Dataset includes all UFC fights 2008 – October, 2013, or 1578 total fights; percentages are rounded.

Physics of the Knockout

Clearly, heavyweights score more knockouts – more than twice as many as the lighter weight classes – and that's a big difference. That means you can bet that a heavyweight fight will end early by strikes and be right slightly more than half of the time, while betting against a lightweight fight ending in strikes will get you paid four out of every five times. Analysis of other promotions revealed very similar patterns, despite a variety of slight differences in environmental variables. So size matters. Period.

One obvious reason for this relationship is knockout power. Some guys have it, and some don't. A key driver of power is how much muscle mass is available to drive the strike. Retired UFC heavyweight Shane Carwin once discussed his power, saying that when his hands touch people, "they go to sleep." His softly spoken words and modest and subtle demeanor euphemized the violence he was describing. The real mechanism for his sleep-inducing strikes is the large amount of muscle mass all over his body, making his heavy hands that much more powerful. Muscles are like engines; they burn energy and convert chemical potential energy into mechanical kinetic energy. The more muscle you have, the more work you can do. The men who compete in the upper echelons of the UFC heavyweight division have a lot of muscle mass, and their fists can do some serious work. The result is that we see a lot of heavyweight fights ending in strikes, and the sleep they cause is anything but gentle.

Isaac Newton determined that force is equal to mass times acceleration ($F = ma$). The simplicity of Newtonian mechanics belies another more fundamental truth: physics is merciless. There's no ancient mystery to this kind of "Force," and there's no magical jewelry you can wear to break its laws or prevent its inexorable, unrelenting truths. The monstrous meat paws of a heavyweight, with correspondingly massive arms, back, hips, and legs propelling their hands forward, are capable of inducing rapid acceleration of a human head on contact. Which brings us to another important equation in collisions: $p = mv$. That is, momentum equals mass times velocity (Force is just the derivative of momentum over time). When the point of impact occurs between fist and head, we're ultimately concerned with how much energy is transferred from the hand into the formerly stationary head, and collisions like this are governed by momentum. Momentum is "conserved," it can neither be created nor destroyed. A direct strike means imparting as much energy as possible from the striker's body into the acceleration of the target's (less massive) head. Both equations rely on mass.

Looking at the other variable in the momentum equation leads us to believe that throwing faster punches should also equate to knockouts. Don't lighter weight fighters have quicker hands, and therefore are able to compensate for the size difference? That may be true, but the much larger mass of a heavy fighter seems to dominate any increase in the quickness of lighter fighters. Larger fighters also tend to be taller, with longer arms. While it certainly takes more energy and time to get a bigger fist accelerated and moving at high velocity, long arms also have a longer runway to accelerate before they run out of room, quickly decelerate, and then finally stop at their maximum reach distance. The shorter arms of a lightweight may snap into movement quickly, but they can't accelerate for very long.

Stylistic Selection

Knowing that their chances of scoring a knockout at lightweight are drastically reduced, smaller fighters have attempted to win on the ground far more often than heavyweights. The physics of the situation has changed the way fights go down. Lightweights attempt more takedowns per fight than larger fighters, and attempt almost twice as many submissions. A compounding bonus for the lightweight submission game is that the percentage of submission attempts that are locked-in tightly is more than double that of heavyweights. The intermediate weight classes line up in these metrics as we'd expect, and thus the performance differences between fighters of varying size go on and on. Suffice to say, if a BJJ submission expert is going to get a chance to wield his skills in an MMA fight, he's going to need some time to get position and work his game.

For lightweights, their increased chance of surviving a few direct strikes along the way means their chances of lasting long enough to develop a finishing position is much greater than for heavier fighters, who may never get that opportunity. When was the last time you saw a heavyweight willing to absorb blows while repeatedly shooting for takedowns? Ultimately, this means that we should see better BJJ practitioners among the quicker, elusive, lighter weights where their skills have a better chance to shine than at heavyweight, where just one crushing XXXL glove makes the difference between awake time and nap time.

The UFC Arms Race
& the Incredible Shrinking Middleweight

In 2005 Kenny Florian made his Octagon debut at the finale of the inaugural season of The Ultimate Fighter. Weighing in at 183 pounds and competing at middleweight, Florian went on to suffer his first (and only) TKO loss at the hands of Diego Sanchez. Then Florian went on a diet, returning to the Octagon later that year 15 pounds lighter as a welterweight, and rattling off two quick stoppage victories. But Florian wasn't done shrinking. In 2006 he dropped another 15 pounds for his lightweight debut. He would stay in that division for four years, amassing an impressive 9-3 record, with his only losses coming in title fights or title eliminators. In 2011, with the lightweight title picture clogged by the Maynard-Edgar battles, Florian tightened his belt by 10 more pounds and moved down to featherweight, now weighing in 40 pounds lighter than in his UFC debut six years prior. When he retired two fights later, the UFC Hall of Famer was the only fighter to have competed in four different UFC divisions. Which got me thinking: how often do fighters switch weight classes, and how has the average size within a division changed over time?

In analysis of UFC fighters from 2002 to 2013 with at least two Octagon appearances, 38% of them had competed in at least two separate weight classes. If we change the sample size to fighters with at least four appearances, then the metric leaps to 56%. That means more than half of all UFC fighters will drop a division if they compete for at least four fights. We know that size is an advantage, and the overall trend in the UFC is for fighters to get better at managing their weight and compete in lower divisions. Consider how quickly the UFC has evolved under competitive forces. Today's top MMA athletes are full-time fighters with cutting edge training camps. They have dieticians and nutritionists, and even supplement sponsors. For fight week they may even have a personal chef to travel with them to help manage the weight cut and rebound. All of this means that the amount of raw athlete packed into each pound that steps on the UFC scale at weigh-in time is as at an all-time high, but could even go higher.

If these forces are real, then we can assume that fighters in prior years may not have been optimizing their size as well as fighters do today. With the right analysis, we should be able to see evidence of that. Here's how fighter size by division has changed over the last decade.

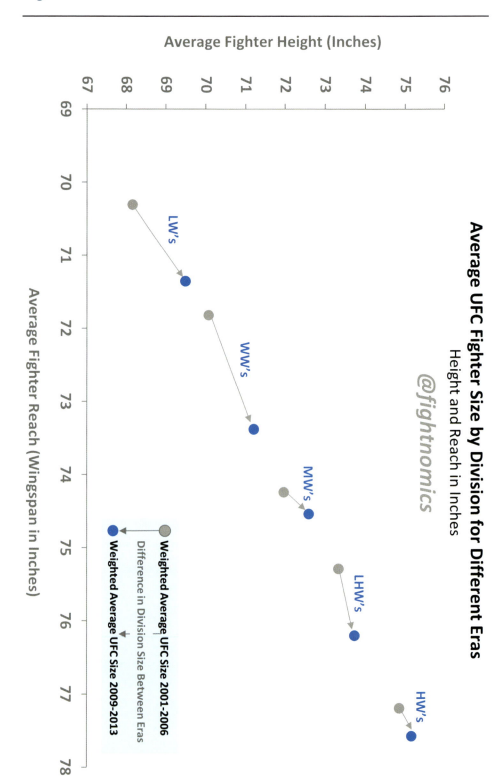

Average UFC Fighter Size by Division for Different Eras

Height and Reach in Inches

@fightnomics

Average Fighter Height (Inches)

Average Fighter Reach (Wingspan in Inches)

LW's

WW's

MW's

LHW's

HW's

Weighted Average UFC Size 2001-2006

Difference in Division Size Between Eras

Weighted Average UFC Size 2009-2013

The graph shows that the average size of each legacy UFC division (that existed before Zuffa's addition of the WEC) has grown in average height and reach over time. I've used a weighted average that simply looks at any fighter appearance in the Octagon by weight class and captures height and reach. The reality isn't just that modern fighters are taller and longer than fighters a decade ago, it's also that the same fighters weigh less. Fighters have shrunk their waistlines, while divisions have sprouted vertically and horizontally – all thanks to the perpetual arms race that motivates athletes to become champions.

Change in Average Fighter Size Over Time

UFC Division	2002-2006		2010-2013	
	Height"	Reach"	Height"	Reach"
Lightweights	68.2	70.3	69.5	71.4
Welterweights	70.1	71.8	71.2	73.4
Middleweights	72.0	74.2	72.6	74.5
Light Heavyweights	73.3	75.3	73.7	76.2
Heavyweights	74.8	77.2	75.2	77.6

The same data is presented here explicitly in order to show the real changes. In smaller weight classes where the weight cut to drop a division is also smaller, we see larger relative changes in size. Lightweights didn't even have a division they could move down to until the WEC merger in 2011, so plenty of fighters who could have competed below lightweight were hanging out in a larger division simply because it was their only opportunity to compete in the UFC. While my analysis used larger sample sizes to ensure the hypothesis was well tested, I've isolated the same size value for even more recent periods like 2011-2013, or just 2012-2013. It seems the divisions aren't done growing. The more recent the period of data I use, the larger the legacy divisions get. It's an arms race, and it's not over yet.

Remember the case of Kenny Florian, who migrated 40 pounds and four weight classes down the UFC divisions with the same-sized frame that was five foot, ten inches tall with a reach of 74 inches. According to the chart, he was a tiny middleweight, but a fair-sized welterweight. At lightweight, however, Florian had a size advantage over the average division opponent, so it's no surprise that he found a home in this division for most of his career. When Florian cut down to the next division, he was huge by comparison. He had a big size advantage over most featherweights who averaged five foot eight with a reach of only 70 inches. Now retired from fighting, but having clued us into an important trend in MMA, I wish Kenny many satisfying meals at all-you-can-eat buffets.

Another benefit of viewing size data graphically is that it can quickly show us patterns at a macro-level, but also highlight where individual data points stand relative to the larger picture. We know size is a relative advantage in MMA, so one would assume that the most successful athletes combine genetic benefits along with their training and skill. So how do UFC champions really stack up to their peers? Let's take the current averages per division and overlay the champions of 2013 (at the time of this analysis) on the same chart. Does the cream really rise to the top?

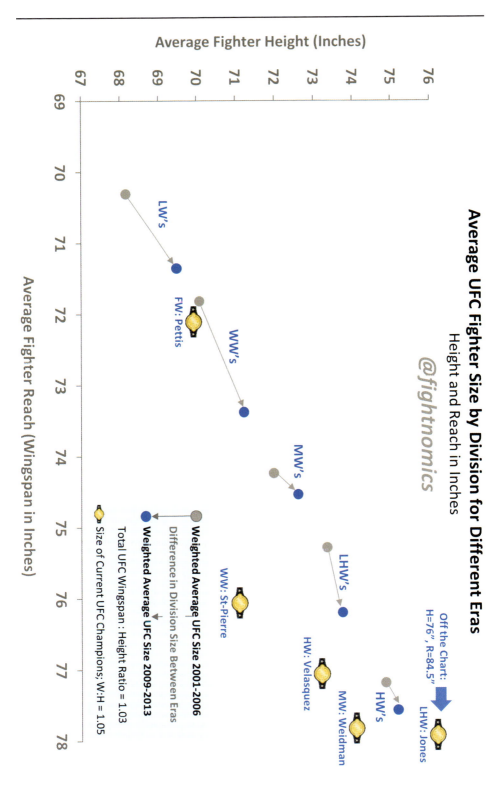

Average UFC Fighter Size by Division for Different Eras

Height and Reach in Inches

@fightnomics

Average Fighter Height (Inches)

Average Fighter Reach (Wingspan in Inches)

LW's

FW: Pettis

WW's

MW's

WW: St-Pierre

LHW's

HW: Velasquez

MW: Weidman

HW's

LHW: Jones

Off the Chart:
H=76", R=84.5"

● Weighted Average UFC Size 2001-2006

Difference in Division Size Between Eras

● Weighted Average UFC Size 2009-2013

Total UFC Wingspan : Height Ratio = 1.03

Size of Current UFC Champions: W:H = 1.05

Consider for a moment Leonardo Da Vinci's "Vitruvian Man." In his famous drawing of the human form surrounded by a circle and square, one of his observations was that "the length of a man's outspread arms is equal to his height." That means the average wingspan (reach)-to-height ratio should be about 1.0 even. Da Vinci was really close, or maybe he was dead on correct for his time, and the relative shapes of human bodies have changed in the 500 years since his observation. Either way, the average for men today is about 1.02, slightly lower for women. In the UFC, we see that the average ratio is actually 1.03 and even higher for the average of title holders at 1.05.

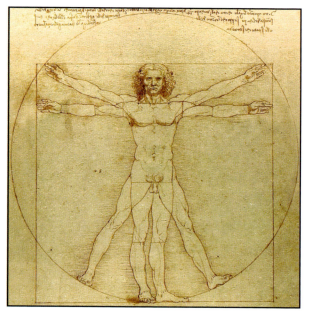

In Leonardo Da Vinci's "Vitruvian Man," he observed that the wingspan to height ration of a human is about 1.0. He was really close. Photo from Wiki Commons.

In many sports wingspan carries an advantage. Basketball is one where long arms are especially advantageous, and the NBA average ratio is 1.06. That small bump above the norm may not seem like a lot, but those few decimals are very significant. In fact, one of the diagnostic criteria for the connective tissue disorder known as Marfan's Syndrome (which Abraham Lincoln was suspected of having), is 1.05. Individuals with this genetic condition tend to be tall and very lanky with overly flexible joints.[1]

Only two UFC champions, Dominick Cruz and Cain Velasquez, could be considered "undersized" for their divisions in terms of reach. One more, Jose Aldo, is little shorter than his division peers but has equal reach. The rest, Demetrious Johnson, Renan Barao, Anthony Pettis, Georges St-Pierre, Chris Weidman and Jon Jones all have reach (and in most cases height) that is longer than their division peers. Some of these champions are physical outliers. St-Pierre and Barao have very high wingspan ratios of 1.07 and 1.06, respectively, while Jon Jones is literally off the chart with his UFC-longest reach of 84.5 inches on a six foot four inch frame resulting in a ratio of 1.11. Jones' wingspan ratio isn't just the longest in the UFC, it's the longest confirmed ratio in MMA history. And while Jones is clearly an extreme case, notice how most champions on the size graph are shifted to the right of the division average trend (and not upward), suggesting that longer reach in general is more important than height.

Controversial heavyweight boxing champion Sonny Liston had the most ridiculous known wingspan for a fighter with his 84 inch reach and 72.5 inch height. His wingspan ratio was 1.16, but wasn't enough to keep him on his feet when he fought Muhammad Ali (wingspan ratio of 1.07) a second time. Ali won by first round knockout and stood over Liston in the famously iconic pose. Now you know that both fighters in that picture had crazy arm length for their heights, which may have been a contributing factor in landing the two in a championship boxing match to begin with.

Fightnomics: Notable Freakish Wingspans in MMA

Rank	Fighter	Reach"	Height"	Ratio
1	Jon Jones	84.5	76	1.112
2	Uriah Hall	80	72	1.111
3	Marcus Brimage	71	64	1.109
4	Mark Bocek	75	68	1.103
5	Miguel Torres	76	69	1.101
5	Paul Daley	76	69	1.101
7	Matt Mitrione	82	75	1.093
8	Gerald Harris	77.5	71	1.092
9	Frankie Edgar	72	66	1.091
10	Rameau T. Sokoudjou	78	72	1.083
10	Muhammed Lawal	78	72	1.083
12	Shane Carwin	80	74	1.081
12	John Lineker	67	62	1.081
14	Brock Lesnar	81	75	1.080
15	Cheick Kongo	82	76	1.079
15	Antonio Silva	82	76	1.079
17	Chan Sung Jung	72	67	1.075
18	Georges St-Pierre	76	71	1.070
18	Court McGee	76	71	1.070
18	Ben Alloway	76	71	1.070
21	Phil Davis	79	74	1.068
22	Rory MacDonald	76.5	72	1.063
23	Mike Brown	70	66	1.061
23	Nam Phan	70	66	1.061
23	Renan Barao	70	66	1.061

A look at the highest ratios in MMA reveals plenty of noteworthy fighters and more than a few champions. The question is, why? Having a long wingspan-to-height ratio makes sense as an advantage if our conclusions about the relative importance of reach over height are true. If two fighters have identical reach, but one is shorter, the shorter fighter can likely pack more muscle into his frame and still weigh-in at the same limit as his opponent. If this is true, fighters who have relatively short wingspans for their height are at a disadvantage in more than just reach, but also probably strength.

Fightnomics: Notable Disadvantaged Wingspans in MMA

Rank	Fighter	Reach"	Height"	Ratio
1	Diego Brandao	64	67	0.955
2	Chris Lytle	68	71	0.958
3	Matt Wiman	67.5	70	0.964
4	Antonio Banuelos	63	65	0.969
4	Issei Tamura	63	65	0.969
6	Ivan Menjivar	64	66	0.970
7	Alex Karalexis	66	68	0.971
7	Andy Ogle	66	68	0.971
7	Mike Wilkinson	66	68	0.971
7	Leonard Garcia	68	70	0.971

Think about the Normal Distribution of height in the human population, which is the kind of shape that is generally referred to as a Bell curve. Most of us fall in the center of the curve around the average value for any given anthropometric. Out on the extremes there are fewer individuals. Throughout history the curve may shift, as it has moved up in height (to the right in the example curve shown) over the last few centuries. Kids are growing up to be taller for a variety of reasons including nutrition, sexual selection, and improved health care. The distribution of these heights, however, maintains a shape that reflects the most popular heights as being the most average while people who are very tall or very short are also very rare.

If we overlay the UFC divisions on a height distribution for American men, we realize that there are more candidates of potential fighters in the central divisions. That is to say, if we figure out what weight class corresponds to the "average" (mean) size of a male, we can correctly assume that there are more potential men out there competing in that division than the ones at either extreme. How many men have a frame the size of an average heavyweight or flyweight? It's hard to say exactly, but it's a lot fewer than men with body frames the size of the average lightweight.

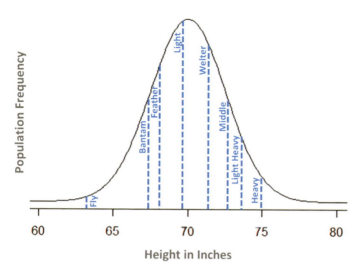

Height distributions for men with mean UFC divisions indicated.

According to the National Center for Health Statistics, the average value for height for men in the United States comes out to five-foot nine-and-a-half inches. If we look back to our average UFC fighter size, we see that this places the average American man squarely in the lightweight division. Numerically, the largest UFC divisions are the lightweight and welterweight divisions (which trade spots for first place depending on the roster and the time of year), with featherweights coming in third. According to the height distribution chart this makes perfect sense, because those divisions offer the most potential candidates from the population at large. On the fringes we can see that there are much fewer men walking around with a height of 63.5 inches, or 75 inches, making the flyweight and heavyweight divisions less populous due to fewer individuals being the right size. The relative infrequency of individuals sized for these extreme weight classes results in few total fighters that are UFC caliber, and therefore small divisions with fewer roster spots if the UFC wants to maintain a high competitive standard for its fighters.

Prior to 2011, the UFC's smallest division was the 155-pound lightweight class, meaning a large pool of smaller athletes went untapped. There was even a time when the lightweights disappeared, meaning the UFC could only offer a home for "above average" sized fighters. When Zuffa merged the smaller WEC divisions (bantamweight through lightweight) into the UFC at the beginning of 2011, they consolidated a broader range of athletes under one roof that enabled the promotion to allocate more roster spots to the most elite fighters across the full spectrum of human sizes. Now thanks to the newest men's division at flyweight, expect to see a few fighters from the more populous bantamweight division drop the extra 10 pounds to compete there. But when it comes to the question of adding a new "strawweight" division for fighters at a limit of 115 pounds, the curve suggests there will be the smallest talent pool yet at that extreme end of the height distribution.

It takes some numbers to build a division, some critical threshold of talent to draw from, and in the case of extreme sizes, some divisions may not meet that threshold. The UFC's newest division is the first one for women. The female bantamweights average a height of 5' 6," which is a little taller than the mean height for women in the core UFC markets. If anyone wants to predict which division will come next for the UFC, in theory, it should be a women's flyweight division, since that one offers the largest population segment in which to scout talent. Sorry, Cris Cyborg, but bringing in a women's featherweight division to the UFC would have been like adding a cruiserweight (220-pound limit) division rather than merging in the WEC featherweights. From a talent availability perspective, divisions closer to the population mean offer a better return.

It's important to remember that the US population curve we used in the graphic is further to the right than distributions for some other countries. That means the men's strawweight division could make more sense for promotions featuring a high mix of fighters from Mexico, or many Asian countries, for example, where the average height is smaller than in the US and Western Europe. Because the UFC has traditionally served English speaking markets, the 5' 9" average has served as the center of mass (or in this case height) for countries in North America, Western Europe, and Australia and New Zealand. Brazil too measures up at 5' 8.5," closely in line with the other current UFC-feeder countries. Should the UFC begin to gear custom content to the large markets of Indonesia (average male height of 5' 2"), India (5' 5"), China (5' 7") or Mexico (5' 7.5"), it may consider focusing on smaller divisions.

The Reach Advantage: The Reality of Range

In addition to weight and height, reach is one of the most basic anthropometric characteristics of fighters, deserving placement on any Tale of the Tape in a combat sport. It's also one of the few aspects a fighter has no control over, unlike speed, technique, endurance, and even muscle mass.

No one improves their reach except by facing shorter-armed opponents.

The term "reach advantage" is used so routinely in combat sports that it's now part of the popular lexicon. As part of the array of hand-me-downs inherited from boxing, a reach differential in MMA is sure to draw immediate attention from fans and announcers alike when viewing the Tale of the Tape. The validity of the reach advantage however, and certainly a quantification of it, has never before been analyzed. Do fighters with longer striking range have a significant advantage over shorter-range opponents? Is the reach advantage real? If so, how real, and how does it work? Time for a data experiment.

We start by creating a trustworthy data set, so I took a large batch of UFC fights spanning 2007 through the summer of 2013 and then filtered out instances where other potentially advantageous factors like differences in age, fighting stance, and height were present. We're left with about 500 modern UFC fights controlled for matchmaking and modern rules, where the two fighters also had similar age and height, and fought using the same stance. I then tagged the fighters who had a reach advantage and calculated the win percentage for the rangier fighters.

At this high level view, longer-reach fighters won 53% of their fights, losing 47% of the time (I cut no contest fights). Not bad, but not something to bet the house on because a six-point swing doesn't make the reach advantage a huge differentiator. However, not all reach advantages are created equal. When I track how much of a reach advantage the fighters have, a better pattern arises, with some more tangible conclusions.

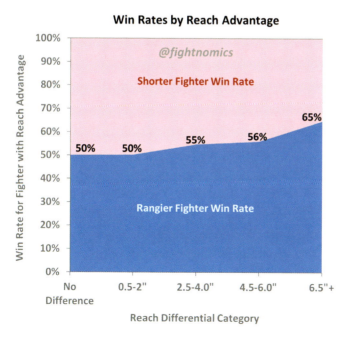

155

Rangier fighters are winning more fights than their shorter-armed opponents, but only when the reach differential is greater than two inches. Those are the first big takeaways: the reach advantage is real, but only when it's at least two inches. Furthermore, the data analysis shows the bigger the reach differential, the larger the effect size of the advantage. Fighters with at least a 6.5-inch longer wingspan than their opponents win almost two-thirds of their fights. Fights with large reach differentials occur less frequently, but in the mid-range categories for reach differentials of 2.5" to 6.0," the advantage equates to over a 10-point swing in win rates.

If the reach advantage really is real, we would also expect fights that are predominantly standing to show a stronger effect. So using the TIP data, I created a filter for fights that stayed standing for more than 70% of the total duration of the fight. Re-running the reach analysis as before produced the following results.

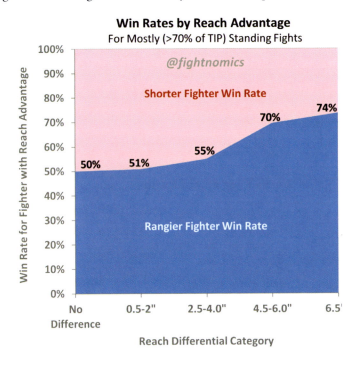

The analysis supports the hypothesis that the reach advantage is strong when it comes to striking, because the effect size is larger when fights stay standing for the majority of the time. The overall win rate for rangier fighters in the primarily standing fights group jumped up to 56% overall and again showed a clearly increasing pattern of effect size correlating with longer reach advantages. That also means that longer reach in a matchup between fighters who like to keep fights standing is an even bigger advantage than usual, with the longest reach differentials resulting in nearly three quarters of fights being won by the rangier fighter. If we remember the more basic rule that a reach advantage starts at 2.5 inches, then calculating the overall win rate for fighters with a 2.5-inch and greater range advantage gives us 60%. We're now at a 20-point swing on win rates for fighters with a clear advantage who keep fights standing. That seems like a lot. This one predictor variable in isolation can end up accounting for a big, big advantage.

So if the reach advantage is exaggerated when fights stay standing, does that mean you can reduce it on the mat? To test this idea I used the same method for filtering fights by TIP data, this time capturing only fights that stayed on the ground for at least 70% of the time.

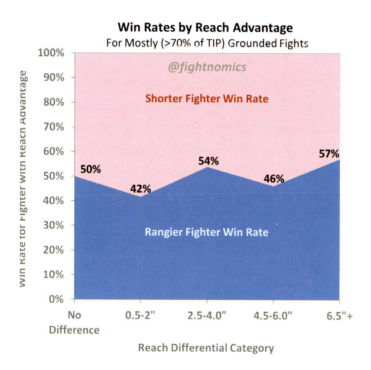

After re-running the analysis, the results suggest that one way to nullify the reach advantage is to keep the fight on the ground. In this group, the overall win rate for longer fighters was only 49%, with increasing reach differentials showing only a slight increase in win rates. The sample size in this group was the smallest of all, which explains some of the volatility, but the conclusion looking at the overall win rate certainly lends credence to the strength of a grappling-first strategy against rangier fighters.

How Reach Works

It's believed that range is critical in striking, and here are two specific reasons why the reach advantage might be such a big deal: A reach differential between opponents creates a perimeter zone where a longer fighter can land strikes, while his shorter opponent cannot. Theoretically, the longer fighter should be able to land strikes more easily than opponents, resulting in higher accuracy. The knockout potential of longer arms in striking may be higher due to a longer runway of acceleration and potential torque, an effect that is boosted if the punch is an uppercut or hook. With these particular strikes, the lever-like action of the arm swinging around a fixed axis (the shoulder) is accentuated by a longer radius from the body. The target of the punch (the chin) also has a lever effect responding to these types of strikes, making the head snap more violently on impact under greater force. Therefore, a long armed hook is more likely to cause a knockout than a shorter one.

So even if rangier fighters are mainly working their more accurate and rangy jab, their power strikes should also cause more knockdowns and knockouts. These hypotheses are testable given the level of detail in the FightMetric database, and any exploration of performance data related to the reach advantage is breaking new ground. Given what we already know from prior analysis, the experiment will only analyze fights with a 2.5-inch or greater reach differential, where the matchup was otherwise even in terms of age and fighting stance. The mix of weight classes in this sample is irrelevant since both groups (the Advantaged and Disadvantaged fighters) will comprise the same relative shares of fighters by division. We're not looking at how these metrics perform against benchmarks, just how the fighters performed against each other when a reach advantage was at work.

Head to Head Striking Metrics
For Fights with a 2.5"+ Reach Differential

Striking Metric	Advantaged Fighters	Disadvantaged Fighters	% Difference for Rangier Fighters
Head Jab Accuracy	32.1%	29.2%	+10%
Head Power Accuracy	26.5%	23.7%	+12%
Knockdown Rate	3.7%	3.3%	+10%
Significant Strike Accuracy	43.2%	40.5%	+7%
Standup Striking Ratio	1.0	1.0	0%

The analysis tested key striking metrics for these fighters where there was a significant reach advantage. The results show the rangier fighters performed better overall in these fights, with higher strike accuracy and knockdown power. Interestingly, standup striking pace was even, although (not shown) longer fighters used a slightly higher mix of power head strikes than shorter fighters. When filtering specifically for the fights where rangier fighters won, their striking performance metrics got even better, while the same metrics for the smaller fighters stayed roughly the same, or even were slightly better in defeat than in the overall sample. That means when rangy fighters put their reach advantage to work, they tend to do better.

When disadvantaged fighters won against the larger opponents, it wasn't thanks to striking. In that group, the smaller fighters actually showed slightly worse striking performance in victory, suggesting their wins were not dependent on striking accuracy and power, but perhaps on other things like grappling. Just because we filtered for fights that spent the majority of the time standing does not mean that some of these fights didn't hit the mat or end by submission.

The research findings presented here are consistent with traditional views of the reach advantage theory. Being the longer fighter is indeed an advantage, one that can be accentuated with increasing reach differentials, and it has a stronger effect on fight outcomes the longer the fighters stay on the feet. The key to using a reach advantage lies in distance striking, while the best path to defeating it is not engaging in a striking war, but rather getting the fight to the ground. The question of pace presents another trend worthy of deeper exploration. When rangier fighters won they demonstrated superior pace. When smaller fighters won, they were the same or worse in striking accuracy and power metrics, but superior to the longer range fighters in pace alone. In addition to grappling, it seems that one way to mitigate a reach disadvantage is simply to outwork your opponent.

The Truth About the "Height Advantage"

As you may have noticed, I've spent a lot of time talking about size, but haven't addressed whether height is an advantage. The answer to this question requires attention to detail. Many have argued that height is an advantage in MMA, just as it should be in other combat sports. Taller fighters can punch downward, and have heads that are higher and harder to hit. Do taller fighters tend to win more often than shorter opponents? Yes, they do. However, the subtlety in answering this question lies in isolating height as a separate variable from reach, and that's where the truth does not conform to popular belief.

Just looking at UFC fighters where one fighter was taller than his opponent by at least two inches or more, I found the win rate for the taller fighters to be 54%. Setting the threshold at three inches or more bumps the win rate up to 56% of the taller fighters. Well, okay then, the height advantage is real. But as I've warned before: not so fast. This lazy setup to analyzing the data neglected to filter out other potentially important factors, the most obvious of which is fighter reach. There are also factors that I was careful to exclude in prior analysis like age and fighter stance. To truly put height to the test as an important advantage in MMA, it must therefore be isolated from all other meaningful anthropometric factors, of which reach has already been proven to be one. Height and reach go together of course, but the diversity of human physiques ensures that sometimes we'll have two fighters squaring off at the same weight, with identical reach, but one will be significantly taller. Those are the fights we need to analyze to really test the hypothesis of the Height Advantage.

After controlling for our additional influencing variables, fighters with a height advantage of two inches or more only won 48% of their fights. Increasing the threshold to three inches actually made things worse for the taller fighters, who only won 46% of fights under that condition. The sample size gets smaller the more specific the analysis gets, but the analysis doesn't support the "height advantage" as a real advantage. If anything, being tall without getting a related benefit from longer arms might even be a disadvantage. It's possible that the driver of this pattern is the frame size versus muscle mass tradeoff. Larger frame size translates to longer reach, which we've proven is an advantage. But larger frames weigh more due to larger bones, meaning that on average larger fighters cannot carry the same amount of muscle mass as their smaller-framed division peers. That means being larger in frame sacrifices some strength, and is only worth that tradeoff if you're getting a reach benefit.

Regardless, when it comes to considering a size matchup we now know a few things. First, **the reach advantage is real, and can be a huge advantage for fighters who can keep a fight standing. But talk of a "height advantage" is actually a myth, one that was born out of the inherent correlation of height and reach, and the dominating effect of the reach advantage**. The conclusion is that height is not an advantage unless it also comes with reach, meaning that there are ways that size matters, and also at least one way in which it doesn't. So the next time you see two fighters that have the same reach, but a several-inch height differential, make sure you remember which one has the real advantage.

Chapter Notes:

1. For more on wingspans, and the "Big Bang Theory of Body Types" read "The Sports Gene" by David Epstein, Penguin Group, New York, New York, 2013.

7

Beyond the Measuring Tape: Rookies, Veterans, and Southpaws

We've now determined how size matters in MMA, and how it doesn't. The Tale of the Tape, however, isn't just limited to size measurements, despite those numbers eliciting the most focus from commentators. Another key data point is a fighter's age, and though it doesn't get included in the on-screen graphics, I'll also add fighting stance as an anthropometric factor that has a storied history in the fight game. Age and stance are second tier factors on the traditional Tale of the Tape, but because we've got this massive database of fights to examine we're going to run these variables through the ringer anyway and see what comes out the other end. In the last chapter we ran analyses which tested the reach and height advantages only after filtering out age and stance differences, so we'll take the same approach here to stay consistent. As much as possible, when analyzing a particular variable we want to identify fights where "all other things are equal."

Whenever a fighter is identified as having a left-hand dominant stance the words "southpaw" and "advantage" roll off of the tongue like "conspiracy" and "theory." The "southpaw advantage" is so engrained in the world of combat sports that few question its legitimacy, though opinions vary on how important it is and how it works. Until now there has been limited research on the details of southpaw versus orthodox stance fighters. It's the Area 51 of the fight game, drawing tons of speculation, and even confident conclusions, but with very little hard evidence. Fortunately for us, razor wire and armed guards are impotent against the FightMetric database and the Fightnomics analytical process. With several years of detailed UFC fight data, we're now going to attack this question and answer it once and for all, trumping all previously published academic research with a bombardment of fight analysis of unprecedented magnitude. Does using a southpaw stance confer a greater advantage than an orthodox stance? Go ahead and place your bets and strap yourselves in because we're pitting lefties and righties in a statistical cage fight.

The Trouble with Lefties

It happens every time two fighters reach out and touch gloves to initiate the first round, but something looks off. One of the two fighters is in a left-handed stance, destroying the natural overlapping symmetry of opposing fighters ready to engage. The commentators remark that the right-handed "orthodox" stance fighter might have some trouble with his "southpaw" opponent. But why, and is it even true?

When I first asked fighters and trainers about the southpaw advantage there was general agreement that the effect was real, and responses about the cause fell mostly into two categories. The first was that natural right handers are accustomed to circling to their right as they fight and when they reset. When facing other orthodox opponents the mutual circling results in a counter-clockwise spin like a hurricane in the Northern hemisphere, constantly moving both fighters away from the power hand of their opponent. Note: if you didn't already know it, a golden rule of fighting is to stay away from the power shot, so if your opponent is right handed, don't circle to your left or you will be moving into his power shot. The same may be observed when two southpaws square off, each circling left in a clockwise spin. We should call these double-southpaw fights "cyclone matchups" like the cyclone's spin in the Southern Hemisphere. But I digress. When there is a mixed stance matchup, orthodox fighters who continue to circle right walk directly towards the power hand of their opponents. They're zigging when they should be zagging. While this could easily be corrected through training and preparation, many rational tactics are forgotten the instant a fight starts in earnest. Or as boxer Joe Louis put it, "everybody has a plan until they get hit." Fighters may recognize the circling threat against southpaws, but they may not be able to adjust their instincts during a fight. Once fists start flying instinct takes over and the fighters resort to the techniques they are most comfortable and familiar with, which may mean a reversion to circling in an unfavorable direction. Unfortunately, this movement isn't (currently) tracked in the UFC, and so we can't confirm that suboptimal circling patterns are leading orthodox fighters astray when they face southpaws.

A more general secondary theory about the southpaw advantage is more testable with the data we have. I've heard lot of comments about the "awkwardness" of facing left-handers, because most training partners are right handed. Left-handers are rare (or "infrequent" technically speaking) in the population and also in the pool of competitors, so if the advantage trend for southpaws is real it would be an example of a selection based on "infrequency dependence." For that theory to be at work here, the more left-handers there are in the population at large, the less of an effect there should be. The effect relies on the infrequency of the key quality, meaning the rarer the quality is, the bigger the effect. It's a simple enough concept, but wouldn't athletes competing at a high level train for this? We can examine fight outcomes as well as performance statistics to test this hypothesis. Basically, if southpaws win more often than not against orthodox stance fighters, then at least we know there is some sort of advantage. Furthermore, if orthodox fighters do worse against southpaws in skill metrics than when they face other right handers, that would also support the idea of infrequency dependence being a mechanism for the advantage.

If southpaws are simply superior to orthodox fighters overall then that could also explain it. Are there any inherent advantages to being left-handed, like in strength or coordination? What if left-handers are just genetically different in key athletic traits? For example, there's a 10% rule when it comes to strength that says your dominant hand is about 10% stronger than the non-dominant hand. That's a good rule of thumb for exercise scientists and rehab therapists, but researchers tested that rule further by separating the sample into right- and left-hand dominant individuals. The findings showed the right handers were indeed stronger in their dominant hands, in fact slightly more than 10% stronger. Left-handers, however, had roughly equal strength in both hands.[1] Prior studies had combined all the results and ended up with a 10% average for everyone. So really the 10% rule of strength differential between hands is only true for right-handers, while lefties are equally (or almost) as strong with their "weak" hand.

The 10% research findings support the idea that left-handers live in a right-handed world and are more versatile than right-hand dominant people. Whether it's zippers, manual transmissions, or just hand shaking, lefties may be a little more dexterous in their non-dominant hands than their right-handed counterparts simply because of how often they manipulate objects with their off hand. Researchers have tested people with different hand dominance by having them write with their non-dominant hand, and to no surprise, the left-handers performed better learning to write right-handed than peers attempting the reverse.[2] That's enough reason to explore whether or not the southpaw advantage is just based on the infrequency of training partners, or the potential for lefties to perform better at basic skills like punching.

So we have several working theories, but we haven't even answered the very first question yet. Is there really an advantage at all? If we can find evidence of the southpaw advantage in MMA then we can go deeper into testing how and why it works. But before we solve the southpaw riddle we need go back in time and understand why we even have different hand-dominance in the first place, and why it might be important to fighting.

A Brief History of Lefties

The term "southpaw" originates from baseball during the late 1800's. Baseball diamonds were constructed to allow hitters to face East-Northeast to avoid sun glare in the late afternoons. Before they pitched a ball, "normal" right-handed pitchers stood on the mound facing north while lefties pitched facing southward, leading one sportswriter to coin the "southpaw" moniker for left-handed pitchers. The nicknaming of left-handers as southpaws was quickly adopted into the boxing vernacular, and the term has survived over a century as synonymous with any left-hand preference, especially in sports. But we're still a long way from understanding why the modern term is associated with an athletic advantage today.

The modern left-handed "advantage" is actually a complete reversal from historical associations with negative qualities. The word "left" comes from the Anglo-Saxon word "lyft" meaning "weak." Zing! The latin word "dexter" meant "right" and was synonymous with manual skill. When we say someone is "ambidextrous" we mean they can use both hands equally, but literally the term means they have two right hands. That's way better than being known as a terrible dancer, or "having two left feet." To this day in the UK to be "cack-handed" (left-hand dominant) is to be clumsy or awkward, and in French the word for left ("gauche") is also synonymous with a lack of tact, elegance, or grace. Parents in some Asian cultures will even force children to use their right hands against their natural inclinations due to superstitions that persist today. For centuries parents had their children "re-educated" to be right handed in an attempt to preempt the whispers from neighbors that their child might be possessed by the devil or inclined towards criminal behavior. Fortunately these flawed members of the population were rare, but even more fortunate is that we no longer care much about, nor stigmatize superficial genetic qualities based on superstition. And yet some bias remains.

An estimated 10% of humans today exhibit left hand dominance, reinforcing the idea that southpaws are a small minority and different from the norm. Various studies of human prehistory have attempted to examine hand preference through our evolution, and while there's some evidence suggesting that millions of years ago hand dominance may have been more even, additional research has found a skew towards right-handedness as far back as 50,000 years. We see hints that more primitive primates show less preference for hand dominance, but that on the human line of evolution clues remain that we started preferring right hands fairly long ago. The research includes prehistoric remains and clever observations of cave paintings and tools showing an early right-hand preference that has not changed in 5,000 years. From an evolutionary point of view, this phenomenon follows our development of lateralized brain structure, and also for increasingly complex social interactions. Speech and fine motor skills that define some our greatest human characteristics may have been grouped together for efficiency in one brain hemisphere, freeing up the other side to worry about other things. Meanwhile, hominids were increasingly cooperating on physical tasks with their newly discovered ability to use tools (thanks to evolving dexterity), and having a preferred hand suddenly became advantageous for the group's overall efficiency.[3]

Okay, fine. We wanted to choose sides, but why the right hand? Again, good theories abound with no firm conclusion either way. One fascinating suggestion is that mothers favored carrying babies with their left arms so the babies could hear their mothers' soothing heartbeat on the left side. This would have freed up the right arm to perform other manual tasks, requiring the right hand to be more coordinated. Or perhaps the mutation and hemisphere selection was simply random, a coin flip of evolution where a tribe of related right-handers became more successful in cooperation and in spreading their genes across the planet. Each subsequent generation inherited a tendency towards one side or another, and for some reason the right-handers won out more often than not. But this is just a lot of armchair science, what's it have to do with fighting?

A lot actually.

The Fighting Hypothesis

Right handers began to rule the world for whatever reason, prompting the question of why did left-handedness remain and survive to modern times? That's where the idea of a "frequency dependent selection" comes into play. Two French researchers specializing in left-hand research, Charlotte Faurie and Maurice Raymond, recently coined the term the "Fighting Hypothesis." Their theory suggests left-handedness survived through human evolution specifically because of the advantage it gave southpaws in combat. There was an "infrequency advantage" at work that gave left-handers an inherent advantage whenever they faced a right-handed opponent, which was most of the time. The rarity of being left-handed meant that orthodox opponents would be less familiar with the approach and style of the southpaw, and would therefore suffer at least a temporary disadvantage in direct competition. The left-hander would perform as usual, facing yet another right-handed opponent, but that small and potentially fleeting imbalance may have been enough of a difference when life and death were on the line.

Consider the evolutionary gene selection experiment known to us as "The Middle Ages." Over the course of a millennium much of Western civilization was at war, and conflict is an excellent driver of selection in evolution as well as culture. Periods of war are where we often find interesting clues as to why we do things the way we do. Consider the small example of spiral staircases in medieval castles. Staircases mostly descended in a counter-clockwise manner to provide optimal sword-thrusting angles for the predominantly right-handed defending forces. Attackers would have been at a disadvantage trying to ascend – unless they were left-handed. Then consider the outlier Clan Kerr of the Scottish borderlands who allegedly had a very high rate of left-handers in their family, and whose name may derive from the Gaelic Cearr meaning left-handed. Sir Andrew Kerr the Southpaw apparently trained his troops to fight left-handed to exploit this advantage in war. However, on the home-front this also required, wait for it, clockwise-descending spiral staircases...boom! Mind blown. Today Scottish expressions like "Kerr-handed" or "kerry-fisted" are still used to describe left-handed individuals.

Professors Faurie and Raymond tried to test The Fighting Hypothesis of the southpaw advantage in conflict by comparing national rates of left-handedness to overall indicators of violence (murder rates, etc.). If they were correct they should find more left-handers in places where there is more direct human conflict. In fact, their study did find a correlation between the percentage of southpaws and violence, with the most violent cultures having a high rate of southpaws, and more pacifistic countries having the lowest. Hypothesis confirmed? Well at least it's not rejected, and the science is certainly interesting, but let's not confuse cause and effect. It's unlikely that left-handers are causing more violence, but rather more left-handers survive in such a volatile environment and pass on their genes, or even that these harsh environmental factors stimulate the epigenetic roots of left-hand preference. Either way, the more competitive an environment, the greater the representation of southpaws.[4] And remember that 10% of the population being left-handed stat I used earlier? It's a little misleading. There's a difference between genders, with men being more likely to be left-handed than women, consistent with plenty of other research that finds men to be more involved in conflict than women. The best number I can find for the male southpaw rate is 11.6%.[5]

Whatever the reason for the development, there's no doubting that hand-dominance is innate and has a real effect on mind and body. Superstitions aside, scientific research has determined subtle, but significant neurological differences between individuals exhibiting different hand dominance. Left-hand dominance has been associated with higher risk of dyslexia and schizophrenia. But on the other hand, in this case literally, we see that left-handers also succeed in a number of ways above and beyond their basic representation in the population. Modern US presidents have frequently bucked the right-handed trend, and more recent studies found an edge for southpaws in post-college earning potential – not to mention the potential difference in visual-spatial awareness that may come with being left-handed.

Sports give us the best proxy we have for researching trends in the head-to-head conflict of our ancestors. In the statistician's favorite sport of baseball, various calculations have found a disproportionately high number of lefties playing in the major leagues, and a startling 25%-33% of pitchers throw southpaw in any given season. Imagine having to face two different pitchers with equal skill and speed, but one is throwing left-handed. The split-second delay in recognizing the pitch from an infrequent approach may be all that's needed to make the southpaw pitcher strike out more batters and get drafted by the big leagues. A wider study of athletes performed by the aforementioned lefty enthusiast Professor Raymond found that left-handers in inter-active sports (e.g., tennis, boxing, baseball) were over-represented at three times the population baseline rate, while there was no over-representation in non-interactive sports (e.g., running, swimming, gymnastics, golf).

We now have several reasons to expect a left-handed advantage in MMA, which combines the findings of the Fighting Hypothesis research and analysis of interactive sports, but we still need to run the numbers to be sure. Are southpaw fighters a clumsy minority, or do they really spell trouble for the orthodox stance majority?

Quantifying the Southpaw Advantage

There are a few ways to test the southpaw advantage. First, we want to look at fighter population and stance in the most competitive pool of athletes to see if they are over-represented like major league pitchers or pro tennis players. Second, we want to see who wins more often when fighters of differing stance are pitted head-to-head. And lastly, we want to look at what performance metrics may differ between southpaw and orthodox fighters, both innately, as well as when performing against each other.

It's important to distinguish between the southpaw stance in fighting and actually being left-hand dominant. For the purposes of this analysis I am using only the stance of fighters, not their true hand dominance. While it would be better to use both variables for separate consideration, based on data limitations I will only be examining fighters who tend to fight in a southpaw stance, regardless of what their true preference may be. All things being equal, we should see a comparably small share of athletes in any sport favoring their left, and MMA should be no different. And really, if pop culture, superstition, and slang etymology are correct that lefties are clumsy and awkward, we would expect to see a lot fewer than 10%. Yet that's not what we see, and the numbers don't lie.

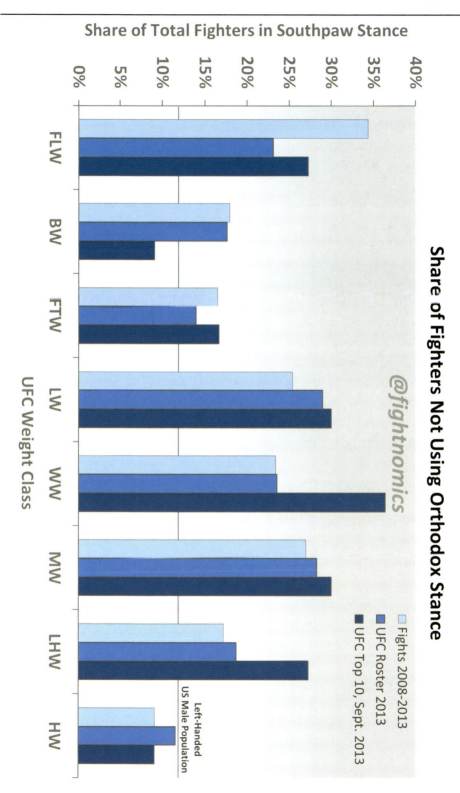

Share of Total Fighters in Southpaw Stance

Share of Fighters Not Using Orthodox Stance

@fightnomics

UFC Weight Class

FLW
BW
FTW
LW
WW
MW
LHW
HW

Left-Handed
US Male Population

Fights 2008-2013
UFC Roster 2013
UFC Top 10, Sept. 2013

171

In over 1,500 UFC fights from 2006-2013, about 20% of the fighters involved fought as southpaws or switch-stance fighters. That's almost double the rate of left-hand dominance in the population at large. Whether or not these unorthodox fighters were truly left-handed individuals is less relevant for this test, because either way they chose to compete as one. Fighters switching stance only made up a small portion of the unorthodox group (~1%), so even without them, pure southpaw stance fighters are still represented above and beyond the population baseline rate. There must be a reason. That number hasn't changed much over time. The UFC roster as of the summer of 2013 showed 22% of fighters using a southpaw or switch stance. What's more, of the UFC's official Top 10 Rankings during the same period, that 22% unorthodox rate held steady. The UFC itself represents the elite of MMA athletes, while the Top Ten rankings represent la crème de la crème. Seeing the rate of southpaws hold at a level way above average as we focus on more and more competitive subgroups of fighters supports the idea that the stance carries an advantage. In the "legacy" UFC divisions that have been around the longest and are thought to be the most competitive, there's actually a clear pattern of increasing numbers of southpaws from historical fights to the current roster to the current Top Ten. That the effect size increases with the level of competitiveness further supports the theory.

We've now seen that there are more proportionately more guys fighting left-handed in the Octagon than there should be, but what happens in the ultimate test of head-to-head competition? I took the same pool of modern MMA fights and isolated just matchups where a southpaw faced an orthodox after eliminating for other potential differentials like age or reach, and found that the southpaws defeated the right-handers 57% of the time. We can conclude that lefties are not only overrepresented in MMA, but also outperform against right-handed peers. So being a southpaw truly does indicate an "Advantage" in MMA when it comes to earning the all-important "W," although perhaps the advantage is somewhat less significant than we've been led to believe. For comparison, a Reach Advantage of more than two-and-a-half inches produces a similar advantage, and is even more advantageous if the fight stays standing. But the simple fact that lefties are disproportionately represented in MMA's premier organization, as well as the fact that they win at a higher rate are reasons enough to keep going. I now want to know how the advantage works.

How the Southpaw Advantage Works

In short: everywhere. For the purpose of this experiment, I've again isolated only fights where one fighter fought southpaw and the other fought in an orthodox stance without other advantages present. I pulled the round-by-round data of key performance metrics. I also pulled the same metrics for fights involving two orthodox fighters, and finally for the rare instances of southpaw-on-southpaw matchups.

The key hypothesis is that the unorthodox standup striking of southpaws gives them the advantage, and certainly there appears to be an edge there. But as it turns out, there was a lot more involved than just differences in striking. During over 1,000 rounds analyzed of lefty-versus-righty competition, southpaws outperformed their opponents across a variety of key metrics in striking, takedowns and grappling on a head-to-head comparison. Southpaws were more accurate, landed slightly more takedowns, and once on the ground, were more successful advancing position. It's almost as if the awkwardness of facing a southpaw striker is the same when that southpaw is passing guard. That the southpaw advantage is real is confirmed when we also compare metrics from pure southpaw or pure orthodox matchups.

Fightnomics Test of the Southpaw Advantage
Performance by Stance and Matchup Scenario, No Reach or Age Differentials

Stance Match Up	Same Stance	Mixed Stance Fight		Same Stance
Performance Metric	Southpaw Fighters	Southpaw Fighters	Orthodox Fighters	Orthodox Fighters
Distance Head Jab Accuracy	28%	31%	27%	27%
Distance Power Head Accuracy	24%	26%	22%	25%
Distance Head Power Share	46%	55%	58%	50%
Knockdown Rate	2.7%	3.0%	2.9%	3.7%
Total Standing Attempts/Min	6.3	4.9	4.7	5.4
Takedown Success Rate	33%	41%	38%	41%
Ground Advances per Takedown	1.01	1.10	0.89	0.99

The trick to this theory is that it's not about southpaws being better fighters per se; it's that **orthodox fighters fight worse when they face the rare southpaw stance**. By that rationale, we should see a drop in performance from orthodox fighters from when they face same-stance peers to when they face southpaws, and that's what this analysis shows. The far right column is a benchmark for how orthodox fighters perform when they compete against each other. Moving one column to the left shows how they perform against southpaws, with a drop-off in most metrics. Notably, striking volume and accuracy both drop, knockdown rate plummets, takedowns are less successful, and when fighters are on the ground they advance position less frequently. While the "why" of the advantage remains debatable, we are clearly seeing the "how" of southpaws outperforming opponents in numerous ways, mainly because those opponents seem to be off their game.

A few nuances in this analysis are also revealed. Look at striking attempts per minute and the power head share metrics. When there's a southpaw versus orthodox matchup, both fighters are more hesitant to engage. Specifically, they use fewer jabs, meaning the portion of power head strikes rises. The awkwardness of a mismatched stance apparently results in fewer overall strikes, but more use of the power hand. In the end the southpaws attempted more strikes, landed more often, and were more active on the ground, which could all support the boost we see in their overall win rate.

The cherry on top of the southpaw advantage is that it's so real that southpaw fighters themselves also succumb to it. **Bolded** and *italicized*, because that was a major knowledge bomb in a book full of knowledge bombs. See how the metrics for southpaws in a mixed stance fight decline when southpaws face each other? When southpaws get a surprise by facing another southpaw fighter, they are in a natural fighting stance pairing, which like orthodox versus orthodox matchups result in more engagement and more use of the jab. However, southpaws find it harder to land their strikes on other southpaws, have lower knockdown rates, and have more trouble landing takedowns and passing guard. All this means that **no one does his best when they facing a southpaw, not even a southpaw**.

Out of the groupings studied, fighters in pure stance matchups end up with the closest scores to each other. Basically, left-handers and right-handers when facing their own stance peers performed very similarly in striking accuracy and ground advances, but it was the orthodox fighters who had the highest knockdown rate. Because these groups are not corrected for weight class distribution as with the mixed stance matchup groups, it's tough to say if there's really any difference at all. But this one additional look at the numbers says that neither group of athletes is inherently better than the other, the difference only materializes when they compete directly against each other.

Given the fundamental nature of fighting stance in MMA, that time had come for this factor to get fully tested. There are plenty of theories about hand-dominance and its neurological roots that remain in question today, but what is no longer debatable is whether or not fighting in a southpaw stance is advantageous. After correcting for other factors **southpaws see a 14-point swing in the win rate overall when facing orthodox fighters, and on a round-by-round basis, cause opponents to underperform in a number of ways**. The mechanism for the southpaw advantage really is the effect of infrequency. **Fighting southpaw isn't really better, but being orthodox against a southpaw is definitely a disadvantage**. This subtlety of these findings support the Fighting Hypothesis.

You're welcome, Professors Faurie and Raymond, and good luck opening the "Leftorium."

The Youth Advantage

Size matters in MMA, but does age? Father time never loses a fight, but at what point does age become a hindrance? When it comes to the Tale of the Tape, that one number signifying years of life can have a greater effect than all others, yet is perhaps the least discussed. In a highly competitive sport requiring incredible feats of strength, endurance, agility, and flexibility, it should be no surprise that youth brings a physical advantage. But experience and maturity are just as critical in MMA as they are in any other strategic competition, and mental factors can heavily influence a fight outcome before fighters even step into the cage. Before even running the analysis I knew this would be an important variable of research, especially given that age is one of the most accurately and pervasively reported data points in MMA. I wanted to know what it's really telling us. Not knowing a formal term, I picked the "Youth Advantage" to describe fighters who were younger than their opponents consistent with other differential advantages and vernacular. So is there an edge in age? Does youth trump experience?

Rookies vs. Veterans

Unlike with most of the Tale of the Tape, age is constantly changing, and there's a pretty disparate range of possible age matchups even at the premier levels of the sport. The first analysis I ran on age was simply a casual glance at how fighters perform in terms of winning percentage at any given age, hoping to see some sort of pattern. This cut of numbers didn't take into account anything other than age, so various other differentials could be skewing the results. Yet even this rudimentary look results in a curve that makes a lot of sense and shows some strong effects through the career lifecycle of a fighter.

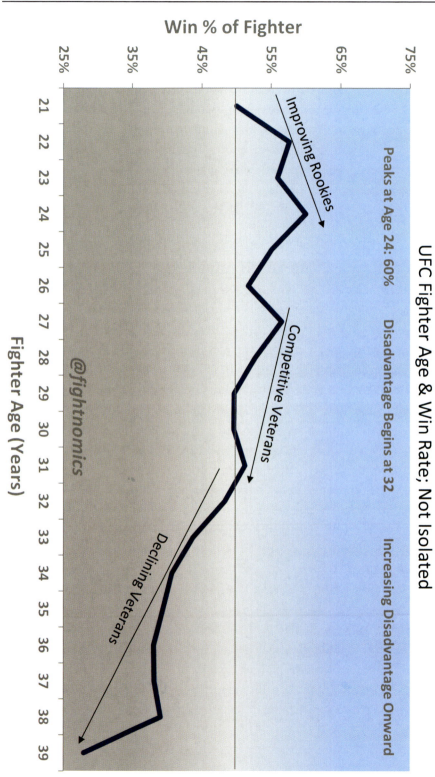

The Youth Advantage:
UFC Fighter Age & Win Rate; Not Isolated

Peaks at Age 24: 60%   Disadvantage Begins at 32   Increasing Disadvantage Onward

Win % of Fighter

75%

65%

55%

45%

35%

25%

Improving Rookies

Competitive Veterans

Declining Veterans

@fightnomics

Fighter Age (Years)

21 22 23 24 25 26 27 28 29 30 31 32 33 34 35 36 37 38 39

This story of how fighters perform through the arc of their careers is compelling. It tells us that young fighters improved rapidly in their early twenties and enjoyed a performance advantage that lasted into their thirties. The tipping point was at age 32, when fighters began a steady decline in performance that eventually dropped off the cliff as they approached 40. A look at the list of current UFC champions reveals that every one of them is 32 or younger. Only two are in their thirties (barely) and the oldest is the longest-reigning active champion who achieved his title status while still in his twenties.

The New Breed: Age of UFC Champions

Weight Class	Name	Age
Flyweight	Demetrious Johnson	27
Women's Bantamweight	Ronda Rousey	26
Bantamweight	Dominick Cruz	28
Bantamweight (Interim)	Renan Barao	26
Featherweight	Jose Aldo	27
Lightweight	Anthony Pettis	26
Welterweight	Georges St. Pierre	32
Middleweight	Chris Weidman	29
Light Heavyweight	Jon Jones	26
Heavyweight	Cain Velasquez	31

UFC Champion Ages as of October, 2013

The new generation of fighters that grew up watching and learning MMA, rather than pioneering it, may already be here. These fighters are elevating the sport to new heights because they are training to elite levels while their bodies are still in peak physiological condition. There will always be exceptions to any rule, like Randy Couture entering MMA at 33 and competing late into his 40's, but Father Time doesn't cut many breaks and neither does science.

Being young carries advantages for fighters entering the Octagon, but it takes two to make a fight (unless you're Tyler Durden), so **instead of looking at just the age of one fighter we can instead look at the difference in age between them**. The generic window of time for a fighter to compete in pro-MMA is between 20 and 40 years old. There are exceptions, but this age range captures the vast majority of fighters who have competed in the UFC. Fighters on the extreme ends of this range are pretty rare and it would be strange to pit the most seasoned veteran against the rawest rookie, so the realistic range for age differentials in UFC fights is about 16 years. Towards the end of that range we're already getting to pretty small sample sizes. I reran the high level analysis of win rates for younger fighters based on how much younger they are than their opponents and the results generated another clear pattern.

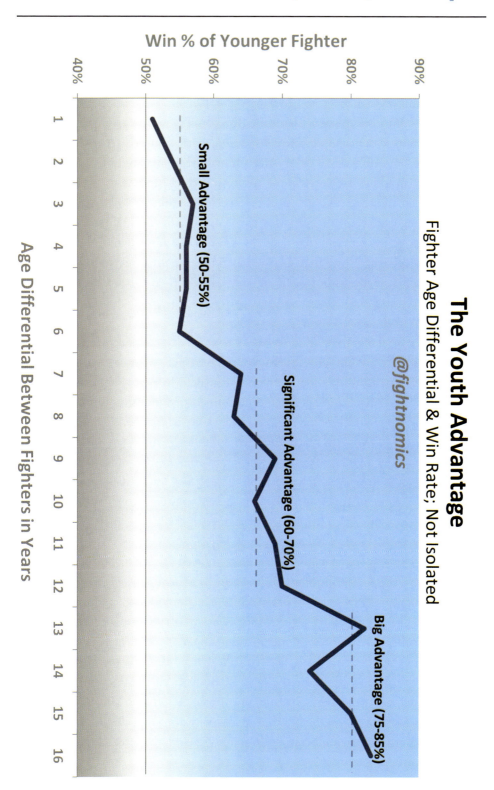

The Youth Advantage

Fighter Age Differential & Win Rate; Not Isolated

@fightnomics

Win % of Younger Fighter

Age Differential Between Fighters in Years

Small Advantage (50-55%)

Significant Advantage (60-70%)

Big Advantage (75-85%)

The upward trend suggests that the bigger the age difference, the better the odds are for the younger fighters. For an age differential of a decade or more, it can be assumed that the younger fighter is still in his twenties, while the older fighter is well into his thirties. This scenario should generally result in a younger fighter who enters the cage in better condition, both from a strength and fitness point of view, as well as in an injury-free (or at least injury-minimized) condition. Both factors would heavily favor the younger fighter, and both are critical to performance in the cage. The question of experience remains; older fighters in the UFC represent a pool of athletes who have survived in the highest ranks of the game long enough to confirm that they are skilled while also having gained valuable competitive experience. Isn't that worth something? It turns out yes, experience is definitely worth something, but we have to dig deeper into the data to find out what.

Father Time's Toll

Generally speaking, we tend to see world records set by athletes in their twenties and early thirties, and in pure measured performance events like running and swimming, it's easy to track athletic trends by age. In MMA several factors blur the attribution of performance to age. First, in a complicated head-to-head competition it's not any single physical metric that determines the winner. Every fight is a fight. And what's more, MMA has not been drawing life-long competitors for very long, such that an older fighter these days may not even be the more "experienced" fighter. Athletes who once watched Forrest Griffin and Stephan Bonnar battle for an Ultimate Fighter contract with their freshmen wrestling team are now among the UFC's champions. Meanwhile, some pioneering Hall of Famers who entered the sport late in life were still competing at high levels until very recently. So the sport itself is undergoing a maturation process as well as a changing of the guard. In addition to these complications in assessing a matchup between ages, science has documented a variety of physical factors affecting athletic performance that change with age, some of which are very relevant to performance in the cage.

As we age, a variety of basic functions deteriorate in performance. But let's be clear; much of this effect is due to inactivity and not just elapsed time because most people don't continue to exercise as they age. Research specifically focusing on *lifelong athletes* has demonstrated that physiological drivers of athletic performance peak during a man's late twenties, then decline slowly with time. Specifically, lean muscle mass, maximal strength, aerobic capacity, reaction time, endurance, and cardiovascular function all decline with age slowly – but surely. Part of this is because of, and in parallel with, declines in testosterone. These effects only occur appreciably after the age of 40, and are gradual and slow declines. Each of these changes affects the body in subtle and cumulative ways until an athlete simply realizes that he is not the force he once was back in his prime. The gradual nature of these effects is such that there's no cutoff point during a normal athlete's expected career where we can predictably and suddenly expect him to "lose a step." These are just the realities of growing older.

Unfortunately for older fighters, they are not just facing stronger, faster, fitter opponents, they're also facing competitors more likely to be healthy and in top form. It's often said that no one goes into a fight at 100% due to the extreme rigors of elite-level MMA training, but **an athlete's ability to recover from recent or pre-existing injuries is much easier in a younger body**. Older fighters simply can't recover fully from training or from injuries, and spend more time "on the bench," and less time maintaining their competitive edge. Older fighters also have longer to accumulate the inevitable laundry list of nagging injuries that stick to them like so many regrettable tattoos. On top of being the best fighters in the world, these are more reasons to respect the grizzled veterans of the Octagon who sacrifice their bodies for the sport they love and for the fans who cheer them on fight night.

We've seen enough preliminary analysis to warrant looking deeper, and there are some plausible causal mechanisms that support the age disadvantage theory. To test the idea that age matters I've taken the large data set of UFC fights and filtered out those where there was a southpaw or significant reach advantage, and tracked fighter age. We're trying isolate the key variable by making "all other things be equal." Given that the sample size at any specific age was smaller due to our controlling filters, I had to lump age into groups of several years. The pattern of high win rates for younger fighters and a steady decline throughout a fighter's career comes through plainly. Once fighters hit their 30th birthday, they're crossing the threshold of disadvantage.

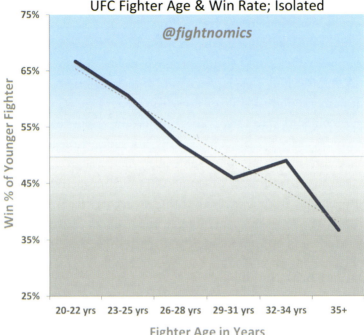

The Youth Advantage:
UFC Fighter Age & Win Rate; Isolated

Clearly it's better to be young. This cut of the data says guys in their 20's win more often than not, but no one in their 30's is beating the 50% threshold. That's a harsh cutoff, and it's interesting, but how much of a direct advantage is youth when we consider two fighters on the Tale of the Tape? Mixed into that data set are plenty of matchups where fighters of similar age faced each other, potentially blurring the results. So using the same set of fight data where there are no stance or reach advantages, I recalculated the win rate of younger fighters based on the age differential. Though the effect isn't as pronounced as our earlier analyses that didn't isolate age from other advantages, the Youth Advantage still comes through as a clear winner. **Overall, when there's at least a four-year age difference and no other advantages are present, younger fighters win nearly 60% of the time.**

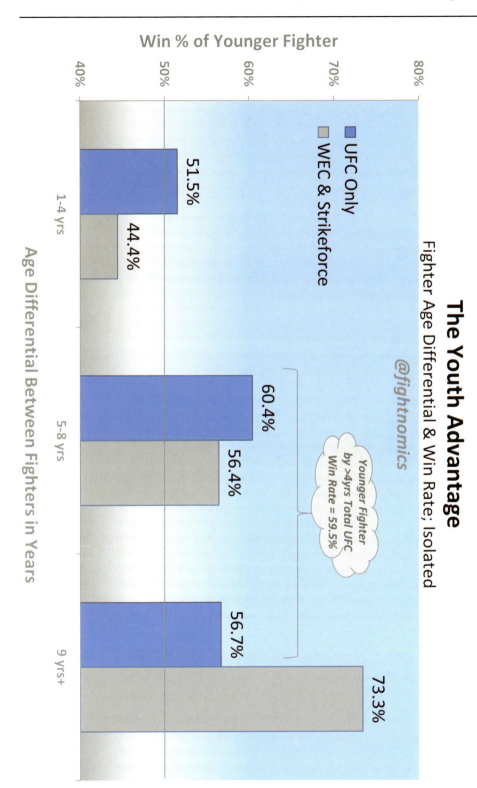

The Youth Advantage

Fighter Age Differential & Win Rate; Isolated

@fightnomics

Win % of Younger Fighter

- ■ UFC Only
- ▢ WEC & Strikeforce

Younger Fighter by >4yrs Total UFC Win Rate = 59.5%

1-4 yrs: 51.5% / 44.4%

5-8 yrs: 60.4% / 56.4%

9 yrs+: 56.7% / 73.3%

Age Differential Between Fighters in Years

Exploring the idea of the "Youth Advantage" at first makes it seem that age is the driver of boosted performances in younger fighters, but upon closer inspection we realize that's not really what's going on. The mechanism is actually more sinister, one that I witnessed take effect first hand.

The Price of Wisdom: Age and Knockouts in MMA

At UFC 129 Randy Couture entered the Octagon for the last time to the cheers of 55,000 fans in Toronto's Rogers Centre, a massive venue normally reserved for major league baseball and Canadian football games. From a dimmed broadcast platform set up in the cheap seats, I watched alongside the cast and crew of the UFC's pre-show team. As Lyoto Machida lined up across the cage, I pointed to my analysis of the matchup, noting specifically that Machida's evasiveness and striking ability were key, as was Couture's age. Randy Couture was 47 years old and a veteran at grinding out victories. His only hope was to neutralize Machida's laser-like strikes via clinching and dirty boxing, possibly even ground and pound, and that just wasn't in the cards. Even from our distant vantage point, we all knew it.

The stat-line on Machida showed extremely accurate striking and similarly excellent striking defense. His takedown defense was also strong, a result of his uncanny ability to maintain distance, which would eliminate any advantage a wrestler might have over him. Couture on the other hand, was a decent striker, but allowed his opponents to land their own strikes with better than average success, indicating poor striking defense. His wrestling acumen led to a good shooting takedown success rate, though surprisingly little success from the clinch. The fight's outcome was right there in front of us on the paper. At betting line of -325, Machida was a strong but not overwhelming favorite at slightly better than three-to-one, and yet that betting line failed to capture how much of an advantage he really had. **The "Dragon" was 15 years younger than the "Natural," an age spread that generally leads to the younger fighter winning the majority of the time**. On top of that, it was clear that Machida, the younger southpaw, was able to keep his distance, meaning he could send his strikes through Couture's loose defense at will.

As the fight began, I watched alongside Kenny Florian and Stephan Bonnar with slight grimaces while Couture pressed forward and tried desperately to get hold of the elusive Machida. During these scrambles Machida landed punches out of nowhere with his typical blazing speed and accuracy. When the first round ended, it was almost a relief that Couture was still standing – a small victory for the grizzled veteran. That relief was short lived; the now famous crane kick that ended the illustrious MMA career of Randy Couture connected with his chin barely a minute into the second round. Couture's head snapped with the impact of the surprise kick, his body immediately crumpling to the mat before the kick was even retracted. Moments after recovering, as Randy stood flashing his Hollywood grin and confirming the retirement we were all expecting, one of his teeth fell out and into his gloved hand.

From the broadcast booth, the excitement from the amazing knockout finish was tempered by the respectful sobriety of witnessing a legend in the act of letting go of his fighting career. "It's time," many said, "he had a great career, but it's time." They were right on both counts. No one expected another return to the cage for The Natural. He was making a wise decision to retire, one that some other fighters have been unable to make even remotely as gracefully. But what was the price of that decision?

The Aging Brain

Despite the age-defying wonder that is Randy Couture's athleticism, why did we all know it was time for him to stop fighting? If fighters are still physically fit late in life, haven't they also gained years of critical experience that might allow them to remain competitive, even if they've lost a step? True, experience is valuable in any vocation, even fighting in a cage. But in contact sports, and especially combat sports, there's also the looming shadow of brain injury that complicates an athlete's ambitions.

The effects of dementia are so common among professional boxers that the medical community even refers to "dementia pugilistica," (named from the Latin root pugil, meaning boxer/fighter) while common slang includes the term "punch-drunk" to describe the slurring of speech and erratic behavior associated with taking too many blows to the head over the years. This is just one of many related neurological conditions associated with deteriorating cognitive and intellectual abilities. When it comes to seeing fighters get knocked out, friends, family, and fans alike would be appalled if they realized their cheers fueled a fighter to push his risk of dementia by fighting past the limits of personal safety. There are simply too many instances of this exact tragedy occurring.

That repeated concussions and even sub-concussive events can lead to long-term neurological problems is not in question. What is in question in assessing MMA performance is whether or not age and/or prior knockouts lead to an increased likelihood of later knockouts. Can a fighter "lose his chin" so to speak? Can a bad knockout make a fighter even more susceptible to future knockouts? Can a quarterback who's been knocked out once get knocked out again from a lighter hit? Physicians specializing in the field of head trauma say "yes," but for now I'll take a big step back and keep things simple.

Let's set up a relevant piece of analysis with a simple question. Does age change the way fighters perform? I've already quantified the "Youth Advantage" in MMA and demonstrated that the younger a fighter is than his opponent, the more likely he is to win. So older fighters are at a disadvantage, but how? How is it, specifically, that the Youth Advantage takes effect inside the Octagon? The analysis here examines UFC fights over a five-year period, excluding the rare disqualifications, no contests or overturned fights. I am showing how fights end by the age of the fighter, first, winners on the left, and then losing fighters on the right. The red area shows fights ending by strikes, the blue shows submissions, and the gray shows decisions. See any difference?

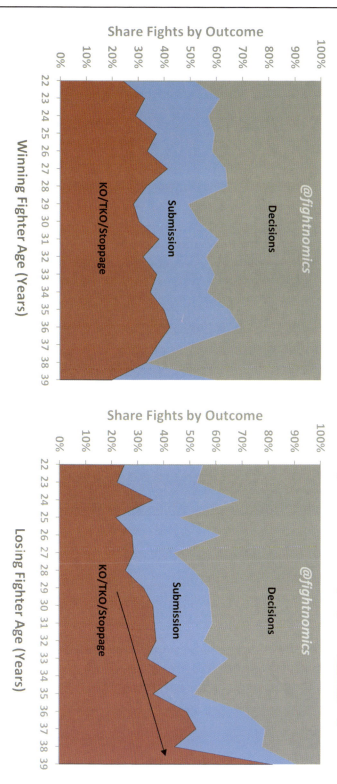

Age doesn't have much of an impact on how fighters win (left graph), but there is a clear trend in how they lose (right graph). The increased likelihood of a knockout loss in older fighters is clear on the right graph, seen by the growing red (T)KO/stoppage area that rises as age goes up. As fighters get older, there's a steady increase in the rate at which they lose by strikes. Specifically, analysis revealed that fighters who are 36-38 years old get knocked out at nearly twice the rate of fighters who are only 22-23. That's a huge difference.

Because finish rates and fight-ending methods are particular to each weight class, I've isolated a single division and aggregated the results by age categories to illustrate the trend. Here's how finish rates evolve with age for UFC Middleweights.

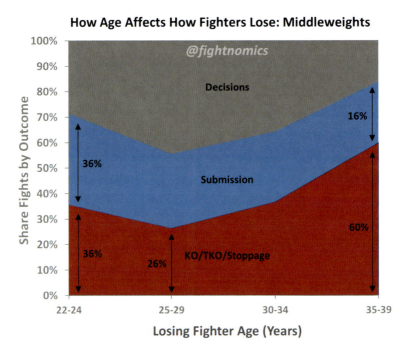

What's also interesting is that **older fighters are less likely to lose by submission than when they were younger. Here, finally, is the advantage of experience – submission defense keeps improving with age and training. Defending submissions isn't necessarily a matter of strength, but of skill**. The best jiu-jitsu practitioners make it look far too easy and may not even break a sweat while their opponents exhaust themselves looking for an opening. The data can be interpreted conversely too: while younger fighters are less likely to lose by strikes, they are more than twice as likely to get submitted as older fighters. Chalk one up for the old guys. The submission game remains the most subtle art within MMA, and is one that favors experience.

It's interesting that TKO losses fall as fighters hit their peak performance zone in their late twenties, then climb rapidly throughout their thirties. This might mean there's a rookie disadvantage in the Octagon when it comes to getting knocked out. It's also interesting that submission losses fall consistently throughout the age range. Again, that's fighter experience adding value in the form of improved submission defense over time. But the steepest pattern of all is still the rising risk of (T)KO with age.

How It Works

In examining this trend I've dug a little deeper on striking metrics and performance with age. Because older fighters tend to lose by strikes, perhaps there's a cause due to the way they fight that leads to those outcomes. At this point we know the "how," we still need to figure out the "why."

Let's consider three potential causes for the rise in knockout losses with age:

1. Older fighters are less accurate strikers, and tend to lose striking exchanges.
2. Older fighters can't keep pace with younger fighters, and so absorb more strikes.
3. Older fighters absorb the same amount of strikes, but those strikes do more damage to them.

To test Hypotheses #1 and #2, I've shown standup head striking accuracy for jabs and power strikes, and also total striking attempts per minute, all by age of the fighter attempting the strikes.

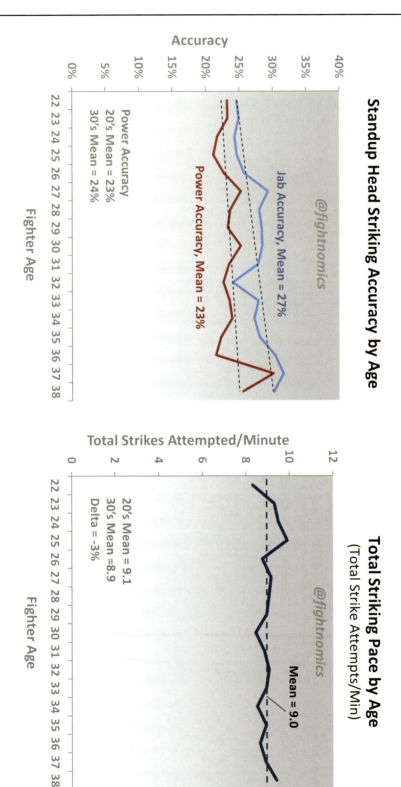

Standup Head Striking Accuracy by Age

Accuracy

@fightnomics

Jab Accuracy, Mean = 27%

Power Accuracy, Mean = 23%

Power Accuracy
20's Mean = 23%
30's Mean = 24%

Fighter Age

Total Striking Pace by Age
(Total Strike Attempts/Min)

Total Strikes Attempted/Minute

@fightnomics

Mean = 9.0

20's Mean = 9.1
30's Mean = 8.9
Delta = -3%

Fighter Age

There's actually a slight rise in striking accuracy with age, and a negligible decline in striking pace. Not much of a difference at all. The slight rise in accuracy could be attributed to increased experience, or even a selection ("survivor") effect that more skilled fighters will last longer in the UFC, and therefore older fighters may be better in skill metrics. So if fighters are still performing well offensively as they age, let's look at the same variables based on the opponent's age to see how that changes things.

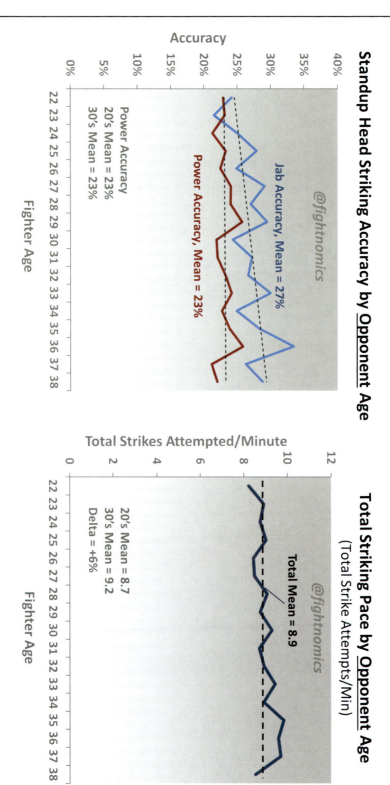

Standup Head Striking Accuracy by <u>Opponent Age</u>

Accuracy

- Jab Accuracy, Mean = 27%
- Power Accuracy, Mean = 23%

@fightnomics

Power Accuracy
20's Mean = 23%
30's Mean = 23%

Fighter Age

Total Striking Pace by <u>Opponent Age</u>
(Total Strike Attempts/Min)

Total Strikes Attempted/Minute

Total Mean = 8.9

@fightnomics

20's Mean = 8.7
30's Mean = 9.2
Delta = +6%

Fighter Age

The only noticeable trend here is that jab accuracy goes up with opponent age. This makes sense, because reaction time deteriorates with age, and jabs are generally shorter, quicker strikes. Thus, older fighters have more trouble defending jabs. But these jabs aren't knockout blows, and **older fighters maintain the same power head striking defense as younger fighters**. Hypothesis #1 doesn't look good.

We also see that it's not necessarily the volume of the strikes either, since striking pace didn't change much with age, or by opponent's age. There's a slight difference in the later years based on opponent age, but it's less than a 10% boost on the total. **Older fighters aren't getting knocked out because they can't keep pace with their opponents and get overwhelmed**. In this view we don't see a strong case for hypothesis #2 either.

That leaves us hypothesis #3. There was a riddle posed by a cartoon owl in commercials back in the day: "how many licks does it take to get to the center of a tootsie pop?" Let's rephrase: how many strikes to the head does it take to knock someone down? The question is a tricky one. Really it only takes only one if you land it right (unless the opponent is taking a dive). We can get a close proxy using UFC data by analyzing how many landed power strikes are required to cause a knockdown on average, and then vary that metric by the age of the fighter receiving these blows. We could answer our question as to "how" older fighters are losing more often by strikes by showing that they cannot withstand strikes as well as younger fighters.

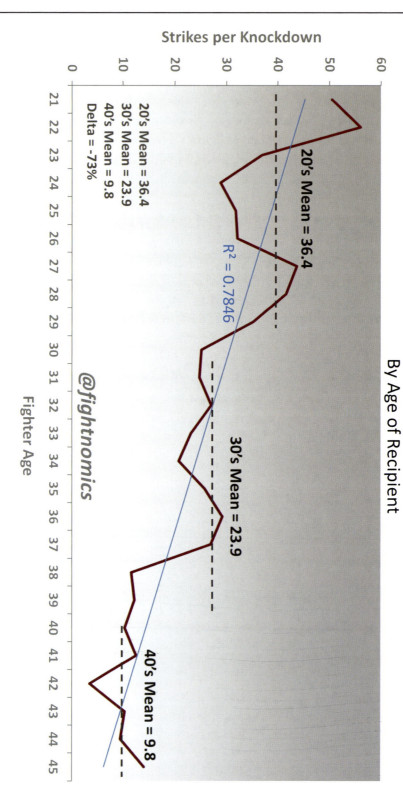

Distance Power Head Strikes Absorbed Per Knockdown
By Age of Recipient

Strikes per Knockdown

20's Mean = 36.4

R² = 0.7846

30's Mean = 23.9

40's Mean = 9.8

@fightnomics

Fighter Age

20's Mean = 36.4
30's Mean = 23.9
40's Mean = 9.8
Delta = -73%

194

Though the data here is somewhat volatile, the basic trend is clear: it takes fewer and fewer head strikes to knock down older fighters. During standup striking it takes a third as many landed strikes to knock down a fighter in his forties than it did when he was in his early twenties. This could be due to one of two basic effects, or a combination of both, depending on our understanding of how knockdowns occur. It could mean the likelihood of a flash knockout, or otherwise consciousness-altering concussion, is higher the older the fighter is. Or it could mean that cumulative strikes do more damage in older fighters, so they can't keep standing as long. Either way, it doesn't really matter. Hypothesis #3 looks compelling: To exploit the Youth Advantage you don't have to throw strikes at a higher pace, or land them with higher accuracy; each blow is simply more likely to knock down an older fighter. Why?

It's the Brain, Stupid

One reason knockout rates may be increasing with age is that the brains of older fighters are less resistant to trauma. Cumulative damage as well as basic physiologic changes with age lead to decreasing resiliency of the brain. Additionally, our brains atrophy over time, so the space between the critical organ and the skull increases ever so slightly. Despite our brains floating in cerebrospinal fluid that essentially acts as a shock absorber within our heads, this protective system isn't enough to prevent trauma in the case of a rapid acceleration (i.e., when a punch lands). As we age, the space in which the brain might bounce off the skull increases; this means that the impact on the brain is harder and more damaging when the head moves suddenly than when our brains were younger, slightly bigger, and better cushioned. It's like wearing a helmet that is too big for your head.

This additional room for brain bouncing increases another more serious risk: "diffuse axonal injury." Imagine that the neurons of your brain are the fibers that hold your memories and intellect together. Squishy brain matter evolved to be resilient and stretchy, much like our imaginations, but there are limits. The more violent a brain injury, the greater the risk of tearing these critical fibers that are the conduits of thoughts and sensations within the brain, or "the infrastructure of your Self." With a larger space at the perimeter of our skulls, the potential for this type of injury goes up as the brain gets compressed and stretched to a greater degree on impact. The tearing of these axons can occur over a wider volume of brain matter and is a serious injury very different from focused bruises. It's also one we don't yet know how to heal. Like striking coach Mike Winklejohn says, "brain damage sucks."

As kids, our more resilient brains protect us from our wildly active and often injurious lifestyles. But as we age our ability to withstand trauma declines, as does our behavioral willingness to put our heads into risky places (unless you're Johnny Knoxville). Whether due to the accumulation of repeated concussions, or the general atrophy and resulting decline in brain resiliency with age, there is an increase in KO/TKO rates as fighters get older. Period. One possible reason supported by medical research is that repeated concussions decrease a person's resiliency against future concussions. An older fighter no longer has to get hit "on the button" to knock him down, as any significant blow to the head could wobble them. It also means that the resilience needed to withstand a few head strikes before reaching a pre-knockdown (or fall down) tipping point degrades with age, for all the same physical and physiological reasons. Hence, **older fighters still perform at high levels, they just can't take a punch like they used to**.

After a concussion, blood on the surface of the brain isn't fully cleared away, and a rusty-colored patch may remain permanently. In autopsies a colorful map of a lifetime's worth of brain traumas might allow researchers to better understand the cumulative effects of these injuries. Age isn't even the real metric of interest here. If we're trying to assess knockout risk based on prior damage, we really should be looking at the totality of a fighter's cage time, training time, and even extra-curricular history. For example, fighters who were football players, especially those who played high-impact positions like defensive backs, could come into the fight game at a dangerous disadvantage. Similarly, **any fighter with a personal tendency to train without head gear, not rest after suffering a knockout, or engage in any other of a variety of poor practices that would accelerate the natural decline in brain resiliency, would be at a disadvantage**. The metric of age then is just a proxy, a heuristic variable that serves as a simple reminder of how long a fighter has been in the game. With greater fidelity of data it might be more valuable to rerun this analysis examining total fights, total knockdowns suffered, years of training and fighting, known concussions, etc.. My guess is that all of these would correlate with increased risk of knockout, but that data isn't readily available. For now, we're left with age.

As with many areas of analysis explored here, when data on new variables becomes available, researchers will work new angles to confirm or reject their hypotheses. In the meantime, the more critical issue in MMA is understanding the frequency of injuries in training versus competition and also how to prevent long-term damage once an injury does occur. Fighters suffering head trauma in fights must absolutely undergo extensive testing and clearance before returning to the sport. And just as importantly, referees, fighters and their cornermen must fully appreciate the importance of stopping a fight when one fighter is clearly out of it. For some older fighters, their offensive skills will keep them competitive, and their submission defense will continue to get better, but when it comes to striking defense a significant age differential means it's no longer a fair fight.

What Have We Learned?

In the Youth vs. Experience battle, youth wins. There is a variety of complex potential drivers of this trend, but at least the pattern is plain enough. And going deeper into the data reveals the differences in how older fighters lose. Specifically, losses by strikes rise with age, while risk of submission falls. While this information may help in forecasting outcomes from the Tale of the Tape, it also adds to the burning need for more medical research into brain injuries from sports and how best to mitigate the risks associated with them. This isn't to say that we, as competitive and athletic animals, should never take risks. It's just that we should fully understand the risks we face in order to make the best decisions.

Sports, even combat sports like MMA, will continue to be a cultural backbone to our modern lives. The passion we feel in competition, even as spectators, is a defining human characteristic, and our lives would undoubtedly feel less complete without these competitive outlets. While sobering research results such as these may lead to that sinking feeling about the weakness of the human condition, we should remind ourselves of the amazing capabilities of our innate athleticism. A gentle reminder of our mortality contrasts sharply with the sometimes surreal invincibility of MMA champions, but it's a healthy exercise to look for balance even amid extremes. MMA fighters are quickly becoming recognized as some of the world's greatest athletes and that is something the sports should embrace, celebrate, but also help preserve.

We're left with a sobering lesson for fighters. While their guts, hearts, or egos may tell them they still have a few fights left, their brains should tell them otherwise. Scientist Carl Sagan once quipped, "I try not to think with my gut." Older fighters would be wise to do the same, and listen to their brains instead. There is wisdom with age, but be careful how much you pay for that wisdom along the way. When the decision to retire becomes all too obvious, chances are the price paid for that certainty was too high.

Chapter Notes

1. *"Grip strength and hand dominance: challenging the 10% rule,"* Petersen P, Petrick M, Connor H, Conklin D., *American Journal of Occupational Therapy,* 1989 Jul; 43(7):444-7.

2. *"Writing with non-dominant hand: left-handers perform better with the right hand than right handers with the left,"* Laskowski, K. and Henneberg, M., *Anthropological Review Vol. 75 (2), 129–136 (2012).*

3. *"Frequency-dependent maintenance of left handedness in humans,"* Raymond, R., Pontier, D., Dufour, A. B., and Pape Moller, A., *Proceedings: Biological Sciences, Vol. 263, No. 1377 (Dec. 22, 1996), pp. 1627-1633.*

4. *"Handedness, homicide and negative frequency-dependent selection,"* Faurie, C. and Raymond, M., *Proceedings of the Royal Society B (2005) 272, 25–28.*

5. *"Sex differences in left-handedness: A meta-analysis of 144 studies,"* Papadatou-Pastou, M., Martin, M., Munafò, M., Jones, G., *Psychological Bulletin, Vol. 134 (5), Sep 2008, 677-699.*

8 Assume the Position: Fighter Position & What it Tells Us

This Chapter in 30 Seconds:

- MMA fights mostly take place with fighters on their feet
- A clear trend is that fighters are spending more time on their feet, and less time on the ground
- While standing, fighters are spending less time in the clinch relative to a distance position
- Of the one-third of average fight time spent on the ground, most is spent in full guard or hovering
- On the ground, more advanced dominant positions like half guard, side control and mount are increasingly hard to achieve, and fighters hold these positions for less time
- The king of all ground positions is back control, which once achieved is easier to hold and offers multiple ways to finish a fight
- Wrestlers aren't "ruining MMA" – fighters on the ground are actually more active in striking and advancing position than ever before, despite spending much less time on the ground overall

Where Fights are Fought

Whether it's on the feet or on the ground, the position of two fighters means a lot in the sport of MMA, and by using Time in Position data we can actually look at how fighters spend their time in the cage. First, at a high level, we can separate distance standing from clinch or ground fighting. Once on the ground we can get into much more detail by examining which exact position the grapplers are in. Do fighters mostly fight on their feet? Or are the grappling arts the dominant share of fights in the UFC?

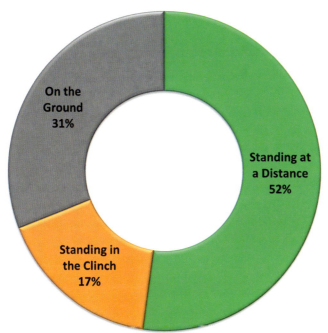

How UFC Fights Are Fought

On the Ground 31%

Standing at a Distance 52%

Standing in the Clinch 17%

*Includes all UFC Fights 2011-April, 2013;
percentages are rounded*

It turns out that UFC fighters in recent years spend more than two-thirds of their time on their feet, the most of which is standing at a distance. The street maxim that "all fights end up on the ground" isn't entirely true when it comes to professionals, but still nearly a third of UFC fight minutes occur with at least one fighter on the mat. Was this always the case? Didn't grapplers once rule the Octagon with unrelenting takedowns, submissions and ground and pound? This view of fight position is a very low resolution snapshot of the sport we like to watch in high-def, so let's look at the metrics again with the additional variable of time to form a more complete picture.

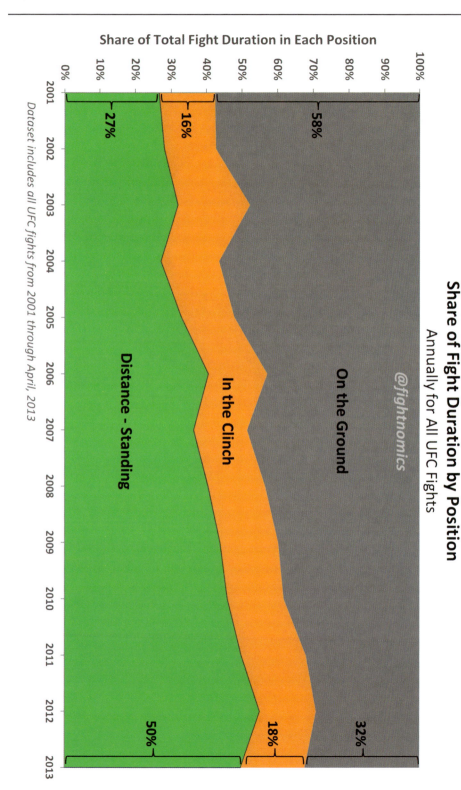

Share of Total Fight Duration in Each Position

Share of Fight Duration by Position
Annually for All UFC Fights

Distance - Standing

In the Clinch

On the Ground

@fightnomics

Dataset includes all UFC fights from 2001 through April, 2013

27%

16%

58%

50%

18%

32%

Again, some patterns are emerging. The last decade of UFC competition has seen changes in many ways, and where fighters are positioned in the cage is one of the most important. Around the time when Zuffa took over the promotion (2001), the majority of all fights took place on the ground. Barely more than a quarter of fight minutes were spent in a distance position allowing fighters to stand and trade strikes. Then in 2004 the game changed, and there was a steady increase in the amount of time that fighters stayed on their feet. The rise in distance fighting was continuous through the rest of the decade until finally hovering around the 50% mark in the most recent years.

All the while the tradeoff with the distance position was time spent on the ground, with ground minutes dropping from 58% of total time all the way down below a third of fight minutes. The trend appears to have stabilized for now, but the landscape of the average UFC fight has significantly changed over the course of a decade. Fighters now spend most of their time on their feet rather than on the ground, which has affected a number of other trend and performance metrics as well.

When looking at time in position and how fights end, it turns out that fights that stay standing longer are more likely to end by KO/TKO, while fights that spend more time on the ground are more likely to end by submission (an obvious observation, but important to point out). In addition to improving submission defense skills of fighters competing at the highest levels, this additional macro-trend is contributing to the slight decline in submission rates versus finishes by strikes. For fans of high-paced standup striking, this is all good news, but sandwiched in the middle of distance fighting and the ground game is a more subtle trend.

The Decline of the Clinch

Clinch fighting is the continuation of striking where boxing or other pure distance striking arts ends, and it is the least likely basic position in MMA. That doesn't mean it can't be critical to determining how a fight transpires, or that fighters don't sometimes differentiate themselves in clinch fighting, it just means that it comprises a small portion of total fight time. Originally making up 16% of fight time back in 2001, clinch time has crept slightly upward to 18% in 2013. That small bump is actually hiding an opposite trend at work, which is that fighters are clinching less, not more. Given that fighters are staying on their feet a lot more often today than a decade ago, how much standing time in fights is spent clinching?

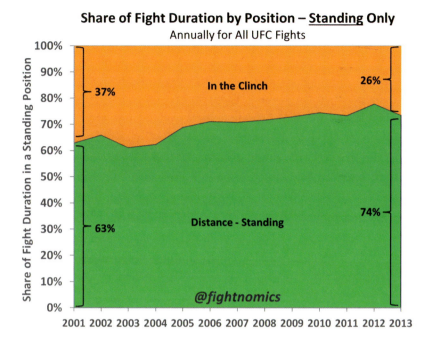

Share of Fight Duration by Position – Standing Only
Annually for All UFC Fights

Clinching is actually on the decline in a relative sense once we account for the increased time fighters are spending on their feet. Historically fighters were clinched for over a third of their time standing, while today that number has fallen closer to a quarter. Part of this trend may be explained by the fact that referees are separating fighters more frequently when there is a position stalemate along the fence. Another explanation is perhaps that fighters are simply doing less in the clinch over all, justifying a separation. Upon closer inspection, however, that doesn't seem to be the case.

Isolating time spent in the clinch on an annual basis and tallying aggregate striking activity and takedown attempts that occur in the clinch, there was not an appreciable drop in overall activity by fighters once they were in this position. Fighters each average about one takedown attempt per minute spent in the clinch, while also attempting eight strikes per minute. These trends haven't changed much in recent years, which means either referees are breaking up clinched fights more frequently, or fighters are choosing to clinch less. I don't have a firm answer given all the dynamics involved, although I do think referees are more empowered to encourage action than they were in the early 2000's. This simple breaking and resetting of fighters has led to more time spent trading from a distance (which fans seem to appreciate).

For fans who believe clinching is stalling or boring, now you know at least there's less of this, relatively speaking. That may also change how fighters compete, accentuating the skills of fighters who have range rather than a strong clinch game.

One missed opportunity in all this is that apparently fighters have not exploited the clinch for more takedowns. Remember, takedown attempts from the clinch have much higher success rates than shooting over open ground. Yet fighters appear to favor distance shooting attempts over clinch attempts. On the flipside, fans of fighters who can expertly leverage a Thai Plumb to land knees to finish their opponent take solace; the clinch game still offers the occasional spectacular finish.

The Ground Game

Historical UFC data from 2002 to 2013 shows that fighters are actually spending more time standing during fights, specifically in a distance standing position rather than in the clinch. While well over half of fight minutes in 2002 were spent on the ground, that number has been declining, and approached only one-third of fight minutes in 2013. There's still plenty of fighting done on the ground, and that's where things get complicated. Contrasting the limited number of physical arrangements that can occur between two fighters on their feet, grappling on the ground presents a diverse tangle of limbs and torsos, sometimes not even aligned in the same direction. Once a fighter is "grounded," the FightMetric system kicks in with a new vocabulary of specific body arrangements, position advances, and determinations of control and dominance. The nuances of these positions often lead to the most confusion by the casual observer, so diving into the details of what happens on the ground should be helpful in understanding the ground game beyond just strikes and submissions. Here's how time is spent on the ground in the UFC.

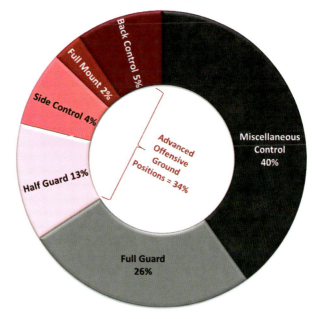

How UFC Fights Are Fought on the Ground

Back Control 5%
Full Mount 2%
Side Control 4%
Half Guard 13%
Advanced Offensive Ground Positions = 34%
Miscellaneous Control 40%
Full Guard 26%

Includes all UFC Fights 2011-April, 2013; percentages are rounded

The black and gray areas represent fairly neutral positions, although one fighter (the one on top) is still designated as being in control. Two-thirds of all time spent on the mat is in one of these conservative positions. Much of the time in "Miscellaneous Control" is actually where one fighter is standing above another who is lying down in the famous "Ali-Inoki" position. Sometimes a fighter is knocked down, falls, is thrown, or just pulls guard and ends up on his back, while the other fighter decides not to pursue the fight to the floor and stands back. Sometimes there are tentative kicks from the standing fighter to the legs of the grounded opponent, as both fighters wait to see if the other will make a move. The stalemate sometimes ends with the standing fighter stepping back and the referee interjecting to ensure a return to a normal distance fighting position. Sometimes the fighter on top will attempt an aggressive move to try to secure a more dominant ground position. Diving over the defensive fighter's legs sometimes works, and sometimes the defending fighter is able to deflect the incoming threat and maintain his defensive posture. Either way, these standoffs end up taking nearly half of all time where at least one fighter is on the ground.

Whether a top control fighter lands a takedown or wades his way into the leg defense of a grounded opponent, full guard is the next most common position. The top fighter is still technically in control, but the position is by no means a dominant one. One-quarter of all time spent on the mat sees one fighter in the guard of another. Some fighters are content to fight with their hands from full guard, while others will attempt to advance position to enable more dangerous attacks. Full guard is being used less and less, as fighters are increasingly choosing to this position. Unlike in Vegas, what happens in the guard doesn't necessarily stay in the guard.

Only one-third of ground time is in a position more advanced than full guard, but these are definitely the times where the fight enters a critical period. As we progress through more difficult-to-achieve positions, the number of those who succeed and the amount of time they spend in these positions falls, which makes sense since many times these positions lead to fight-ending submissions or prompt the fighter on the bottom to try harder to escape. The uptick in time spent in back control is thanks to situations where a fighter skips directly to grabbing the back of an opponent while in the clinch or in a scramble. More ways to achieve this valuable position means it gets more attention than other intermediary positions.

As with other position metrics, it's likely that the rapidly evolving sport of MMA has seen changes with ground positions as well. So let's consider a historical view on an annual basis to determine what trends are underlying ground fighting in the UFC.

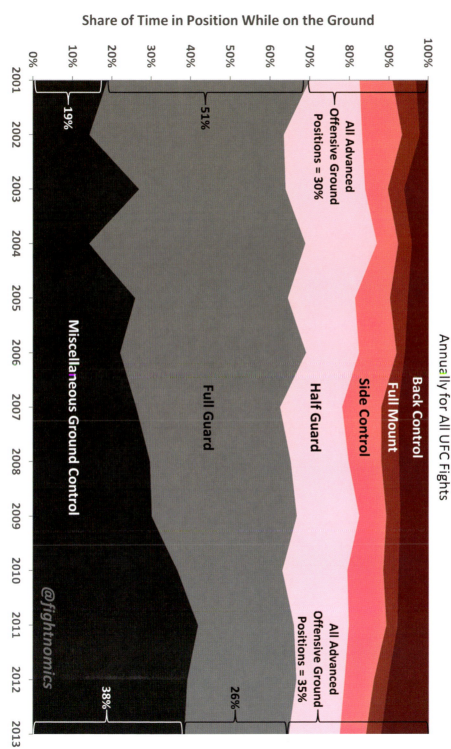

How Fights Take Place on the Ground
Annually for All UFC Fights

Share of Time in Position While on the Ground

All Advanced Offensive Ground Positions = 30%

Back Control
Full Mount
Side Control
Half Guard
Full Guard
Miscellaneous Ground Control

All Advanced Offensive Ground Positions = 35%

@fightnomics

207

Full guard isn't a great place to be. While you're technically in top "control," you have few weapons at your disposal, and you remain susceptible to submissions since many grapplers actually prefer to fight off their backs. So it's no surprise that fighters are spending less and less time in this position. But fighters can't just decide to advance position, those achievements must be earned, and all fighters continue to improve their grappling skills simultaneously. From a historical standpoint, we don't see much improvement in time spent in dominant positions, although we do see a trend of more fighters getting (or keeping) back control.

The King of All Ground Positions

So if passing guard is still difficult, but fighters want to avoid staying in the full guard of opponents, what's left? Fighters are spending more time in the "miscellaneous ground control position," which mainly includes a hovering stance. Some experienced grapplers will practically invite their opponents to take top control by "pulling" or "giving up" guard, for example, in attempt to draw a striker into a grappling match. Fighters in the UFC are wise to the dangers of waltzing into the guard of an experienced submission ace, and are generally more hesitant to spend any time there at all.

Another look at the ground data considers the likelihood of achieving each position for fighters in control. By correcting for takedowns landed (not perfect, but a good enough proxy), the data provides the likelihood of a controlling fighter achieving each position. Here's how it shakes out.

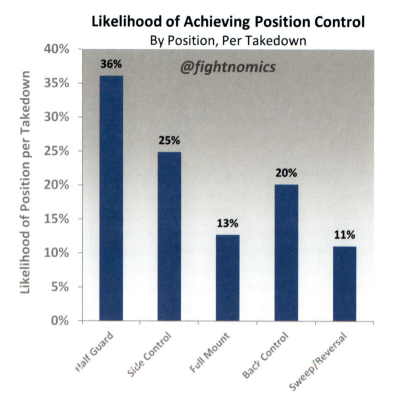

Likelihood of Achieving Position Control
By Position, Per Takedown

@fightnomics

There's a similar trend of increasing difficulty to achieve more dominant positions, with another slight boost for back control as some fighters also achieve this position with the benefit of a takedown first, or skip directly to this position after scoring a knockdown. What's surprising is that less than half of all takedowns will ever proceed to half guard. Although some fighters may get to side control directly from a takedown, even the combination of those two numbers implies that plenty of takedowns stall out in full guard.

The last look at this data divides time in position by the number of positions achieved, and tells us something interesting about how fighters defend against advancing opponents. If dominant positions are inherently more valuable to the offensive fighter, wouldn't they tend to spend more time in better positions?

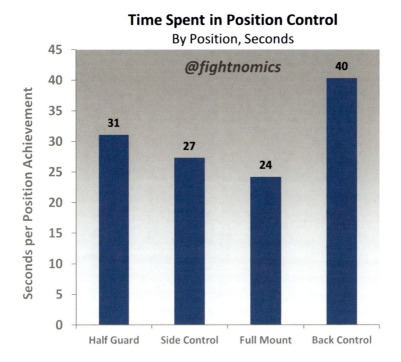

Time Spent in Position Control
By Position, Seconds

Apparently, **more dominant positions are harder to maintain**. The defense rate for each position is actually very similar; about one third of all position advances will eventually be reversed or escaped from by the bottom fighter. So calculating the time spent per position achievement tells us how long fighters are staying there, and by proxy, how quickly fighters are defending it. As it turns out, more advanced positions are harder to hold, with the exception of back control, which trumps them all. We've already seen how successful the rear naked choke is compared to other submission types, and now we another reason why: a fighter taking back control is really hard to shake. Fighters in this position of control spend much more time there, and can set up their submissions without worrying about strikes from the defender. Many believe that the full mount is the best position to achieve, but the data reveals that it is also the most difficult position to hold. Indeed, **back control is the king of all ground positions, and the data confirms it**.

Gunnar Nelson demonstrates the king of all ground positions before he would submit DaMarques Johnson by rear naked choke. Photo by Martin McNeil.

Are Wrestlers Ruining MMA?

Long before there was modern MMA, there was wrestling, and despite the rapid increase in popularity of MMA and even jiu-jitsu in the US, the most popular combat sport offered by American high schools and universities is still wrestling. After college many wrestlers are left with a truck load of skills and no outlet for them, so it's no surprise that a common career path to the UFC shoots across numerous wrestling mats of the American Midwest. Regardless of the demonstrated success and numerous UFC titles won by former Olympic and NCAA wrestlers, there are many who claim that "wrestlers are ruining MMA."

It's almost cliché at this point, but it must be confronted. The accusation permeates the message boards, gets screamed from the stands during live events, and tossed out as fact by the guy next to me at the sports bar in a skullified t-shirt triple-fisting lite beer bottles completely unaware that there are more efficient and delicious ways to catch a buzz from the taps of the establishment. But I digress. The claim has been made and it must now be put to the test. Considering that I am not currently under the employ of any MMA promotion, I will be mounting a defense for the sport of MMA pro bono. I assert that wrestling is not ruining MMA.

First, let's acknowledge the premise: traditional wrestling in and of itself cannot result in direct victory in MMA. Well, that's not entirely true thanks to one of the most gloriously ridiculous anecdotes of UFC-lore. At the inaugural UFC 1 event, Royce Gracie got Art "One Glove" Jimmerson to tap due to a full mount position. The smothering helplessness that the boxer felt under Gracie's top position did technically finish that fight, as there were no other metrics other than a takedown and mount to consider as the fight ending move. In case you're wondering, Jimmerson tapped the mat using the hand without the boxing glove on it. The case of Art Jimmerson remains an exception to the rule. There's no doubt that wrestling lacks the finishing potential of striking or submission disciplines, and yet being able to control your opponent and establish dominant position can eventually set up finishes by strikes or submissions. So what do the numbers say? Are wrestlers making MMA boring?

If wrestlers were truly taking over the sport, we should see an increasing amount of time spent on the ground in positions where they are most experienced, and less time standing and striking where a wrestler would be more vulnerable. Yet that is not the case. In Chapter 5 we saw that takedowns are occurring at a consistent pace through time, while their success rate is actually going down. Despite the addition of many high profile wrestlers to elite MMA ranks (especially in smaller weight classes), these trends don't support an influx of wrestlers attempting to wrestle their way to victory.

And in case you've forgotten the lesson of the prior few pages, **fighters are spending less time on the ground overall, and even less time working from a conservative guard position once they're there**. Again, one would expect a wrestling outbreak to cause more ground fighting, not less. So if there are more fighters on the UFC roster with wrestling experience, they're either unable to fight to their strength, or simply choosing not to. Either way it contradicts the notion that wrestlers are boring fans to tears while stalling out on the mat at an increasing rate. However, most criticism of wrestlers focuses not on whether they take opponents down, but on what happens after they're on the ground.

Staying Busy

When a fight hits the ground, position is extremely important, and controlling an opponent is a clear path to grinding out a decision victory. So if "boring-ass wrasslers" (as Junie Browning might say) are truly ruining MMA with heavy ground control and little action, we should look at offensive activity metrics once fights are on the ground to see if there's proof of that claim. Let's consider all the different things that fighters "do" once they're on the ground: striking, submissions, position advances, and eventually standups or escapes. Inversely, it's implicit that all these things must be defended as well, which adds to the amount of action overall on the mat.

Evolution of Ground Fighting
Average Activity per Minute by Era, Change between Periods

Ground Metric	2003-2005 Average	2011-2013 Average	Change
Submission Attempts/Min	0.31	0.27	-13%
Ground Strikes/Min	13.73	14.26	+4%
Position Advances/Min	0.62	0.66	+6%
Dominant Positions/Min	0.34	0.40	+15%
Standups/Min	0.35	0.48	+28%

Ground fighters today have been more aggressive than previously in advancing position, while still taking time to attempt strikes as a higher pace. The tradeoff has been fewer submission attempts. And if the overall increase in action isn't enough, you'll need less patience than ever before as the average takedown lasts much less time than in earlier years. So really, wrestlers are not ruining the sport by any means. We should also remember that wrestling is actually a martial art in itself, and therefore deserving of inclusion in Mixed Martial Arts.

I know what logical fallacies I'm up against here: arguments from exception, confirmation bias, false dichotomies, or just simply hasty generalizations. A hidden bump in the road to mainstreaming MMA as a popular sport is the education of new fans who were not the early adopters to begin with. Some of these fans came reluctantly, perhaps giving up on sports like boxing and unfairly translating their expectations of what fights should look like from one sport to another. As MMA continues to evolve into maturity, we should appreciate that the level of skill continues to climb. Fights are more competitive than ever before. Sure, there are occasional snoozers that seem to stall out on the ground, and live spectators are within their rights to vocalize displeasure. But as the fanbase grows more and more, "new" fans are filling the ranks who may not have experience in combat sports, or may not fully appreciate what they're witnessing. More educated fans are equally within their rights to explain (politely) the nuances of grappling. Let's remember that fighters are risking a lot to enter the cage, all for our entertainment. So we should appreciate that fighters as a whole have actually elevated their game and boosted their offensive skills in recent years, and most certainly are not ruining the sport.

MMA Betting Lines: The Odds Are Good, but the Goods Are Odd

This Chapter in 30 Seconds:

- *Betting lines are generally an accurate predictor of who will win a fight*
- *Still, 32% of the fights with a clear favorite and underdog result in an upset*
- *Only 12% of UFC fights are an even "Pick 'Em"*
- *The more extreme the betting line, the more likely there will be a finish*
- *A "puncher's chance" is around 10-15%*
- *Main Events have the lowest rate of upsets at 23%, likely due to bias in casual fans created by hype*
- *Macro-trend analysis can help you identify value in betting odds*
- *Anything can happen in a fight, and that's why we watch*

The Game Outside the Game

For as long as people have competed in any athletic endeavor, people have enjoyed watching them and dissecting the competition by the numbers. Sports fans are constantly bombarded with data and information, even in a nascent sport like MMA. As any sport grows, the metrics that measure it and the statistics that report it all evolve and advance, but there's one set of numbers that are omnipresent from the birth of almost any game or sport: the betting odds. Oddsmakers price the potential outcomes of sports and give observers a chance to participate in the contest by betting, which many are all too happy to oblige. Given the financial implications of this "game outside the game," humans always strive to perfect the art of odds making to ensure a fair market, and to keep themselves in business. In a free market economy a big score on a risky bet can be a shortcut to financial security.

Han Solo famously demanded never to tell him the odds before he was about to attempt the improbable. Yet betting odds can be an amazingly informative piece of information from an analytical perspective, even if just to allow the casual viewer to understand who to root for as an underdog. In MMA the Tale of the

Tape summarizes the basic physique of each of the fighters, while their records summarize their performance history within the sport. These are important pieces of information, as we have seen, but it's the betting line that provides the most reliable predictor as to what will happen when the cage door shuts. The latest evolution of televised UFC broadcasts has gone so far as to present betting odds to viewers via onscreen graphics, a pioneering and innovative maneuver for mainstream media to trump the legacy taboo of gambling innuendo. So let's take a closer look at what the odds can tell us about MMA, matchmaking, and upsets. Hey, Han, "earmuffs."

Running the Numbers on the Odds Makers

In an academic sense betting lines are basically the market price for a certain event or outcome. These prices can move according to betting activity leading up to the event, and when a fight begins, that betting line is the public's final guess at the probability of each fighter winning, with roughly half of bettors picking each side of the line. Many experts make bold and confident predictions about fights, and they're all wrong a good portion of the time. But what about the odds? How do we tell if they're right? And what can we learn from looking at them in aggregate?

The fact is that only a small portion of fights are truly evenly matched according to odds makers. So called "Pick 'Em" fights (with some small margin of allowance) make up only 12% of all matchups in the UFC, with the rest of fights having a clear favorite and underdog. UFC President Dana White occasionally mentions these betting lines to help build the story around matchups, often to point out why a particular fighter might be a "live dog." White is correct to play up that possibility, because upsets occur in roughly 32% of all fights. That's a key stat to understand because it implies that just picking favorites will lead to a wrong conclusion nearly a third of the time. So the next time you look at a fight card expecting no surprises, just remember that on average there will be several upsets. A 10-fight card with only one pick em' matchup should still result in three upsets.

I'll be using "Moneyline" odds here for straight up fight winners, so my apologies to any readers unfamiliar with the system. For moneyline odds, a negative sign in front of the line value denotes a favorite and the value is the amount of money you would have to risk to win 100 units (in this case I'll use US dollars). So a line of -200 equates to a two-to-one favorite in which you would have to risk $200 to win $100. Underdogs are denoted by a plus sign, and the value indicates how much you would win with a 100 unit bet. So a +200 dog gives one-in-three odds, such that if you bet $100 you could win $200 more with an upset (and, of course, your risked money back). Whenever possible I'll be translating these odds to an "implied win probability." The implied win probability is essentially the percentage of bets you would have to win for a certain line to break even in the long run. If you always bet those -200 favorites, you would need to win two-thirds of the time in order to win enough to offset your losses, so the implied win probability for those matchups is 67%.

There's a variety of other ways to bet on fights, including the over/under (betting when the fight will end), and "prop" bets where you can bet on a particular outcome like a fighter winning by submission, or winning in a certain round. A favorite bet of mine is the "inside the distance" or "ITD" bet, which we'll get into later.

First, let's just look at how fighters match up in straight-up betting odds. They are extremely valuable in sports, just as they are in business, as they represent the market's prediction of who will win. According to the "wisdom of crowds" theory, lots of people making a prediction about something will generally be more accurate than small groups or individuals will be in the long run. That especially goes for the lone wolf throwing down his life savings on a hunch or a movie line like "always bet on black." Because betting lines "float" like stock prices, the market will determine the final price of a predicted outcome, with about half of the market falling on each side of the bet. Ultimately, it's not the accuracy of the odds makers, but rather the betting lines that get moved by the public that we'll be testing.

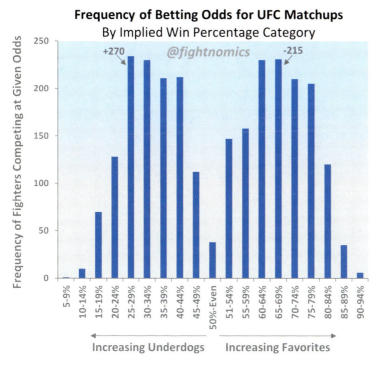

Frequency of Betting Odds for UFC Matchups
By Implied Win Percentage Category

The most common betting lines for UFC underdogs are around +270, which suggests an implied win probability of 27%. The equation to calculate implied odds of underdogs is 100 / (100 + the moneyline), or in this case 100 / 370 = 27%. The most common favorite lines are around -215, implying a win probability of 68%. Let's say that makes the "average" favorite reflect 68% confidence by the betting market. That implied win percentage calculation for favorites is the moneyline / (the moneyline -100), which is -215 / -315 = 68%.

As the graph suggests, fighters going into fights generally fall into one of two camps: a clear favorite, and a clear underdog. People love to pick sides, and even in betting it's rare to see a true pick 'em with an nearly 50% win probability for each fighter. The distribution of fighter odds ends up fitting a bi-modal distribution, peaking where the typical favorites and underdog are valued. The shape of this distribution also suggests that extreme betting odds in either direction are very rare. People may be generally over-confident, but in a financial market extreme or irrational confidence can be punished harshly.

According to these odds, almost every fighter competing in the UFC since 2008 has had at least a 10% chance of winning. Only 1 out of 2,588 fighters analyzed was given less than a 10% chance. That was Yaotzin Meza, who was knocked out by Chad Mendes one minute and fifty-five seconds into their fight. Impressively, Meza still won his next UFC fight as a +200 underdog . . . "impossible is nothing!" The next most extreme line in recent history was Stephan Bonnar at +800 against Anderson Silva. It was said that Bonnar had "a puncher's chance," and the market gave him just an 11% probability of victory. Looking for the few betting lines of similarly extreme underdogs **we can estimate a puncher's chance to be about 10-15%.** An important concept to remember when it comes to betting lines is known as "the vigorish," or just "the vig." This is the margin of profit that is built into the betting lines by the bookmakers in return for offering the contest to begin with. No one is expected to provide services for free. The vig is also a buffer, a small margin of error that ensures that in the long run "the house" always wins. At the beginning of this book I used the analogy of how the green zero in roulette makes betting black and red ultimately a losing proposition. Sure, you can win a 100% profit on a single spin, or play both colors for a long run of games and keep your balance whole. But sports betting, like casino games, always favor the house in the long run. Eventually that green zero will get you. Betting on fights also has a green zero that many people forget about, the draw. In fighting there are winners, losers, and occasionally "neithers," and between the small probability of a draw and small margin of the vigorish, gamblers must understand that the odds are literally stacked against them.

When it comes to betting, the trick is to try to be less wrong than the market, and with enough margin of return to cover the vig that normally prevents us from breaking even. The bookmakers make a living on volume, not on making bets themselves, so it's the market that has to pay to play. In thermodynamics the three fundamental laws can be summarized as "1. You can't win. 2. You can't break even. 3. You can't get out of the game." Gambling comes frighteningly close to this system, in that if you choose to enter the game, just breaking even becomes extremely difficult. The longer you play in a system where odds favor the house, the more you will lose.

That said, we're still going to play this game (on paper). Sports betting is big business, and glitzy events like the Kentucky Derby, the Super Bowl, and championship "prize fights" all make compelling attractions for the occasional sports gambler. From our view as spectators and fans of MMA, understanding betting lines can also help us understand the sport. For the more adventurous (or just risk averse), you might also learn a few tricks from the analysis that could help you at least minimize your losses in the long run, or recognize a "good bet" when you see it.

What Do Odds Makers Know?

In a macro sense, cage fighting is inherently difficult to predict for a variety of reasons. Competitors in the young sport are individuals, without teammates who could pick up slack or help cover for their mistakes. On a football field there is a safety to cover the cornerback when he gets burned deep, but in a cage the fighter is all alone. These individual competitors only fight mere minutes per outing, and, if they're lucky, only a few times per year. And let's not forget the raw and primal forces at work in the cage, where a single strike or positional mistake can end the fight in seconds.

The volatility of these factors means there is absolutely no such thing as a guaranteed win when you're allowing one trained competitor unmitigated access to do violence on the other. The sport is completely dynamic, often intense, and has only a few round breaks to reset the action. These are also the reasons we watch and love the sport: it's fast, furious, and anything can happen. It's the polar opposite of the true statistician's game of baseball.

Given how difficult MMA might be to predict and quantify compared to other mainstream team sports, it could be very revealing to look at how accurate odds makers have been over the last few years of UFC events. To run the test we'll compare actual performance to implied, expected performance. If ten fighters were each listed as slight underdogs with a 40% implied win probability, we should expect four of them to win, and six to lose, if the odds were indeed accurately set. Hence, we can compare fighters grouped by the odds they fought at to their actual win rate and see what difference there is.

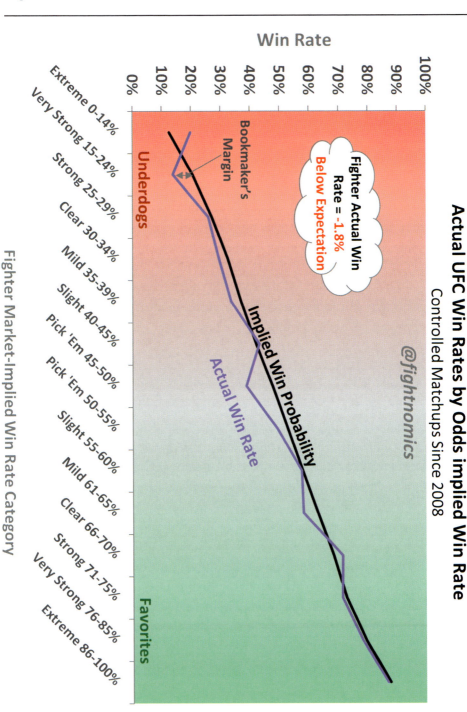

Actual UFC Win Rates by Odds implied Win Rate
Controlled Matchups Since 2008

@fightnomics

It turns out that odds makers (and ultimately the market) have been pretty good at assessing the likelihood of fight outcomes. The odds-based predictions closely match the actual outcomes of the fights. Historically, the actual win rate clings closely underneath the betting line implied win rate, but rarely touches or surpasses it. Basically, reality has a hard time matching up to the implied win rate of the odds, illustrating the margin built in for the bookmakers. Chalk up another one to the wisdom of crowds. The exception to this occurs at the extreme end of the spectrum where very heavy underdogs have been over-performing by winning more fights than expected over heavy favorites, but the sample size for this group is the smallest one of all. Don't go betting your life savings on long shots just yet – but never count anyone out either. If you don't believe me, here are ten reminders never to count anyone out of a fight.

Top 10 UFC Upsets

Rank	Winner	Loser	Outcome	Event / Year	Odds
1	Joey Beltran	Rolles Gracie	TKO, R2	UFC 109, 2010	+625
2	Frankie Edgar	BJ Penn	Un. Dec.	UFC 112, 2010	+620
3	Joe Lauzon	Jens Pulver	KO, R1	UFC 63, 2006	+610
4	Junior Dos Santos	Fabricio Werdum	KO, R1	UFC 90, 2008	+560
5	Matt Serra	Georges St-Pierre	TKO, R1	UFC 69, 2007	+550
6	Frankie Edgar	Tyson Griffin	Un. Dec.	UFC 67, 2007	+525
7	Tito Ortiz	Ryan Bader	Submission, R1	UFC 132, 2011	+500
8	Chan Sung Jung	Mark Hominick	KO, R1	UFC 140, 2011	+475
9	Jamie Varner	Edson Barboza	TKO, R1	UFC 146, 2012	+460
10	Drew McFedries	Alessio Sakara	TKO, R1	UFC 65, 2006	+455

At face value, there's no particular betting line where outcomes are drastically different from the expectation set by the odds, but we also know that generally almost a third of fights will not end as the masses predict. There are no guaranteed outcomes in MMA, with the ever-present potential for a spectacular finish to every fight. That's what makes for such an exciting sport.

Patterns in the Chaos

The betting line allows us to view fights through the lens of how evenly matched the fighters are. In theory, if betting lines are accurate (and they seem to be), then more extreme spreads mean the fighters are mismatched against each other. Conversely, when two fighters are very evenly matched, it's rare to see one dominate the other. What does the evenness of the matchup mean for how fights play out?

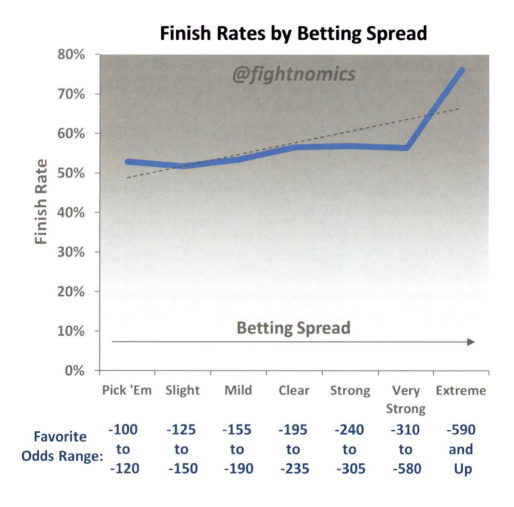

Finish Rates by Betting Spread

	Pick 'Em	Slight	Mild	Clear	Strong	Very Strong	Extreme
Favorite Odds Range:	-100 to -120	-125 to -150	-155 to -190	-195 to -235	-240 to -305	-310 to -580	-590 and Up

There's a pattern that emerges for wider betting spreads, which is a proxy for increasingly mismatched fighters. When fighters are more mismatched, finish rates go up. It's only pronounced for the extreme lines, but still there's an upward trend for increasing odds. This makes sense, because either the favorite truly is much better than his opponent, and hence more likely to finish him, or the underdog's only hope for victory is a miraculous move that finishes the fight. The result is that the stronger the differential of market expectations between two fighters facing each other, the less likely those two fighters are to go the distance.

Now look back at the Top Ten UFC Upsets list. Notice anything? Eight of those ten upsets were finishes, and seven were in the first round. It could be argued that Ortiz only got the submission after dropping Bader with a punch, so in eight of ten of the biggest UFC upsets of all time, strikes from the underdog made all the difference. Of course, this is MMA, and no fighter is ever more than one strike away from a finish, regardless of how great an underdog he is. Every fighter has a puncher's chance.

Speaking of upsets, how does our benchmark for UFC upsets change with other factors like weight class, card type, or even the position of a fight on the card? We can calculate the upset rate for various scenarios to see if any are more upset-prone than others.

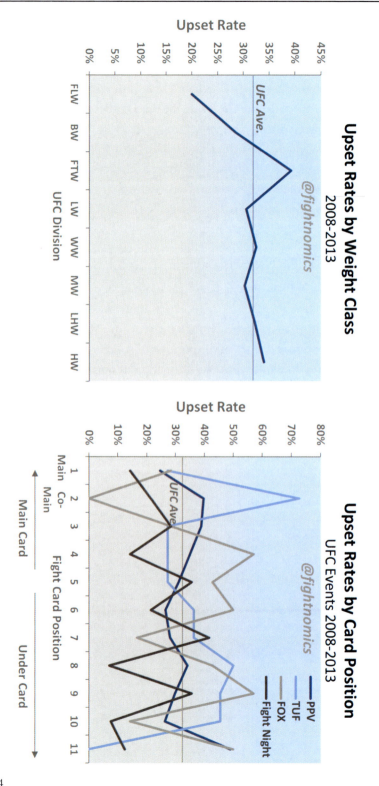

Upset Rates by Weight Class — 2008-2013 — @fightnomics

Upset Rates by Card Position — UFC Events 2008-2013 — @fightnomics

Pattern seeking on these could lead us astray. In the first graph, there's more volatility in the weight classes with smaller sample sizes leading to the wild fluctuations in the UFC's newest divisions. In the core divisions with the largest sample sizes (lightweight through middleweight) the upset rates closely hug the UFC overall average. We might imagine that heavyweights with their dangerous knockout ability could see more upsets, but their rate isn't far from average either. If you're hunting for upsets, using weight class as a guide is probably not the way to go. With more data (fight time and fights) we might revisit the smaller weight classes to see if their volatility (in either direction) holds.

Using card position to predict upsets may look noisy, but actually shows a little more promise. To hunt for trends I used groups of UFC events, separated by the type of televised event that it was. Using card position as the changing variable, we can see what upset rates look like based on where fights take place in the pecking order. In this case, "1" is the main event, "2 is the co-main event, and so on down the line until you get the earliest preliminary fights on the card down around 11-13. Because many cards don't have a 12th or 13th fight, I cut the graph to focus on numbers where there's more complete data.

The amount of volatility in the card position chart makes it messy, but it was important to cut the data into different groups to ensure that whatever pattern the upset rate formed was consistent and not random. As with weight classes, I don't think you can predictably bet on upsets occurring above the market rate for any certain scenario. For each spot on the fight display order there are events that see upset rates above and below the UFC global average. When isolating only main card fights where presumably the fighters are better known than on undercards, odds performance against actual performance was remarkably consistent in aggregate, but became volatile when separated into event types. Across the entire main card however, regardless of the type of event, the betting lines matched reality and each time maintained the small 1-2% edge in favor of the house.

The only variation on the fight card position rule is in the all-important main event. As it turns out, **upsets are rare in main events, a pattern that is true for all types of UFC fight cards**. It's not a huge difference, but something about being in the main event pushed the likelihood of upsets significantly below the overall average. So the natural next question is whether or not betting odds have properly accounted for that trend. When comparing favorites to betting lines in just main events, it turns out that the market is leaning too heavily on underdogs.

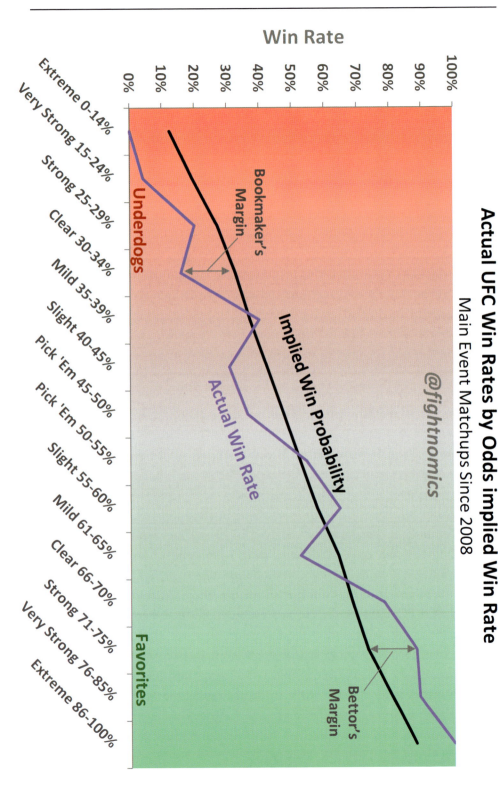

Actual UFC Win Rates by Odds implied Win Rate

Main Event Matchups Since 2008

@fightnomics

In the long run, betting lines are hard to outsmart. But that changes when you only consider the main events. We know that there are low upset rates in main events, and now we see that the market improperly accounts for that that trend. That spells opportunity. Taking a strategy of betting on the underdog in main events would be even more of a losing proposition than blindly picking at random. On the flipside, sticking with only favorites would have outperformed betting lines for most categories. According to the analysis, clear favorites (-195 moneyline) or better, are smart bets that outperform the market in the long run. I'll propose an explanation for this.

The Power of Hype, and Why It's Profitable

In the sport of baseball entire geographies show consistent perennial support for a certain team out of loyalty, but MMA fighters don't live in that world. Major league sports teams are around year after year, with guaranteed fresh starts against the same teams and bitter rivals. No matter how bad a team's performance is, their devoted season ticket holders continuously demonstrate the completely irrational expectation that "next year is our year." And they'll even do this amidst losing-streaks that would make Bob Sapp blush.

We know loyalty is an extremely powerful force. The citizens who live near a certain team can watch the exact same game with fans from another city and reach completely different conclusions as to who should have won or how fairly the game was played. The force at work is academically known as "in-group bias," the tendency for people to favor members of their own city/school/team/religion/etc. over outsiders regardless of any tangible evidence regarding the true nature of the individuals. The behavior can be irrational, but it's also evolutionarily justified and long predates our species. Notre Dame students exemplified multiple aspects of this bias by selling "Catholics vs. Convicts" t-shirts prior to a critical football game pitting their "Fighting Irish" against the University of Miami Hurricanes in 1988, a contest between undefeated teams that would ultimately determine the national champion.

In fighting, the lack of geographic focus or any "teams" reduces inherent favoritism for individual fighters. Fighter nationality is certainly a factor in influencing MMA fans, or more subtlety, fighter training camps (reflecting smaller regional loyalty) or fighting style (boxers generally support strikers). And it doesn't really matter who Georges St-Pierre fights in Montreal, the crowd is always going to be on his side.

But in-group bias has its limits when clear affiliations are stripped away. Few athletes are as naked, literally and figuratively, as the MMA fighter. There are no shirts or jerseys to signify their team or nation while they compete, just fight shorts with assorted sponsor logos. So what then accounts for the lopsided fan support of Urijah Faber, even against fellow American fighters on his home soil? The answer is a blend of the fighter's identity as a person and competitor, but also the hype that has been generated by promoters on his behalf. Hype, like loyalty, can also be powerful, and one can be used to generate the other in a synergistic cycle. The UFC literally makes a living off hype, and it could be responsible for irrational betting behaviors in the market.

Quick Science Lesson: The Case for Bias

In psychology the term "Halo Effect" refers to positive bias awarded to individuals with some perceived attractive condition. In short, the "fair-haired boy" or the attractive lady can do no wrong. People will perceive attractive people, or people with impressive titles or affiliations, to be superior in ways that are unrelated to judging criteria. Some people get the Halo around their heads for whatever reason, and we judge them more favorably forever after.

The opposite phenomenon is known as the "Devil Effect," or the "Horn Effect" (which I prefer). Imagine the Horn Effect as tainting someone who is related to a criminal, or who has been part of a company or team during the time of a notorious scandal. Even if the individual had nothing to do with the scandal or crime, he will be judged as guilty by association. The broader application of this bias to material things is known as "contagion," which can be positive (wearing a shirt signed by a celebrity) or negative (a chair that a killer once sat in).

A common example cited is when jurors treat attractive defendants more favorably, as if looking nice makes someone more inherently trustworthy, or at least less likely to commit crime. Defendants always want "character witnesses" to essentially say nice things about them in an attempt to persuade the jury to ignore hard evidence in favor of personal testimonials from friends and family. In a brilliant experiment, lecturers who were introduced to a crowd with impressive (yet fictional) titles and credentials were judged as smarter and funnier (and even taller!) than the very same actors delivering the exact same speech to an audience that didn't receive the same pre-lecture hype. The effect of this bias can be strong, and pervasive. We'll insist it can't happen to us, but it does – all the time. To say that you are biased is not meant to be insulting; it simply means you're human. We are all full of psychological and cognitive biases that affect us in many small, but often powerful ways, and that's just the reality of the human condition. Whether you like it or not you employ in-group bias and are susceptible to the Halo Effect. These same **biases can be amplified with hype**.

Why is this relevant here and now? In sports we often bias our perception of players based on their prior teams or college programs. Though we could readily examine a wide receiver's 40-yard dash speed and completion rate, we may consider him to be inferior when coming from a Division III program compared to an identically speedy and dexterous athlete coming from a perennial Division I powerhouse. In soccer, research has suggested a Halo Effect may be inflating salaries of players from Brazil in the British premiership due to the locally perceived superiority (and fear) of Brazilian players. In MMA, having UFC credentials means being part of the elite of the fight game. Being a former champion (no matter how fleeting the title reign was) is an accolade that follows a fighter the rest of his career. That's the Halo Effect at work. Veterans with greater fan-visibility and corresponding fame nearly always benefit from the Halo Effect of prior hype, regardless of how they performed. This is why there are grounds for bias in multiple directions, and nowhere is it more pronounced than for main events.

Main events are the subject of the majority of media attention for any MMA card, regardless of the promotion. The UFC generally shows "deep" fight cards featuring matchups fans want to see, even numerous fights that may have important implications on the state of their divisions. That is in sharp contrast to the current state of boxing, for example, which essentially focuses on a single main event for broadcast purposes. But when it comes to marketing a fight card (even in MMA), and the media's reporting of it, there's no question the majority of attention goes to the main event. Competing for limited attention spans and wanting to maximize the appeal of an event means marketers have to be focused on the stars of the show. So that's where we want to focus our attention too, because there is probably a causal relationship between hype and odds. I believe the hype for main events is likely leading to market imbalances in predicting outcomes.

Main events generally have the best known stars of the sport. In the UFC's case, main events mostly include title fights, primarily on PPV and FOX TV cards. In the cases of title fights, one person competing in the main event is already a superstar, and the other is a challenger. Common sense in the entertainment industry says people should be less interested in watching a fight if they already know the outcome. The Halo Effect works against the promotion's desire keep things interesting. In order to entice the audience to watch, there must be a compelling case why the matchup is a good one. Fans love underdogs and generally hate consistent winners (like the Yankees or the Duke Basketball team). As much as we succumb to the star power of champions above and beyond their close peers, we also want to see others slay those very same kings. Hence, the thesis of each marketing campaign for a fight card is usually a story about why the challenger has a chance to defeat the champion. In the case of a non-title fight with a clear favorite, the effect would be the same. Promoting an event where a champion will take on an opponent with very poor chances for an upset (sometimes called a "squash match") isn't compelling for fans, which translates into a low pay-per-view buy rate. There must be some question that has to be answered. Like knowing the ending of a movie or book before reading it, wanting to spend time watching it all transpire is less enticing when you believe you already know the outcome of a sporting contest.

So if promoting fights must normally focus more on hyping the challenger than the champion, isn't it possible that some of that hype influences the opinion of fans? That is the point after all, to create a sense of mystery about the outcome of the fight, that this challenger is the one that will dethrone the king. It's going to happen this time, and you want to see it when it does! If marketing is at all effective in influencing the fan base (and if it isn't, why are they spending money on it?) then **it is reasonable to conclude that the public's perception of the fairness of a main event matchup will generally be irrationally skewed towards the underdog**. And that's all it takes, folks, a little irrationality in an otherwise historically efficient market.

The effect of this hype-driven bias could easily trickle into betting markets, especially because main events generally draw more betting action than more obscure fights on the card. The casual bettor, or just the guy who happens to be in Vegas on fight weekend and wants to make a fun bet, is therefore skewed toward betting on underdogs, specifically in main events. Because betting lines float, they will drift towards the underdog to reflect the market's expectation of the outcome. The outcome, of course, is agnostic of the marketing or hype that went into it. Hype is an "exogenous variable," a pollutant to the handicapper or sharp sports bettor. A documentary could present a two-hour cavalcade of outsider opinions demanding that you believe a challenger has a better-than-average chance to topple an incumbent, and yet it does nothing to change the a priori probability of that fighter actually winning. There is now a small disturbance in the force applied by the Invisible Hand, an incongruence between expectation and reality.

The second the cage door closes the two fighters compete to the best of their ability and condition. The results from the modern era of the UFC are that main event favorites outperform the market's expectations, and all those guys hanging out at the club holding onto losing longshot underdog betting slips toss them away and forget about them. **But you, the readers of this book, now know not to put your money where your bias is!** Thanks to a variety of other biases, the same people who lost money hoping for the underdog upset will quickly forget about their mistakes, perhaps clinging to the memory of the one that came through, and will be influenced by the next hype cycle once again believing that this is the challenger who will do it. The more rational "sharps" will always bet against a psychic to win the lottery, or against sports team "curses," as these irrational impressions are contradicted by harsh realities. Always bet against hype, because hype doesn't matter once the referee says "fight." The simple rule of betting main event favorites historically has done very well, so let's see how quickly this book causes the market inefficiency to be competed away.

Not So Quick on the Draw

A remarkably juicy yet oft-overlooked betting prop is omnipresent in every UFC matchup. Betting on a fight to end in a draw typically offers a monster payout. In a recent sample of betting lines for a UFC event, the average line on a draw was +9,000. That line can vary as low as +7,000, and as extreme as +15,000. For the average money on a line draw, a $100 bet on a draw would pay out $9000 (plus your money back) in the event the fights goes to the judges' cards and results in a tie. With a ridiculous payout like that, it's worth considering a strategy of betting on draws. With a smart $100 bet, you could pay for one hell of a weekend in Vegas.

Unfortunately, predicting a draw is an inherently tricky business thanks to the current scoring system where judges almost always score rounds 10-9 in favor of one fighter. Because there are always an uneven number of rounds (three or five) in MMA, that means even fights where each fighter gets the upper hand for some of the match, there will still be a winner on the score cards. Most draws fall into two categories, neither of which is easy to foresee. First, if a fighter wins two close but clear rounds out of three, but also commits a penalty resulting in a referee point deduction, then the fight will end in a draw. This happened most recently to Cheick Kongo in a fight against Travis Browne at UFC 120, when Kongo had a point deducted for repeatedly grabbing Browne's shorts. Despite winning two out of three rounds, the result was a draw.

In the second scenario, one round may receive an unusual score of 10-8 or 10-10, where the other rounds even out the score for a tie. Judges rarely deviate from the 10-9 standard, but it can happen if a round is extraordinarily lopsided (10-8) or completely even with little action (10-10 or 9-9). This scenario happened to BJ Penn and Jon Fitch at UFC 127 when their main event fight ended in a majority draw. In the cases described here, it's hard to bet on a normal fight being punctuated by such a rare scenario as a strangely-scored round or a referee point deduction. The rare and fluky natures of these scenarios ultimately make predicting draws a game of random chance. But is chance enough?

We already know from Chapter 2 that Draws are rare. Like, less than 1% rare. Since 2008, fights ending in a draw only account for 0.6% of all UFC fights. If we take a generous case for odds on a draw to be +10,000 then the implied hit rate is 1%. That means betting on draws is a losing strategy in the long run. You would need to see odds of +18,000 or more just to break even, assuming the trends of the last six years carry forward. Conversely, you could bet against draws with lines like -25,000. But with such extreme lines you would have to wager massive amounts of cash to win small amounts, which is directly contrary to our natural risk aversion as a species. And if you do that math, that betting line says draws won't happen 99.6% of the time – which is 0.2% too much. Yet another deck that's stacked against you.

A Few Simple Betting Strategies That Will Get You Paid

I'll be the first to say that prediction is not the objective of my analysis here, but no matter how firmly I assert that, everyone wants to know how to bet using stats. Unfortunately, macro-trends (the kinds detailed in this book) are not reliable in a single fight. Micro-trends will dominate instead. A great striker with tons of statistical and anthropometric advantages over his opponent only needs to eat one punch for victory to escape his grasp. When this happens, I sometimes say that a fighter "broke my spreadsheet," but I know it can happen on any given fight night. So the best thing to do is to bet macro-trends based on weight class or finish rate patterns that are reliable in the long-term, or bet when the market odds have been influenced by hype.

Inside the Distance

Betting inside the distance makes for an interesting macro-trend bet. Because finish rates show a clear pattern by division, we can set thresholds on betting lines to represent the average finish rate by division. We know that 51% of all UFC fights end by submission or KO/TKO, so an even betting line of +100 (implying 50% win rate) would almost accurately reflect that expectation, with a tiny margin in our favor. However, we also know that finish rates vary predictably by weight class, with larger divisions finishing more fights. In theory, we can establish a better betting line threshold that accurately reflects the finish rate for each division. It would look something like this.

Betting "Inside the Distance" Decoder

Weight Class	Finish Rate	Implied Odds
Flyweight	38%	+160
Bantamweight	49%	+105
Featherweight	39%	+155
Lightweight	51%	-105
Welterweight	51%	-105
Middleweight	59%	-145
Light Heavyweight	58%	-140
Heavyweight	74%	-285

First off, I'm aware of the blip around the featherweights and bantamweights. I'm also aware that flyweight finish rates don't drop off as we'd expect them to moving down in weight. In fact, if I were to use the most recent fight cards that occurred while writing this book, the flyweight finish rate would jump to nearly 50%. It's possible that (a) the smaller divisions haven't been around very long and therefore have smaller and more volatile sample sizes, or (b) there's some basic lower limit to finish rates for UFC caliber fighters around 38-40%, or perhaps both. So while this table represents a straight up mathematical conversion of the finish rate into implied odds, I would urge caution and a little rationalization before ever putting your money at risk. **Finding betting odds that are significantly different than the implied odds threshold for a certain weight class makes for an interesting play. Other factors could help make the case for an inside the distance play, like fighters with good finishing skills, poor defense, or simply older age.**

Basically, whenever you see odds that imply a much lower or higher finish rate than the macro-trend for that division, you should get suspicious, and you should also consider playing the opposite way. Of course, there will always be exceptions to general rules. At UFC 166 for example, Daniel Cormier fought Roy

Nelson with inside the distance odds not just a little higher than the heavyweight average of -285, but at plus money for a finish! A decision bet only paid -165. So the market was saying these two heavyweights were more than likely going the distance, despite the fact that this division finishes 74% of their fights. However, it was a reasonable expectation based on the fact that neither fighter was likely to be finished, and the heavy favorite (Cormier) was unlikely to TKO Nelson with his hands. A submission finish by either fighter was equally unlikely. In the end, the minus money line on a three-round decision was a wise play, and ended up coming to fruition as Cormier dominated the fight but never threatened to finish it.

On the flipside, on that same UFC 166 card, heavyweights Gabriel Gonzaga and Shawn Jordan squared off with an inside the distance line of -230, suggesting these two were more resilient or less capable than other heavyweights of finishing a fight. In fact, both these guys had finished every one of their opponents in their UFC victories, and had also been previously finished in losses. Regardless of who won, the fight was likely to be over long before round three, and hence the inside the distance play was a good one. On fight night, it only took Gonzaga one minute and thirty-three seconds to secure the upset KO victory, and cash a reasonable return on the ITD bettors.

Seeing odds that are implying a high threshold for a finish relative to the fighters' division makes a reasonable play for a "Goes to Decision" bet. If the fighters are experienced (but not too old), and have shown good resiliency in the past, that further buoys the case for a three-rounder. Understanding the critical cutoff specific to the division, and making multiple plays using a disciplined loyalty to the macro-trends should pay off in the long run. Just remember that odds are generally well set, so you won't see opportunities often. But now at least you know how to recognize them when they present themselves.

Betting the Youth Advantage

In Chapter 7 we saw that older fighters are less likely to lose by submission, but much more likely to lose by strikes. If you're betting against an older fighter, consider adding value with a prop bet for a TKO finish rather than a submission finish. Specificity always lowers the likelihood of a given prediction, but it also adds value for the same reason. Knowing that age changes the way fighters lose can help steer you towards more intelligent prop bets on finishes.

Slippery Submissions

The macro trends of submissions make for interesting betting opportunities. You know that few fights above middleweight will end by submission (only 16% for light heavyweights and heavyweights), so picking that finish method for larger fighters is a bad call. Even in the smaller weight classes, submission finishes only occur one fifth of the time. So when you're considering a submission finish, make sure the odds are long enough to reward the risk you're taking, otherwise short that bet (bet on another finish method, or against submission).

Alternatively, live betting makes these trends even more pronounced. As we saw in Chapter 5, submission success rates fall sharply towards the end of fights. If live betting odds don't reflect the dropping likelihood of a submission finish, then there's another opportunity to short (bet against it like a inflated stock). Finally, the next time a guy goes for a low probability Guillotine or Ankle Lock and the overeager fan at the bar thinks it's all over – quick! – bet him the next round of drinks that there's an escape. And then cheers. Understanding the differences between submission success rates will help you understand when the fight is really in jeopardy and when it's not.

The Pace Advantage

Back in Chapter 4, I presented the idea of the "Pace Advantage," meaning fighters who average a high volume of output in terms of Significant Strike Attempts per Minute. Fighters with high output tend to win more often, and fighters with low pace tend to lose a lot more often. That makes for an informative predictive variable about who will win in the long run, but it's possible that betting lines and the market they represent have already accounted for this. Actually, they haven't.

The high-pace group of fighters outperformed betting lines with actual wins 5% higher than their implied win probability. The middle group closely matched their expected win rate with a very slight underperformance that is consistent with the built-in "vig." The low-pace group underperformed market expectations by a large 18% margin. That means they only won 82% of the fights they should have won if the moneyline odds set by the market were accurate.

I have found many scenarios that imply the market is not perfectly "efficient" when it comes to predicting MMA outcomes, despite being very accurate in a macro sense. In this case, a little math is all that's required to identify market mispricing of a fighter's chances. As a rule of thumb, just avoid betting on fighters with low average pace, because otherwise you will lose more money in the long run than by just betting at random. Due to the larger gap in performance of the

Low-Pace group, betting against them would be the most profitable strategy.

I include each fighter's pace on all of my Uber Tale of the Tapes (see Chapter 14), but the data necessary to calculate a fighter's average pace is readily available on their profile page at FightMetric.com, and the math required you already learned in the 3rd grade.

The Agnostic Bettor and the True Tale of the Tape

Before you go placing a bet on your lead pipe lock of the night, make sure you've (correctly) appraised the Tale of the Tape first. You now know that younger fighters tend to do well, Southpaws have a slight advantage, and Reach is a real benefit, especially if the fight is likely to stay standing. If you find fighters with these advantages who offer a reasonable return on investment, you can feel more confident in pulling the trigger on a bet. Conversely, if your favorite fighter is at a clear disadvantage by one or all of these factors, you should strongly consider passing on the play.

Lastly, avoid the hype train when making your picks. This should be obvious, but a fight is not a popularity contest and it's never a question of which athlete you like more. If you really want to get diligent, avoid watching pre-event shows marketing the main event, or just choose to side with the favorite in every main event. Remember, you're biased, and that's okay. It's why your friends stick by your side even after you acted like a jackass last weekend after an especially raucous fight watch party. We're only human, and that's still a pretty awesome spot to be in. Admit when you're at risk for influence, but when your money is on the line stick to the numbers and the long view.

Fistful of Dollars: Fight Night Bonuses

A Brief History of UFC Fight Night Bonuses

Just how big is a big bonus for doing your job well? In March of 2013, I was in Montreal for UFC 156 and made a bewildering financial observation. The UFC's typical Fight of the Night bonuses for that card were $50,000 each, which actually sounded small for a pay per view event. At least they were "low" when put into historical context, and they've been that way ever since. Bonuses are a valuable tool in any business and the UFC is no different. Most fans know who the frequent bonus winners are – guys like Joe Lauzon, who not only pulls off skillful submission finishes, but has an exciting never-say-die fighting style that leads to bonus-worthy performances even in defeat. The UFC is one of the only organizations where you can actually get a bonus while technically failing.

Topical money-related news always gets the media and fans frothing. Let's take a step back and look at the big picture, as well as the first graph in this book to use dollars as a unit of measure. Here's the official fight night bonus amount published for Fight of the Night (FOTN), Knockout of the Night (KOTN), and Submission of the Night (SOTN) at numbered UFC events since UFC 61 in 2006 through UFC 166 in 2013.

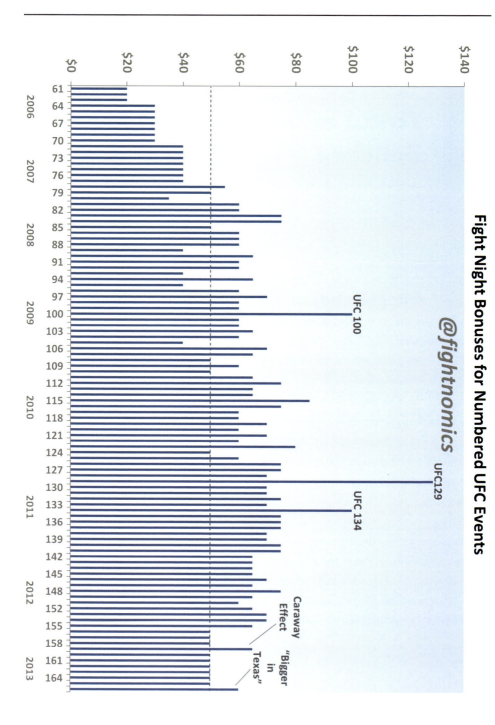

Fight Night Bonuses for Numbered UFC Events

@fightnomics

The Rise of the UFC in the Mid-2000's

Let's put this in context by going back in time. The end of 2006 was a great time for the UFC. In addition to launching seasons three and four of the smash hit reality series, "The Ultimate Fighter," they closed out the year with a defining moment in UFC 66. Headlined by future hall of fame superstars Chuck Liddell and Tito Ortiz, the event drew more than one million pay-per-view purchases, a first for the still maturing organization.

It may then come as a surprise that Liddell and Ortiz each only received a $30,000 bonus for their Fight of the Night performance. If we consider that there's a lag between success and financial reward, then this isn't surprising at all. These same fight night bonus amounts would double by UFC 81 just over a year later when they hit $60,000 for the first time. For part-time fighters on the undercard only making "three and three" back then (i.e., $3,000 to fight and another $3,000 to win), a $60,000 bonus was ten times what they made for a winning performance alone, and was potentially a life-changing windfall. For heavyweight Pat Barry at UFC 104, a Fight of the Night performance was capped off with a KO of the Night bonus for his back and forth battle and eventual knockout of Antoni Hardonk. The resulting double-bonus check of $120,000 dwarfed his show-money for the evening, just $14,000. Leading up to the fight Barry was allegedly so broke he had been surviving on ketchup and rice, and was just days away from eviction. Windfall indeed! And like the UFC itself, bonuses weren't finished growing yet.

The Highs

The biggest ever bonus winners came at UFC 129, with bonuses appropriately set at $129,000 each. With an estimated 55,000 attendees, it was the largest UFC show in history. The event also had two title belts on the line with Georges St-Pierre defeating Jake Shields and Jose Aldo outlasting Mark Hominick. It was also the first and last time fight night bonuses would exceed $100,000.

Two other events hit the six-figure bonus mark, each one a special occasion for Zuffa. The first time UFC fighters saw bonuses of $100,000 was the summer of 2009 at the blockbuster UFC 100 event. Again, two belts were on the line for the historic (but not exactly 100th) UFC event, with Georges St-Pierre successfully defending his belt against Thiago Alves and Brock Lesnar unifying the heavyweight title via a TKO of Frank Mir. Amazingly, future champion Jon Jones also competed on the card, but was buried on the prelims in what was at the time only his third UFC appearance. Talk about a stacked card.

Most recently, Zuffa awarded $100,000 bonuses at UFC 134 in 2011 at the highly publicized return to Brazil. The card was stacked with high profile fighters and capped off with an Anderson Silva striking clinic against Yushin Okami, which signified a new Zuffa commitment to the booming Brazil market. But it was also the last time bonuses would ever come close to six figures.

UFC 156: Flat Is the New Up

Since 2011 fight night bonuses have been consistently above $60,000, and more typically in the $65,000 to $75,000 range, but since the beginning of 2012 the trend has been downward. Why the kitty failed to gain ground in recent years is a mystery that has yet to be resolved, but may be tied to the maturation of the core US market. It was spring of 2013 at UFC 156 in Montreal that the official (and surprising) news came: all UFC event bonuses would be $50,000 going forward. If bonuses are an indicator of the strength of a company, then this news may have pressed some financial panic buttons. For bonus-seeking fighters, this normalization meant that there was no longer any downside to competing on lower profile (i.e., TUF Finale, FuelTV) fight cards. But it also meant that the occasional $75,000 or even $100,000 windfalls that changed the lives of some exciting fighters were gone. Many in the US have already dealt with the realities of stagnant growth: "flat is the new up."

Notable exceptions include what we may call "the Caraway Effect," and "things are always bigger in Texas." These were the only blips in bonus amounts since the new policy took effect. The first was at UFC 159 when (allegedly) Bryan Caraway convinced Dana White to boost bonuses to $65,000 to match the last time Caraway fought at UFC 149. That comment was based on the fact that Caraway won the FOTN bonus at UFC 149. In a strange twist, Caraway went on to win a Submission of the Night bonus at UFC 159 only thanks to a positive drug test by Pat Healy. Coincidence? Or genius?! More recently at UFC 166, fighter Tim Boetsch prodded Dana White to increase the bonus in honor of the fight card's return to Texas, "because everything is bigger in Texas." The dare worked and several fighters received a $10,000 boost to the normal bonus rate. Mr. Boetsch, however, was not among the winners despite being victorious. Thanks for taking one for the team though, Tim, you may have a bright future as a collective bargainer.

The normalization of bonus amounts regardless of the event type (e.g., a Fight Night on FOX compared to a Pay-per-View event) was a secondary effect of the decision to make a standard bonus amount. The less reported trend that different events had very different bonus amounts was overshadowed by the selection of the amount that would become the standard. From a fighter's point of view, event normalizations may have been the more important aspect of the decision because it allowed everyone to compete for the same bonus amounts. Consider this analysis of average bonus levels based on the event type prior to the launch of FOX Sports, just for 2012 events.

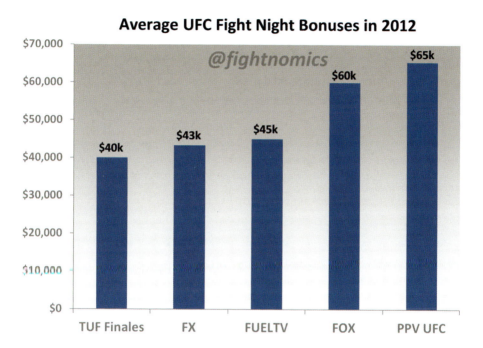

There has always been a clear pecking order in the importance of UFC events depending on where they are aired and historically the bonus rates closely mirrored this status. Fighters who were recent cast members from The Ultimate Fighter or were in the smaller experimental weight classes frequently found themselves competing on UFC cards of lesser importance. There are pros and cons to this, of course, as free television meant potentially larger audiences than pay-per-view card if their fight was aired, which could translate into bigger sponsorship money. But it also lowered the bonus ceiling for an exciting performance. Now that's no longer an issue, as a fighter competing on FOX Sports 2 is vying for the same $200,000 bonus pool as fighters on the more important FOX or PPV events. The playing field is now level.

Mandatory disclaimer: we are only talking about bonuses here, not salaries, and this information clearly doesn't capture all fighter compensation. Zuffa can, and often does, compensate fighters above their listed salaries and Fight Night Bonuses via what is referred to as "locker room bonuses." We should keep in mind that Zuffa ultimately pays most of its fighters more than they've agreed to pay them contractually whether it's reported in the media or not. This is unusual and generous by the standards of most occupations, despite the low average pay of fighters compared to more mainstream sports. Such is the nature of a sport struggling for wider audiences and mainstream acceptance. The data presented here represents concrete payouts and in aggregate remains worthy of analysis as it reflects the trends of the organization's growth.

Who Wins Fight Night Bonuses?

Bonuses have been on the MMA media's watch list since 2006, and today social media users light up with references to the FOTN, KOTN and SOTN bonuses even during live events whenever spectacular performances happen in the Octagon. Fans, fighters, and even celebrities use Twitter to convince Uncle Dana to award a bonus to a certain favored son of the moment. So which favored fighters are we talking about?

Given what we already know about the differences in fighters based on size, a natural question about who wins bonuses could be answered by weight class. By calculating the rate at which any given fighter wins a bonus based solely on his division and the type of bonus, several simple questions can be answered. A more subtle question that lurks amidst UFC events has always been around weight classes that may or may not be exciting. Bonuses specifically reward excitement and superlative finishes, so using them as a proxy we can attack the question of which division is the most exciting.

There are usually 24 fighters (give or take a pair) who compete on any given UFC card, to which only four bonus awards are typically made. **Divvying up two FOTN, one KOTN, and one SOTN awards leads to an overall chance of 17.5% for any given fighter to take home an award.** Here's how the divisions stack up to the financial measure of excitement.

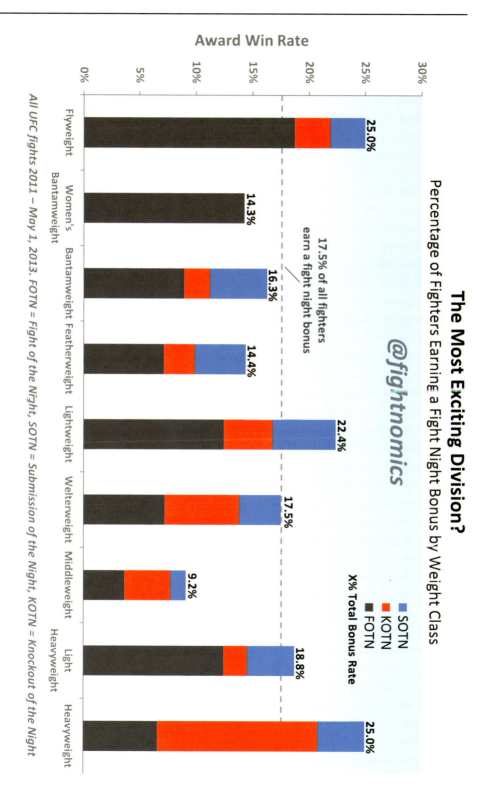

The Most Exciting Division?

Percentage of Fighters Earning a Fight Night Bonus by Weight Class

Award Win Rate

17.5% of all fighters earn a fight night bonus

@fightnomics

X% Total Bonus Rate

- SOTN
- KOTN
- FOTN

Flyweight — 25.0%
Women's Bantamweight — 14.3%
Bantamweight — 16.3%
Featherweight — 14.4%
Lightweight — 22.4%
Welterweight — 17.5%
Middleweight — 9.2%
Light Heavyweight — 18.8%
Heavyweight — 25.0%

All UFC fights 2011 – May 1, 2013. FOTN = Fight of the Night, SOTN = Submission of the Night, KOTN = Knockout of the Night

The first takeaway is that every division wins a decent share of bonuses, but there isn't any correlation between size and win rate of bonuses. In fact, the two extreme ends of the division, the flyweights and the heavyweights are tied for the highest bonus-winning rate at 25%. And anchoring the very middle of the divisions, the lightweights come in as a very close next runner up. In between these high performers are the rest of the divisions with varying rates of bonus winning performances. But if we differentiate more broadly between smaller and larger fighters, a few patterns emerge.

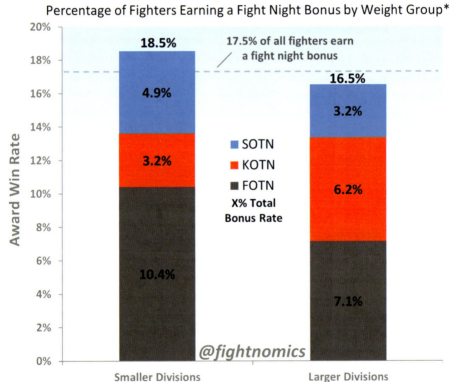

Pulling Their Weight

Percentage of Fighters Earning a Fight Night Bonus by Weight Group*

All UFC fights 2011 – May 1, 2013.
FOTN = Fight of the Night, SOTN = Submission of the Night, KOTN = Knockout of the Night.
*Smaller Divisions here include Lightweight and below. Larger Divisions include Welterweight and above. Number of fights occurring in each group is roughly equal over the period analyzed.

The difference in knockout power is again reflected in this analysis when we take size into account. The larger divisions on the right side of the graph win KOTN bonuses at a much higher clip than the smaller divisions to the left, which is consistent with the underlying likelihood of causing knockouts to begin with. All of the numbers are starting to gel now into a bigger picture. But interestingly, SOTN bonuses are fairly evenly distributed among the divisions, at least relative to KOTN bonuses. Despite finishing the fewest fights by submission, heavyweight and light heavyweight fighters still earn the SOTN at a reasonable rate. Though lighter fighters do earn more SOTN bonuses, the averages by group are much closer than for knockouts.

When it comes to arguably the most important bonus of all, the FOTN, the lighter fighters are winning more often, and it's the lightest fighters of all who take the cake. When any given flyweight fighter enters the Octagon there's a 25% chance he'll end the night with a bonus of some kind. Flyweights have managed a few finishing bonuses, but more impressively they've been winning FOTN awards two at a time after simultaneously putting on exciting performances in the Fight of the Night. Guys like John Dodson, Ian McCall, and of course Demetrious "Mighty Mouse" Johnson were brought into the UFC with some controversy and doubt from MMA fans. Yet **the flyweights have pulled their weight, and then some. Pound for-pound these have been the most exciting fighters to date**.

But Who Really Wins Fight Night Bonuses?

Fight night bonuses are here to stay, which is great news for perpetually exciting fighters like Joe Lauzon. Bonuses incentivize performance, spread the wealth, and reward fighters who give their all for the fans. Bonuses are also an official metric for justifying their place on the UFC roster – and who doesn't need a little job security these days? Our look at bonus rates by division was mildly revealing, but that's just one layer of the statistician's onion. There's another bit of analysis that shows a more powerful predictive pattern.

What I've graphed here is the percentage likelihood of a fighter winning a Fight Night Bonus based solely on card placement. The card placement number goes in reverse order of appearance on the broadcast, so main events (on the left side of the graph) are "1," co-main events are "2," all the way down to the Facebook-aired preliminary fights (on the right side of the graph) in the 11, 12 or 13 spots. The lower the number is, the more important the fight. Remember, the overall likelihood of any given fighter winning a bonus at an event is roughly 17.5%. Some of these results may not be surprising, but the reasons for them may not be as clear.

It Pays to Fight Last

Percentage of Fighters Earning a Fight Night Bonus by Fight Order*

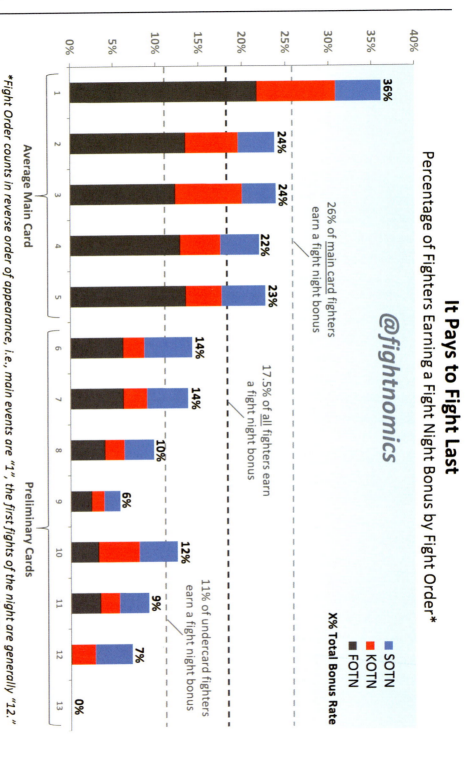

@fightnomics

X% Total Bonus Rate

- SOTN
- KOTN
- FOTN

Average Main Card

26% of main card fighters earn a fight night bonus

1 — 36%
2 — 24%
3 — 24%
4 — 22%
5 — 23%

17.5% of all fighters earn a fight night bonus

Preliminary Cards

6 — 14%
7 — 14%
8 — 10%
9 — 6%
10 — 12%
11 — 9%
12 — 7%
13 — 0%

11% of undercard fighters earn a fight night bonus

*Fight Order counts in reverse order of appearance, i.e., main events are "1", the first fights of the night are generally "12." FOTNs award two fighters at a time, hence the overall rate of these bonuses is roughly X2 KOTN and SOTN.

What does this prove? **It pays to fight last. Fighters competing in the highest profile spots on the fight card are the most likely to win fight night bonuses**. It is fair that (presumably) the highest paid fighters also get more than their share of bonus money? If you're fighting in a main event you have more than a one-in-three chance of winning a bonus of some kind, with most of those bonuses not requiring a finish, or even a win. Whereas towards the bottom of the preliminary card, fighters average only a one-in-ten chance of taking home a bonus, and more likely require a win inside the distance to do so. Is that how a true meritocracy should play out?

Not so fast. One theory is that the bump in bonuses on the main card may be a reflection of the higher skill level of the fighters who compete there. Basically, knocking a guy out who is highly ranked (and highly skilled) is inherently more impressive than finishing an undercard newcomer or fading veteran. Bonuses, therefore, may reflect the level of difficulty that increases as the event approaches its conclusion, and reward that same difficulty in performing at a high level against better competition. When the rich get richer, it may just be because they're that much better.

This may be the driving factor. Certainly a Fight of the Night bonus requires not one, but both fighters to be in great shape and able to fight through a skillful back-and-forth war. In theory, main events feature the most talented fighters of any given card, and correspondingly result in a whopping 36% of those fighters taking home some form of fight night bonus on top of other compensation. **A fighter in any given spot on the main card will average a 14.7% FOTN bonus rate, while being on the prelim card results in a measly 3.2% FOTN average**. That's a huge drop, and a far larger drop than knockout and submission averages across the card.

The main card bump in finishing bonuses may also be a reflection of other factors. First, larger fighters are more likely to command main card presence. This may be due to their higher finish rates, or fan's general appetite for bigger, better, faster. Bigger fighters sell tickets and generally deliver for the fans by scoring more knockouts. This may be an additional factor in the KOTN average being 6.4% for main card fighters, but only 2.4% for fighters on the prelims.

The same trends of weight class and card placement may also work in reverse for submissions, which are the most stable bonus type across the board. Main card fighters take home 4.6% of these bonuses per spot, while prelim fighters average 3.5%. Not a huge drop. Overall, submissions are less common than KO's, so sometimes the selection of a SOTN winner is easier and limited to a single option. And perhaps the idea of a skillful submission is also better able to stand alone in our minds, regardless of card placement, allowing undercard fighters a fairer shot at the bonus.

The bonus-rate boost for main card fighters could also be a side effect of the spotlight. If the UFC is going to spend a lot of money convincing a lot of people to watch you fight then it stands to reason that you're going to live up to that hype and fight your ass off. These fighters are also better paid, and will have better sponsorships allowing them to train full-time and afford the luxuries of state of the art training camps. Main card fighters could therefore be better trained and more motivated to turn in a memorable performance. It's possible. But solving the riddle of why main card fighters win so many bonuses is all about looking a little further down the card.

Consider the #5 and #6 spots on the card more closely. **Despite nearly identical rates for finish bonuses, rates for the more subjective FOTN bonuses drop from over 13% on the bottom of the main card to just 6% at the top of the preliminaries**. Is there really that much of a difference in quality and skill of fighters between those two positions on the card? Are fighters in the sixth spot on the card less than half as exciting as the very next pairing of the night? Probably not. So what is causing such a noticeable chasm between the main and preliminary cards? Isn't there some incentive for the final fight of the UFC preliminary card to be stacked with exciting fighters to boost pay-per-view purchase rates? According to the data, these guys aren't anywhere close to being as exciting as the lead-off fighters for the main card. So what's driving this sudden spike in bonus-worthy performances? Watch out folks: science!

At the end of the night, what stands out in our minds? Was it a devastating 10-second KO on the Facebook prelims, or was it a highly ranked fighter getting unexpectedly TKO'd by a new contender? Our tendency to remember more recent events is most commonly described as the "Availability Heuristic." **Basically, what comes to mind when we try to recall things is the information and memories that are most readily available to us. And that means most fresh in our minds. More specifically it's called "Recency Bias,"** and I believe that bias is a powerful underlying cognitive and psychological influence on the end-of-night decision to award bonuses. There's a limit to how much we can keep in our heads, especially short-term recent memories. New memories always crowd out older ones. When it comes time to decide bonuses (immediately following the main event), not all fights will come to mind equally.

This bias is why entertainment programs always try to "end with a bang," or in the UFC's case, the main event. It's why cruise ships save their best dinner for last, why bands play their biggest hit as an encore, and why Disney World has fireworks every single night. When searching for superlative memories (the best or worst of an event) it's always easier to remember the things that are most fresh in our minds – and that means most recent. In the case of MMA events, most recent means the last few fights of the night. We'd like to think that everyone has a fair shot at fight night bonuses, but that's unrealistic, if only because the people who decide who wins them are human after all. **Being later on the card, therefore, boosts your chances of being remembered beyond otherwise objective comparisons of performance**. While fighters themselves might like the "idea" of bonuses, they're also working off an incorrect assumption that they all have an equal shot at winning them.

As with any managerial decision it's always good to run the numbers while exploring options. Let the matter of "Who Wins Fight Night Bonuses" now be settled: it pays to fight last, for clear (if potentially irrational) reasons. The next question might be whether this system of reward is the right one. The concept of compensation and motivation is complex enough that entire classes are taught at business schools on the subject, and some professional consultants make their living advising businesses just on this one aspect of strategy. Various ideas have been suggested for UFC bonuses, like getting rid of bonuses to increase base pay, or the more marketable idea of fan-based voting for awards. Unfortunately, the first attempt at a fan-vote approach backfired when Georges St-Pierre took home a huge $100K Fight of the Night bonus on a home town card with a less than-noteworthy performance at UFC 124. If fans, like fighters themselves, want to ensure that UFC fighters with low pay get taken care of then they certainly blew their best chance. But hey, perhaps MMA fans are more educated now? If you've made it this far into this book, then that should be the case.

11 World Cup of MMA: Breaking Down Fighters by Geography

S ince UFC 1 the Octagon has been a "cage of nations" and earned a reputation for being the melting pot of global combat sports. Some countries have traditionally been over-represented at the highest levels of the game, while others still have yet to earn their first UFC win. Since inception the UFC has employed fighters from 48 different countries, although the distribution of fight card appearances isn't nearly as uniform as you might think. Just five countries have made up 90% of all fighter appearances in competition. Geography hasn't been cool since the sixth grade (it was cool then, right?), but if you're an MMA fan it's worth exploring the geographic roots of UFC fighters if only for home-town bragging rights. We don't just want to know who is fighting; we want to know who is winning, how often, and even which ones have excelled in specific aspects of the fight game. Welcome to the World Cup of MMA.

Where Do UFC Fighters Come From?

The first question we need to ask is who is playing? Which nations have captured the most UFC roster spots over the years? Of 1,103 fighters who competed in the UFC by October of 2013, here are the Top 20 countries that have been represented, including how many fighters have come from each nation. It's time we introduce some new phraseology. I'll refer to the "Big Five" of MMA as the five countries that have been represented the most in the sport. These are the USA, Brazil, Canada, United Kingdom, and Japan in order of representation.

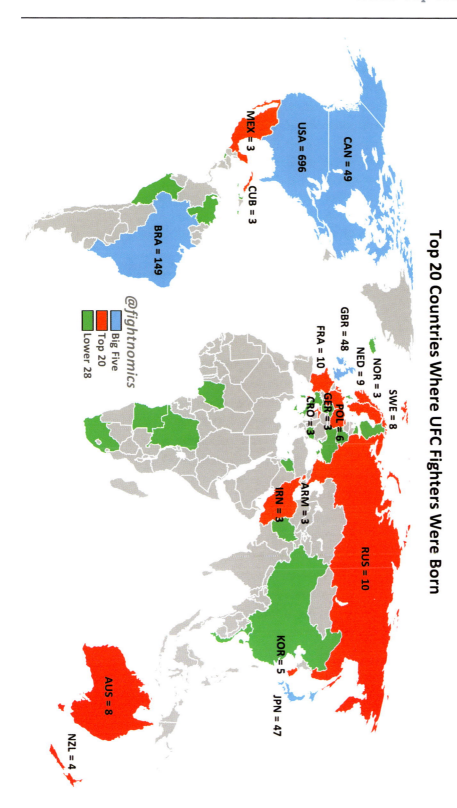

Top 20 Countries Where UFC Fighters Were Born

@fightnomics

Big Five
Top 20
Lower 28

MEX = 3
USA = 696
CAN = 49
CUB = 3
BRA = 149

GBR = 48
FRA = 10
NED = 9
NOR = 3
SWE = 8
GER = 3
POL = 6
CRO = 3
IRN = 3
ARM = 3
RUS = 10
KOR = 5
JPN = 47
AUS = 8
NZL = 4

The "Big Five" countries collectively make up a 90% lion's share of historical UFC roster spots, as well as 90% of the fighter appearances through the years. The Top 20 nations shown in the map account for 98% of the total; another 28 nations (the "Lower 28") have sent only one or two fighters to the UFC to date. As far as other mainstream sports go in the United States, this reflects a massive amount of diversity for one sport, despite 63% of the athletes coming from within the US.

Now that we know where UFC fighters come from, let's look at how they've performed inside the Octagon. After isolating fights where there was a winner and loser (no draws or no contests), and where the two fighters were not from the same country, here's how each nation fared overall throughout UFC history. This list only includes countries with at least ten fights.

World Cup of MMA
Win Rate in International Fights by Country

Country	UFC Win Rate
New Zealand	72.2%
South Korea	68.2%
Belarus	66.7%
Denmark	64.7%
Russia	64.1%
Brazil	57.6%
Sweden	56.5%
Netherlands	56.4%
Poland	54.5%
France	53.5%
Bahamas	52.9%
Canada	48.3%
USA	48.2%
United Kingdom	47.3%
Mexico	46.2%
Australia	46.2%
Italy	42.9%
Croatia	39.1%
Armenia	38.5%
Japan	37.8%

@fightnomics

UFC Win Rate

Topping the list is **New Zealand with a win rate of 72%, the highest of any country with at least ten fights**. The Kiwis have been winning nearly three-quarters of their fights thanks to a small but powerful roster of Mark Hunt, James Te-Huna, Dylan Andrews and Robert Whitaker. New Zealand has a population of just 4.5 million, roughly equivalent to the state of Kentucky, yet they've already landed four fighters in the UFC who racked up 13 wins in their first 18 appearances. New Zealand is also the undisputed king of international rugby, so maybe there's some testosterone lacing the water supply down there.

Not far behind are South Korea and Belarus with win rates of two-thirds or better. These nations haven't sent many fighters to the UFC, but the ones that made it have won twice as often as not. The Korean team of five competitors has achieved an overall record of 15-7 in the UFC, led by recent featherweight title contender "The Korean Zombie" Chan Sung Jung. The Belarusians only had two fighters in the UFC, both old-school success stories who arrived early and managed to amass wins over a 13-year period. Andrei Arlovski and Vladimir Matyushenko represented the small nation of only eight million and collectively went 16-8 in the UFC, having both competed for a UFC title. Perhaps more impressively, both fighters are still active as of 2013 at the respective ages of 34 and 42, despite neither fighter still being in the UFC. Matyushenko is so "old-school" that he was actually a member of the Soviet National Wrestling Team. Coincidentally, the Belarusians actually faced each other at UFC 44 in 2003, and it was the larger Arlovski who came away victorious with a first round knockout.

Rounding out the top five most efficient national teams, Denmark and Russia have both fared well in the UFC with win rates above 64%. Notably, the highest performing nations have only competed in limited numbers, and none are among the "Big Five." When it comes to racking up Octagon victories on a larger scale, it's the Brazilians who lay claim to the top performing spot of the Big Five. With an overall win rate of 58%, they are the only nation of the Big Five to win a majority of their fights. The most frequent losers on the list are the Japanese, who round out the bottom of the Big Five in terms of frequency of competition, as well as with their win rate of just 38%. It's strange that a country with a long history of combat sports culture would perform poorly on a consistent basis, but perhaps there are other disadvantages at work, such as less of a tradition of weight cutting.

Way down in the extreme of small sample sizes, the only country with a perfect 100% win rate to date is Iceland, thanks entirely to the 2-0 performance of Welterweight Gunnar Nelson. That's right...Iceland is undefeated in the

UFC. Time will tell if Iceland can move its way up the ranks into World Cup contention, but at least they're off to a better start than Ukraine, Finland, Angola, Austria, and Puerto Rico, that have yet to taste victory in the Octagon (all are 0-1).

There's one more takeaway from this analysis regarding the life cycle of competition. Groupings by UFC size representation can be aggregated, and here's how they perform collectively.

National Records

Group (by Size)	Win Rate
Big Five Countries	49.6%
Rest of Top 20	55.5%
The Lower 28	38.7%
All 48 Nations	50.0%

The up-and-comer nations that make up the rest of Top 20 of the list behind the Big Five have an average win rate of 55%, outperforming the Big Five and the Lower 28. The Big Five has an overall win rate of 49%, heavily influenced by the American win rate. But as we just saw, only one country of the five most represented has broken the 50% win barrier in the long run. The up-and-comers include some nations – and fighters, obviously – to keep an eye on in the future as the sport continues to mature in new UFC markets. The Lower 28 has fared worst of all. Each nation has sent at most two fighters to the UFC's Octagon, but collectively they are barely winning more than one fight in three overall.

Best Overall Finishers

I get this question a lot: which nation's fighters finish the most fights? There's a lot bias loaded in the question, beginning with the assumption that there should be any difference at all. What do the stats say? Which country finishes more fights than its peers, and are you sure you want to know?

Here are the finish rates (winning performances only) for the top three nationalities that comprise 80% of all fights in the UFC. "All Other" nationalities are lumped together for a fourth category for reference. For this analysis I used all UFC fights from 2008 through mid-2013. The most important data manipulation is that we have isolated each weight class, because we already know that size matters when it comes to finish rates.

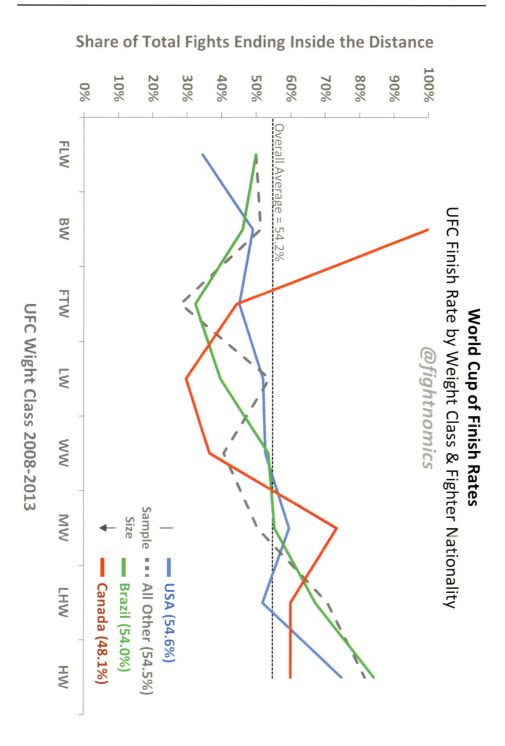

World Cup of Finish Rates

UFC Finish Rate by Weight Class & Fighter Nationality

@fightnomics

Share of Total Fights Ending Inside the Distance

UFC Wight Class 2008-2013

Overall Average = 54.2%

Sample Size

— USA (54.6%)

∎∎∎ All Other (54.5%)

— Brazil (54.0%)

— Canada (48.1%)

An experienced bettor would probably have guessed that there isn't much difference between fighters of different nationalities finishing fights, at least not reliable differences. Most fighters have joined mainstream training camps and although matchmakers may book fighters to compete in certain events based on their home countries, that's only after they've already made the cut for a UFC contract to begin with.

At a glance, the numbers show that Brazilians finish more fights overall (59%) than any other group. "All Other" fighters are next by finishing 58% of their aggregate wins. Americans (53%) come in just below the UFC average (54.5%), while Canadians bring up the rear (47%). Brazilian fans can rejoice in knowing their fighters are most likely to end a fight in the Octagon "inside the distance." American fighters are the most common competitors in the UFC, and ride a consistent finish rate through the weight classes that parallels the overall UFC benchmarks for those divisions (because for the most part, they are the benchmark). Canadians, however, have a volatile finish rate that is high for small and large fighters, but low for fighters in the middle weight classes. This should push their overall average finish rate downward, since lightweight and welterweight divisions are the two largest (in terms of roster size) and most frequently competed.

Surely, haters of George St-Pierre will conclude that he's responsible for dragging down the average of his countrymen, and indeed, he only finished two of nine fights during the period of analysis. Removing his fights from the sample however, might boost the Canadian finish rate for the welterweight division, but the overall finish rate would only climb to 49%, a bump of just a little more than one percent that still leaves the great white north at the bottom of the heap.

This is Fightnomics, so there are more layers to solving this riddle. First, Canada has the smallest sample size of the bunch, and therefore its data is inherently more volatile. The high finish rate for the bantamweight division is from four fights, while the perfect scores at light heavyweight and heavyweight are from just one fight each. Canada's low average in the center of mass divisions could mean that there will be a regression to the mean in years to come. Secondly, and more importantly, Canada has the fewest fights of any group above lightweight, where finish rates are higher.

Brazilians, on the other hand, have the most fighters competing in the larger divisions, which is inflating their overall finish rate average. "All Other" countries have the most biggie-sized fighters of all and also see a slightly higher finish rate than average. And the largest sample size of all, the Americans, sits right in the middle in terms of their share of larger fighters and also very closely align with the UFC average.

So can we conclude that there is a national pecking order to UFC ferocity and finish rates? No, not really. What this analysis shows is that in a macro-scale, there aren't many differences between international fighters in how they finish fights. Most importantly, the allocation of roster spots among the weight divisions is a stronger driver of overall finish rates.

More revealing than overall finish rates would be performance metrics in striking, wrestling and submission disciplines. In these specific areas we might see more pronounced differences by nationalities, but the sample size will be even more volatile. What do you think? What country has the best striking? Who has the best wrestling skills or submission game?

Best Standup Strikers

A quick data experiment looking at performance metrics on a national basis is interesting, although we'll have to temporarily suspend our normal critical desire for smooth data and equal sample sizes, because there are a lot of factors that make this experiment unequal. You can't have your cake and eat it too. I won't spend too much time on this, since it's really a hypothetical experiment, but I'll run the numbers anyway just for giggles.

For the first experiment, I've calculated average performance metrics for several key striking attributes, accounting for accuracy, pace, cage control, knockdown rate and standup striking defense for each country's fighters. I then compared each nation to the average to get a composite score of who outperforms, and who doesn't. The scores here were normalized from 0-100%, but had an average of 64%.

Fightnomics Striking Assessment

Rank	Country	Score
1	New Zealand	73%
2	France	71%
3	Russia	70%
4	South Korea	68%
5	Brazil	66%
6	Denmark	66%
7	Poland	66%
8	Netherlands	66%
9	Canada	65%
10	Mexico	65%
11	Sweden	64%
12	USA	63%
13	Croatia	63%
14	United Kingdom	63%
15	Australia	63%
16	Germany	63%
17	Japan	62%

UFC fights since 2007, relative various striking metrics
Countries with at least 100 minutes of fight time

And the winner is – New Zealand again? Huh. Their superior performance may explain why we saw New Zealand showing up with such a high win rate (72%) to date. Nipping at their heels were the Frenchmen. It turns out that fighters like Cheick Kongo, Cyrille Diabate, and Francis Carmont have all excelled in their striking metrics. Kongo alone actually accounted for almost half of all French fight time, skewing the stats towards his high knockdown rate and good accuracy. You would think The Netherlands would be higher in the table with its rich kickboxing tradition and dense per capita population of kickboxers, but it comes in at Number 8. Still, that's a little above average in the UFC.

Of the Big Five, Brazil again performed the best, showing that they're not just training jiu jitsu down there. Canada managed to stay just above average, while the rest of the Big Five came in below the benchmark. Down at the bottom we see Japan and Germany, which both had fighters lagging far behind their peers in a variety of striking metrics. Again, this performance in striking could explain why Japan and Germany have fared poorly in the UFC in terms of overall win rate at 38% and 22%, respectively.

Best Wrestlers

Taking the same approach as with striking metrics, I ran the numbers on each country with respect to takedowns landed, takedown accuracy, dominant positions on the ground, and sweeps, as well as defensive metrics for each. I used this method only because cauliflower-ear-per-capita data was unavailable. The scores were again put on a 0-100% scale, and in this case ended up with a 48% average.

Fightnomics Wrestling Assessment

Rank	Country	Score
1	South Korea	61%
2	Russia	58%
3	Denmark	53%
4	Sweden	52%
5	New Zealand	52%
6	Mexico	51%
7	Australia	50%
8	Brazil	50%
9	Canada	49%
10	Netherlands	48%
11	Japan	47%
12	Poland	47%
13	France	47%
14	USA	47%
15	United Kingdom	44%
16	Croatia	42%
16	Germany	39%

UFC fights since 2007, relative various wrestling metrics
Countries with at least 100 minutes of fight time

The South Korean team is the top performer in wrestling, making them a true all-around threat in cage when we remember their fourth-place finish in striking metrics. Russia also has done well on the mat, likely thanks to their national passion for the grappling sport "sambo." And the Germans have fared worst of all. But once again the Brazilians and Canadians performed above average, while the rest of the Big Five lagged behind.

Best Submission Artists

When it comes to submissions there's no arguing with results. Here is the submission win rate and submission success rate for countries that have secured at least four victories by submission since 2007 in the UFC.

Fightnomics Submission Assessment

Rank	Country	Win Rate by Submission	Submission Success Rate
1	Australia	47%	36%
2	Denmark	44%	20%
3	Sweden	38%	33%
4	Poland	33%	33%
5	Netherlands	29%	17%
6	Brazil	27%	26%
7	France	24%	42%
8	USA	23%	20%
9	Canada	20%	19%
10	United Kingdom	19%	16%
11	Japan	10%	11%

UFC fights since 2007, countries with at least 4 submission victories
Share of wins by submission (ranked), and submission attempt success rate

This time it's Australia that jumps to the top of the list by finishing almost half its Octagon wins by submission, and by enjoying a healthy 36% submission success rate on each attempt. The average success rate was 21% overall, and the average submission finish rate for wins was 23%, so the Australians are well ahead of the pool in both categories. This is likely thanks in large part to lightweight BJJ black belt George Sotiropoulos, who has tallied four submission wins in the UFC. Sweden also demonstrates why it is making noise as a European nation to be respected and Brazil also pops up as above average to no surprise.

All in all, the Big Five nations didn't do that well in our World Cup of MMA, but perhaps that's due to another macro-trend of fighter population and legacy. Fighters from countries already established in the sport may find it easier to get into the upper echelons thanks to assistance from well-connected camps and managers. This could speed up the career progression for fighters from Brazil and the US, for example, while fighters from smaller and less represented nations will have to work harder to get noticed. The net effect could be the that fighters making enough noise in obscure regional promotions in New Zealand or South Korea are more skilled than newcomers coming from American or Canadian fight camps. This is all speculative, but they are certainly plausible explanations that would be supported by these findings.

Since 2007 the Big Five countries have held the vast majority of the roster spots in the UFC, and yet have actually performed slightly below average. A dilution of talent from these large national pools could be the reason. Perhaps we'll know for sure with a few more years of data and a few more fighters from the far corners of the earth making their way to the biggest stage of the sport. It is inevitable that another small country like Iceland is home to a future top prospect awaiting the spotlight. In the meantime, up-and-coming fighters from those under-represented geographies should feel confident in their potential to compete at high levels, and although the MMA cage may be unforgiving, it is also a great equalizer.

Where Do American Fighters Come From?

Given the huge number of American competitors in the USA, and due to my own national bias, I couldn't walk away from this geographic analysis without answering the question of American fighter origins. Since the dawn of the UFC and all the way through October of 2013, 696 American-born fighters have stepped into the Octagon. For 670 of them, we also know what state they were born in.

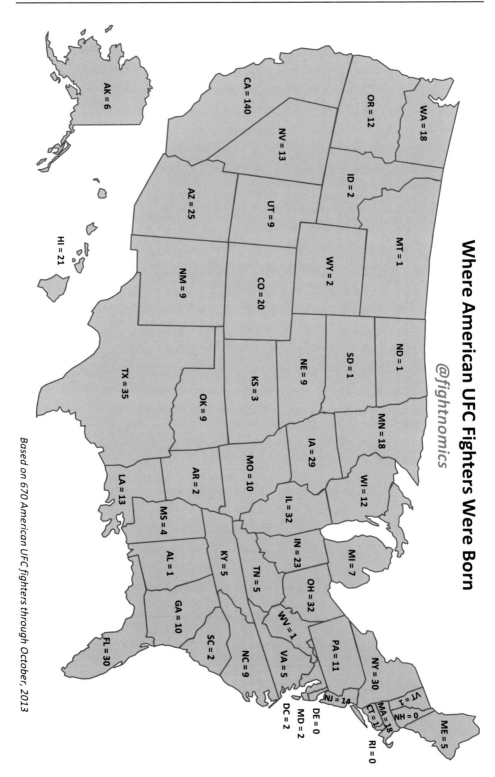

Where American UFC Fighters Were Born

@fightnomics

Based on 670 American UFC fighters through October, 2013

AK = 6
CA = 140
OR = 12
WA = 18
NV = 13
ID = 2
AZ = 25
UT = 9
MT = 1
HI = 21
NM = 9
CO = 20
WY = 2
ND = 1
TX = 35
OK = 9
KS = 3
NE = 9
SD = 1
MN = 18
LA = 13
AR = 2
MO = 10
IA = 29
WI = 12
MS = 4
AL = 1
KY = 5
IL = 32
IN = 23
MI = 7
GA = 10
SC = 2
TN = 5
OH = 32
WV = 1
NC = 9
VA = 5
PA = 11
NY = 30
FL = 30
NJ = 14
DC = 2
MD = 2
DE = 0
CT = 3
MA = 18
VT = 1
NH = 0
RI = 0
ME = 5

These numbers represent how many UFC fighters come from each state, but like most population statistics in the USA, are clearly skewed towards the most populous places. California is home to 140 fighters, and is also the most populous state. The next most populous state is Texas, and it shows up with the second most UFC fighters at 35, after a drop of more than 100. Plenty of less-populous states have sent only a few fighters to the UFC, but how do we tell who is really sending more, on a citizen-per-citizen basis? We can account for population by calculating UFC representation per capita. Actually, I'll use a "Fighters per Million" metric to keep the numbers simple. So where do fighters really come from? What's the pound-for-pound most fightin'-ist state in the whole Union? Now this one really did surprise me.

Fightnomics: Where American Fighters *Really* Come From

Rank	Row Labels	Total Fighters	State Population	Fighters Per Million
1	Hawaii	21	1,392,313	15.1
2	Iowa	29	3,074,186	9.4
3	Alaska	6	731,449	8.2
4	Nebraska	9	1,855,525	4.9
5	Nevada	13	2,758,931	4.7
6	New Mexico	9	2,085,538	4.3
7	Colorado	20	5,187,582	3.9
8	Arizona	25	6,553,255	3.8
9	Maine	5	1,329,192	3.8
10	California	140	38,041,430	3.7
11	Indiana	23	6,537,334	3.5
12	Wyoming	2	576,412	3.5
13	Minnesota	18	5,379,139	3.3
14	District of Columbia	2	632,323	3.2
15	Utah	9	2,855,287	3.2
16	Oregon	12	3,899,353	3.1
17	Louisiana	13	4,601,893	2.8
18	Ohio	32	11,544,225	2.8
19	Massachusetts	18	6,646,144	2.7
20	Washington	18	6,897,012	2.6
21	Illinois	32	12,875,255	2.5
22	Oklahoma	9	3,814,820	2.4
23	Wisconsin	12	5,726,398	2.1
24	Missouri	10	6,021,988	1.7
25	Vermont	1	626,011	1.6
26	New Jersey	14	8,864,590	1.6
27	Florida	30	19,317,568	1.6
28	New York	30	19,570,261	1.5
29	North Dakota	1	699,628	1.4
30	Texas	35	26,059,203	1.3
31	Mississippi	4	2,984,926	1.3
32	Idaho	2	1,595,728	1.3
33	South Dakota	1	833,354	1.2
34	Kentucky	5	4,380,415	1.1
35	Kansas	3	2,885,905	1.0
36	Georgia	10	9,919,945	1.0
37	Montana	1	1,005,141	1.0
38	North Carolina	9	9,752,073	0.9
39	Pennsylvania	11	12,763,536	0.9
40	Tennessee	5	6,456,243	0.8
41	Michigan	7	9,883,360	0.7
42	Arkansas	2	2,949,131	0.7
43	Virginia	5	8,185,867	0.6
44	West Virginia	1	1,855,413	0.5
45	South Carolina	2	4,723,723	0.4
46	Maryland	2	5,884,563	0.3
47	Connecticut	1	3,590,347	0.3
48	Alabama	1	4,822,023	0.2
49	New Hampshire	0	1,320,718	0.0
50	Rhode Island	0	1,050,292	0.0
51	Delaware	0	917,092	0.0
	Grand Total	670	313,914,040	2.1

It's not all surfing and mahalos out in Hawaii. Apparently underneath the famously peaceful island-living is a warrior culture, which makes more sense if you've ever listened to the stories of BJ Penn or Kendall Grove. Twenty-one UFC fighters were born in Hawaii, leading to a dominant position atop the UFC roster when we adjust for population size. None is more famous than Penn, one of the few men to hold a belt at two different weight classes, and as I write this, is cutting weight to compete in yet another.

Next on the list is Iowa, a state that couldn't be more geographically different than Hawaii. This one is no surprise given the pedigree and sheer numbers of wrestlers that the state pumps out with every graduating high school class. Legend has it that there are bars in Iowa that won't even let a man in the door if he doesn't have cauliflower ear. True or not, it makes a great story about a state with a reputation for being tougher than nails.

After correcting for population, California barely makes the top ten, while Texas is actually below the average line. If it's true that everything is bigger in Texas, then perhaps weight cutting is preventing Texans from getting into the UFC. Three states have yet to see a native son (or now daughter) enter the UFC. Given how small New Hampshire, Rhode Island, and Delaware all are, it might be some time before they do. But if you're a young fighter from one of these states, go and ahead remind UFC scouts that this country was founded upon the idea of representation for everyone. So if you're trying to break barriers, best of luck!

12 For the Record: Settling the Biggest Debates in MMA (for now)

You can tell me all day that the sky is falling, but when the barometer holds steady, the anemometer doesn't move, and Doppler radar shows no rain or any significant change in any atmospheric condition then I'm just going to call you Chicken Little. Numbers don't lie and utilizing them correctly enables us to tackle big questions that can be boiled down to simple metrics. The real question is "why didn't we do so from the beginning?" But that would be living in the past and this book is all about using numbers to predict future outcomes. Now that we have more robust data available to us, let's consider some of the most common questions about MMA and run them through the statistical grinder.

The Truth About Finish Rates

Haven't you heard? Guys aren't finishing fights. They're just "playing it safe." At least that's the ugly rumor. It's one thing to boldly make this proclamation in a bar after a closely contested yet lackluster main event, but mentioning the UFC's declining finish rates at a press conference will certainly rouse the ire of those involved in the sport. It's not as if guys aren't trying to finish their opponents. So what's the real story? Are guys really playing it safe in the brighter spotlight of a sport experiencing rapid growth? Or is something else changing the fundamental nature of MMA's top promotion?

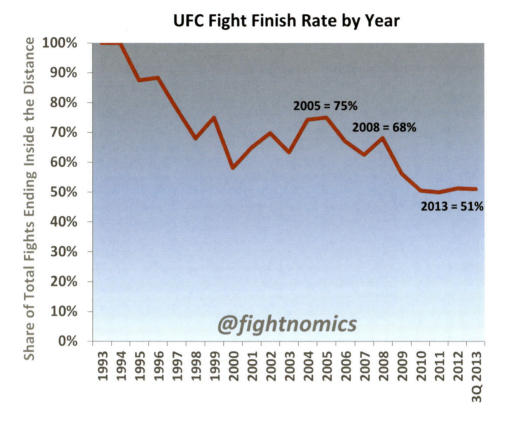

A quick look at the statistics is certainly damning. If this were Wall Street, you'd be scared. However, let's remember that in the early years of UFC competition, rules were significantly different and stylistic imbalances led to few decisions. All eight fights at UFC 1 lasted less than 14 total minutes, and the 36-minute long draw between Royce Gracie and Ken Shamrock at UFC 5 was the first fight to technically go the distance. As higher-skilled athletes compete under the Unified Rules of MMA, you might expect fewer lopsided finishes of the kind that defined the early years of the sport. However, even if we generously mark the first season of The Ultimate Fighter show in 2005 as a starting point for the "Modern Age of MMA," you still see finish rates dropping precipitously in the years since, despite standardized rules and consistent matchmaking. The 76% of fights finished in 2005 is now down to just over 50%. The question is: "Why?"

Annual UFC Fights by Fight Outcome Type

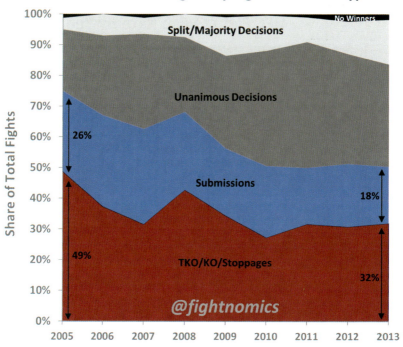

Cutting the cake a different way shows the layers of filling hidden inside. By looking at the data differently, we see that the method of finishes is falling at different rates, with a bigger drop off in striking finishes than submissions. We've already uncovered reasons for part of this: TKO finish rates correspond to body mass. Bigger fighters have a lot more knockout power – and a little bit worse striking defense – so size is a great predictor of overall finish rates in MMA. The overall "center of mass" in the UFC has shifted towards smaller divisions, with more fights being competed in smaller weight classes than ever before. But that doesn't explain why submission rates are falling too. If smaller fighters are filling up fight cards in greater numbers, shouldn't the submission rate go up? Smaller fighters, after all, do average more fights ending by submission than larger fighters.

Isolating each weight class and also separating finishes into those by strikes versus submissions should point us in the right direction for falling finish rates. We'll consider two time periods: 2004 to 2005 during the recent peak in finish rates, and then 2012 to 2013 for the most recent trends, and we'll correct for weight class by focusing just on the legacy divisions because the lightest weight classes have not been around long enough to make the data consistent.

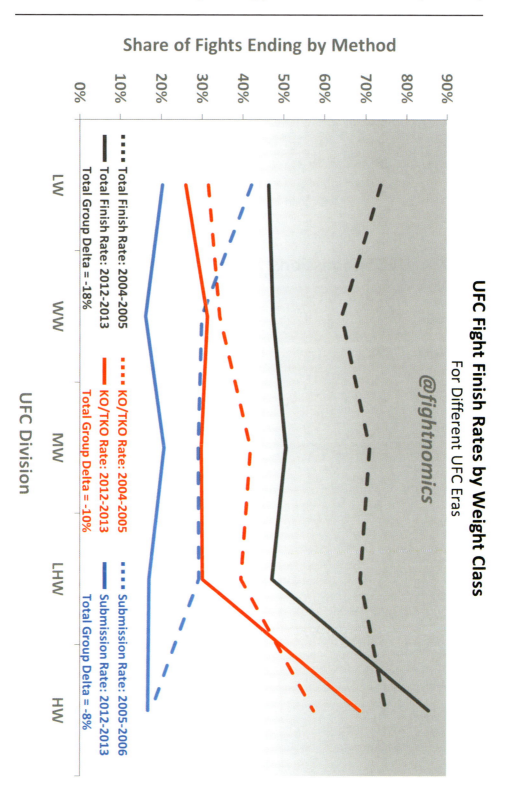

UFC Fight Finish Rates by Weight Class
For Different UFC Eras

Share of Fights Ending by Method

UFC Division

@fightnomics

- ▪▪▪▪ Total Finish Rate: 2004-2005
- ▬▬▬ Total Finish Rate: 2012-2013
- Total Group Delta = -18%

- ▪▪▪▪ KO/TKO Rate: 2004-2005
- ▬▬▬ KO/TKO Rate: 2012-2013
- Total Group Delta = -10%

- ▪▪▪▪ Submission Rate: 2005-2006
- ▬▬▬ Submission Rate: 2012-2013
- Total Group Delta = -8%

The results of this analysis reveal some interesting patterns. First, finish rates overall have dropped 25 percentage points from 2004 to 2013, but when we isolate the group of legacy weight classes, we see a drop of only 18%. That means about a third of the overall drop is simply due to the arrival of new, lighter weight classes that have fewer finishes than heavier divisions. Pound-for-pound there's still a downward trend, so two-thirds of the trend is left unexplained . . . until now. So first, let's try to see how submissions have been trending through the years for the same five legacy divisions of lightweight through heavyweight. We'll take 2005 as the reference point, and look how the metrics changed relative to that year.

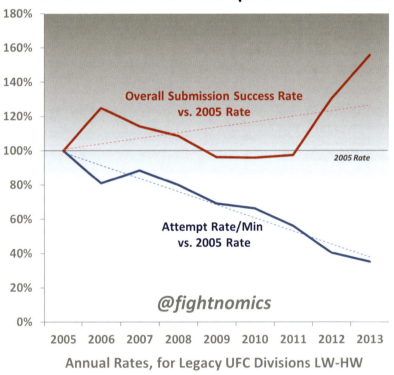

UFC Submissions: Attempt & Success Rates

Annual Rates, for Legacy UFC Divisions LW-HW

Bad news for fans of submission finishes. It turns out that submissions are being attempted less and less, despite the mix of fighters shifting to smaller divisions. There's one definite reason for this, and the rest is still speculative. Remember from Chapter 8 that fights are spending less time on the ground? Well, this means fighters are standing and striking more often rather than grappling and attempting submissions.

According the graph, fighters are attempting barely a third as many submissions per minute of fight time than they were in 2005. That's a huge, market-crash kind of a drop. The decline in attempts is greater than drop in fight time on the ground (which fell by less than half), so a second driver of this downward trend is also that fighters are attempting fewer submissions even when they are on the ground.

Overall submission success rates declined slightly, but then rebounded in the most recent years to be better than they were in 2005. So **submission defense rates are not explaining the drop in overall submission finishes, because most recently they've actually gotten worse**. Fighters are just as effective at using submissions as they've ever been, they're just spending less time at close range and attempting fewer techniques once they get there. The combination of all of these forces is driving submission rates down, and contributing to the drop in finish rates overall. This is an unintended consequence of the overall trend of fighters standing and trading more often, which is further exacerbated by smaller fighters choosing to strike when they may be more dangerous on the mat. But we haven't explained the whole drop in finish rates just yet; we also need to examine standup striking more closely.

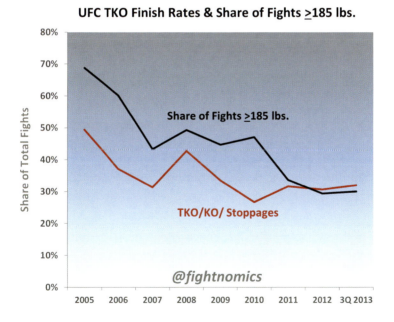

UFC TKO Finish Rates & Share of Fights ≥185 lbs.

At first, I thought the declining share of heavier divisions would explain the drop in striking finish rates, but after more analysis, I realized this only explained a portion of the macro-trend. This chart follows the corresponding decline in striking finishes. However, after isolating just legacy divisions, we still saw a drop of ten percentage points in striking finishes, despite fighters standing and trading longer. So what's causing this discrepancy? Are fighters landing fewer strikes (improved defense or lower output), or are the chins of the recipients more durable than they were years ago?

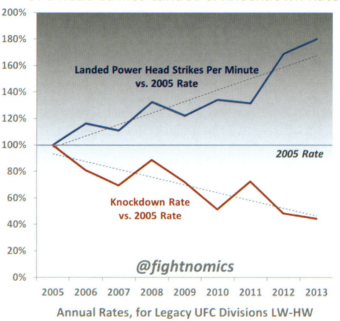

With more time standing, landed power head strikes – remember, these are the most dangerous of all strikes – have been skyrocketing. Currently fighters are landing 80% more of these strikes than they did in 2005, which should result in a lot more knockdowns overall. Except that the knockdown rate is trending in the opposite direction. **Fighters are standing more, landing more, but knocking down less**. So how does this key metric of knockdown rate fare on a pound-for-pound basis?

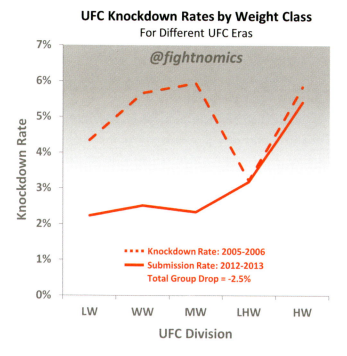

UFC Knockdown Rates by Weight Class
For Different UFC Eras

@fightnomics

- ···· Knockdown Rate: 2005-2006
- ── Submission Rate: 2012-2013
- Total Group Drop = -2.5%

Here we finally flush the fox out of his hole. Knockdown rates in three of the primary UFC divisions are half what they were during the 2005 peak. Despite fighters standing longer and landing more strikes, those same strikes just aren't doing the damage they once did. Perhaps part of this is reflected by the new breed of talent in the UFC that has bubbled up over the last eight years. I calculated the average age of fighters competing in 2005, and the 2013 roster is on average one-year older. So youthfulness is not the cause of the sudden increase in chin resiliency. Something else is going on. Perhaps modern fighters have had better medical care or simply awareness in training, and have been smarter about minimizing head trauma in the gym. Or perhaps striking defense has improved such that fighters are "rolling with the punches" better than in 2005. Statistics have helped identify and isolate a key trend in the sport, but we're still left without a final causal mechanism.

Understanding this underlying trend should hopefully set our expectations differently. Finish rates have indeed declined, but it's not for lack of effort. It's due to a combination of lack of size, diminished time on the ground, and an improved ability to take a punch. Each of these sub-trends is actually a good thing for MMA, as the amount of talent and athleticism in the sport is at an all-time high. Most recently the finish rate has stabilized, as has the mix of weight classes. Perhaps we're entering a period of steady performance that won't whet our appetite for blood like the sluggers of 2005. New fans and old should appreciate the sport for what it is, and not what it once was.

The Home-Cage Advantage

Let's say you're a young up-and-coming UFC fighter fresh off a quick win. Your phone rings and it's a UFC matchmaker offering a new opponent on a big card. Immediately visions of another win, a monster payday, and a sponsorship deal (maybe even a bonus) all dance through your head. Then he drops the bomb on you: the fight is in Brazil, and you'll be fighting a popular hometown guy with a rabid following. Your heart drops. You know what this means. The Home-Cage Advantage is about to end your win streak.

The idea of home-field advantages in sports is nothing new, but to MMA it was the year of 2011 when we saw this phenomenon take brutal effect inside the Octagon as the UFC established a new and recurring presence in Brazil. The initial results were startling. When a Brazilian fighter fought a foreign fighter in Brazil, the local fighter tended to win more often. And not just a little, but lot more often. So I calculated the UFC home-cage win rates for fighters facing foreign opponents since 2007. For fun, I've added the home-field win rates for other major US promotions from the book "Scorecasting."

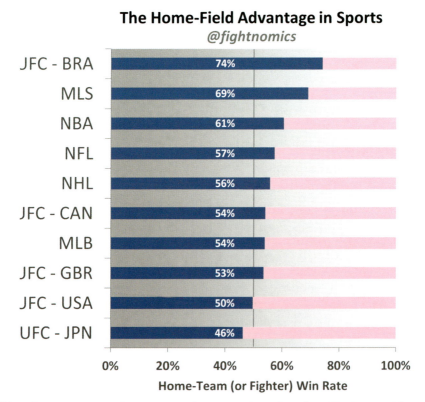

UFC home-country win rates from 2007 through October 10th, 2013. Non-UFC home-field advantages cited from "Scorecasting" by Toby Moskowitz and Jon Wertheim.

From the looks of the data, foreign fighters being invited to a Brazilian UFC event against a local fighter should be terrified. The chances of them leaving Brazil with a "W" is only one in four. The Brazilian home-cage win rate peaked at over 80% during the early summer of 2013 and has been trickling downward ever since. But still, **the Brazilian home-cage advantage dominates the home-cage win rates for other major UFC host nations, and even all other US major league sports**.

Win rates for Brazil, Canada, and the United Kingdom all get a boost above the baseline. American fighters don't see any advantage, but also not much of a disadvantage either with a win rate of 49.7%. The American cage is the most common cage, and perhaps the internationally diverse crowds in the US simply don't provide much of an advantage to local fighters. Or maybe Americans just don't take sides when it comes to nationality, preferring to support their favorite fighter no matter where he's from. In Japan the observation is trickier because we know that Japanese fighters only win 38% of their total fights. So at first glance their home-cage win rate of 46% looks like a disadvantage, but it is actually better than their usual performance. **So across the board, the home-cage is helping fighters win more often than they do as a whole, or on foreign soil**.

But does the market know that? Not according to betting odds at fight time. Aggregating all home-cage fighters resulted in an implied win rate of 51%, the exact same as number as away-cage fighters. Remember that there's a tiny margin of error built into that implied win rate, such that we should only expect fighters to actually win 50% of the time. In reality, the home-cage fighters won 53% of the time, and away-cage fighters won only 46.5% of the time. So **just betting on home-cage fighters versus foreign opponents would be profitable in the long run, while favoring the visitor would be a losing long-term strategy**.

There are several possible explanations for a home-cage advantage in MMA, some of which are present in other sports. The best documented effect is in soccer, both globally and in the US major leagues. Because soccer is a low-scoring game where penalties can have a big impact on whether or not a goal is scored, it is a ripe environment for referee bias to affect the outcome. The bias isn't likely to be intentional, but is an artifact of the crowd. According to a 2003 study by Thomas J. Dohmen of German premier league soccer games, there was evidence that **social pressure from crowds led to decisions by referees that were more often than not advantageous to the home team**. In a fascinating subtlety, the proximity of the crowd altered the effect size. The closer the crowd is (and in this case, the lack of running track that might distance the crowd from the field), the stronger the effect on referee decisions.

Other sports show evidence of real-time bias in officiating. Referees in the NBA are less likely to call fouls when a game is on the line, and much less likely to call a 6th foul on a star player. Non-calls in sports can have every bit of an effect as disciplinary action but without the usual repercussions from players and fans. In baseball, the strike-zone "shrinks" when a hitter already has two strikes against him. Allowing a close pitch through puts the umpire on the spot to call a strikeout, or to allow the hitting sequence to play out on its own. In these cases the inaction of the official in attempting to allow the game to resolve itself is still a bias that affects the game. Fans more quickly forget a non-call, and are therefore more forgiving. But all of these trends demonstrate that sports officials are people too, and they are just as susceptible to social forces as anyone else. Video reviews have the potential to lower the probability of error, but in the end human fallibility is a constant part of every sport.

In MMA there are more than just two individuals involved in any given bout. There's also a referee, and three judges. Each of these additional players can affect the outcome of the fight. Referees must decide when to break action and reset fighter position from the ground or in the clinch, which always neutralizes whatever advantage the controlling fighter had. In a hostile environment, a fighter from another country who's methodically working his top control may quickly draw the "boos" of the crowd, shortening the time until the referee decides to reset the position. In more extreme cases the referee must decide whether or not a barrage of strikes is enough to warrant a stoppage, a threshold that is easier to cross with a wildly cheering crowd than with a silent or booing one.

Judges, despite their name, also show some bias. What's interesting about MMA is that the judges in Brazil are rarely Brazilian, and are often imported from the US. But what's more certain is the intensity of the Brazilian crowd, world-renowned for being the loudest and liveliest of any on the planet. Any judging bias is not nationalistic, but it can easily be social in nature. Imagine a back-and-forth striking duel where each time a fighter lands a clean strike there is silence, but when the home-town favorite comes anywhere near his target the crowd erupts with "ooohs!" We've already seen that judges reward volume over effectiveness, which suggests they can't really tell what's landing during rapid striking exchanges. The home-crowd soundtrack provides a boost to the perception of one fighter's strike effectiveness over the other.

When I dove deeper into the Brazilian home-cage advantage, I found that the local fighters were usually the favorites. So despite betting odds underpricing their performance, it's clear that in terms of matchmaking, Brazil already had a small edge. But that doesn't explain why the local fighters then went on to outperform market expectations. This phenomenon was true for fights ending inside the distance as well as those by decision.

A twist to this story is exemplified by Japanese audiences, known to be the most silent of all. Yet despite the lack of raucous fans loudly celebrating each strike of a native fighter, Japanese fighters have still performed better at home than abroad. So the social influences of crowds may not be the only benefit to fighting on home soil. It's likely that environmental and dietary familiarity can minimize external inconveniences and stressors during fight week for competitors at home, or that performing in front of their countrymen provides an additional boost of emotion required to power through difficult situations. In Brazil, the frequent chant of "Vai morrer!" (you're going to die) could have an adverse reaction on foreign competitors trying to stay focused on the fight at hand. So there are other plausible explanations for the home-cage advantage beyond those documented in officiating by other sports.

The Balance of Power

Some guys swing for the fences as often as possible. Others use a meticulous jab to outpoint opponents and minimize risk. Which one is the better strategy? As it turns out, neither. I've heard the theory that "Jab Artists" who don't fully commit to standup striking lead to boring fights, and that these same fighters are playing it safe to ensure the win. This theory begs the question – are fighters who employ a jab-heavy attack actually winning more often? As I've done elsewhere in this book, I took the approach of classifying fighters into basic groups and then ran fight outcome analysis on each group to see how this basic factor affected win rates. The UFC average power ratio for standup strikes is almost even (see chapter 3) at 51%, if we calculate power strikes as a share of total standup striking. In this case, I separated fighters into three categories:

1. Standup power ratio of 67% or more (High Power).
2. Standup power ratio above 33% and below 67% (Neutral).
3. Standup power ratio of 33% or less (Low Power).

Here's how those fighters performed in terms of wins in the Octagon.

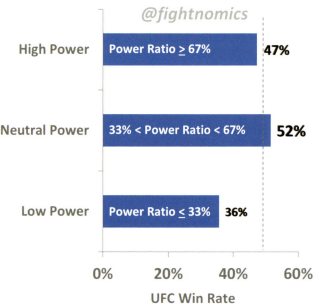

The Balance of Power
Win Rate by Share of Standup Power Strikes

@fightnomics

High Power	Power Ratio ≥ 67% — 47%
Neutral Power	33% < Power Ratio < 67% — 52%
Low Power	Power Ratio ≤ 33% — 36%

0%   20%   40%   60%

UFC Win Rate

The results in this case may surprise you. It turns out that being a balanced fighter is a more successful trait than either relying on too many jabs or swinging heavy hands more often than not. The myth of the Jab Artist is busted. That group of fighters fared worst of all, winning barely a third of their fights. High powered sluggers were much closer to the average win rate, but still lagged slightly. The biggest sample size of all – the Neutral or balanced strikers – did the best, winning slightly more fights than the baseline fighter population without including this factor.

The idea of a conservative striking approach being a savvy way to get the better of opponents is definitely not true. In fact, isolating just fights that ended in decision, the Low Power group still did worst of all. Granted, this is a very rough experiment, one that could have been more detailed in isolated fighters facing other styles. But as a quick and dirty look at this one trait that tends to draw attention from fans, it looks like we have a good answer.

Missing More Than Just Weight

Fighters don't miss weight very often in the UFC, which judging from the usual reaction from Dana White is a good thing. But it still happens, and when it does the implications are beyond just a fighter about to get an angry earful from his boss. Missing weight puts the legitimacy of a bout at risk as well as costing the overweight fighter part of his payday (and I'm not talking about the candy bar). In the rare case of missing weight for a title fight – as Travis Lutter did when he challenged Anderson Silva at UFC 67 – the championship nature of the contest is lost.

Fighters are granted a one-pound allowance over the stated weight limit of each weight class, except in the case of a title fight where the limit is more strictly enforced. Even when fighters weigh in too heavy they are given one or two hours to drop more weight, and try again. Despite these final gray areas at the end of a strictly regulated process of weight management that professional fighters undergo, missing weight still happens. When the fighter cannot, or chooses not to make weight at a second weigh-in, the result is most commonly a 20-25% deduction of pay that is then awarded to the opponent, assuming he is willing to still compete against the heavier fighter. The fight then moves forward as a "catchweight" bout.

From a predictive standpoint, it would be interesting to test whether or not missing weight suggests an advantage or disadvantage in the cage. Given the typically small weight difference involved, carrying a couple of extra pounds into the Octagon doesn't seem like a huge advantage. Conversely, it could be a big disadvantage. Going through the often extreme process of cutting weight for a fight and still falling short suggests the fighter has pushed himself to the brink of severe hydration just 24 hours before attempting a major athletic feat.

Missing weight could also be a clue to an underlying problem facing the fighter. Perhaps an injury prevented a proper training camp, or perhaps distractions outside the gym impacted nutrition, or just boosted the amount of stress a fighter had to endure. Stress hormones make weight loss even harder than it already is. Fighters at the top of the game come from experienced professional training camps which are seasoned veterans at making sure fighters hop on the scale at the right weight, sometimes starting to drop the weight as far as two months out from weigh-in day. So missing weight is a clear signal that something might be wrong. For these reasons, examining the performance of fighters on fight night seems a worthy exercise. This analysis will only include fighters who did not make weight after being given a second opportunity, not those who missed at first, but made weight later.

The **analysis reveals that fighters who missed weight won only 39% of their fights, a pretty huge disadvantage in the world of MMA**. That means missing weight is the same as having a big reach disadvantage. Perhaps this is one reason opponents should choose to accept the match, given their odds of success just went up.

The importance of nutrition for professional fighters cannot be overstated. Ultimately, missing weight is expensive business. In some cases it costs the UFC in the form of fight legitimacy and concern about future matchmaking. But for fighters, the cost is more than just a penalty deduction of salary; it's also more often than not a win bonus and a "W" on their UFC record, which has further-reaching effects. Fortunately, fans are likely aware by now of many nutritional consultants like the Dolce Diet or FitnessVT, and the UFC has even gotten behind their own branded UFC Fit for the mass market. Considering the downsides of missing weight, utilizing the help of professionals in maintaining optimal weight and managing the weight-cut process seems a worthy investment for elite fighters.

What About the Extra Pound at Weigh-Ins?

It was one of the first questions I remember overhearing when I attended a live weigh-in. A fighter steps on the scale, weighs in one pound over the limit (legal for non-title fights), then his opponent comes in right at the limit. "Aha! I wonder if that extra pound will give him an edge," someone says. Well, that is, as we say, a "testable hypothesis." I've run the numbers on UFC fighter outcomes since 2007 based on weigh-in weight, and **there's actually no significant difference in performance between fighters who hit the exact limit and fighters who take the extra pound.** Both groups go on to win almost exactly 50% of their fights.

There's another group, however, where I do see a change in outcomes. **Fighters who weighed-in one pound less than their division limit went on to win only 43% of their fights.** So when it comes to weigh-ins, you can forget about any advantage that may come with an extra pound. If a fighter weighs in a little light though, that's when you should take notice.

Octagon Jitters

When a fighter makes his debut in the UFC, announcers often discuss whether he has "Octagon Jitters" or any nervousness related to his first appearance under the bright lights and on the biggest MMA stage. This phenomenon is pretty easy to test. **Fighters making their first appearance in the UFC win only 44% of their fights**. So that's about the same effect as a mild reach disadvantage. But differentiating the card position of the debuting fighter is more revealing.

If the stress, nerves, logistical unfamiliarity, etc. of performing for the first time is impacting fighters in any way, then it would be reasonable to assume that card position could magnify the effect. This **additional analysis found that fighters debuting on the main card won only 41% of their fights, while those debuting on the preliminary card won 45%**.

It's also possible that new prospects get over-hyped, which could contribute to the larger effect size on the main card. Undercard newcomers don't generally have much hype behind them, so their consistent (albeit slight) underperformance is likely real. Main card newcomers by definition must have some hype behind them to warrant such a placement in their debut, and so perhaps that inflates the level of perceived competition by matchmakers

The effect isn't huge, but the 10- to 20-point swing in win rates is as material as some significant anthropometric disadvantages. Given that every UFC fighter has to make a debut sometime, it's interesting to see this effect align with expectations. Since 2007, the data set included over 600 fighters, the majority of whom made their debut on the undercard. After the fact, these fighters who tested the waters of the UFC under the radar were the wise ones, and they had a slightly better chance of starting their careers off with a win.

Is Ring Rust Real?

"Ring Rust" is a term that gets thrown around quite a bit on fight night when a competitor enters the cage after a long layoff from competition. Originally a boxing term, Ring Rust can also be translated to "Cage Corrosion," but I'll stick with the traditional terminology here. Either way, the implication is that a fighter has been sitting idle for too long, his skills getting rusty.

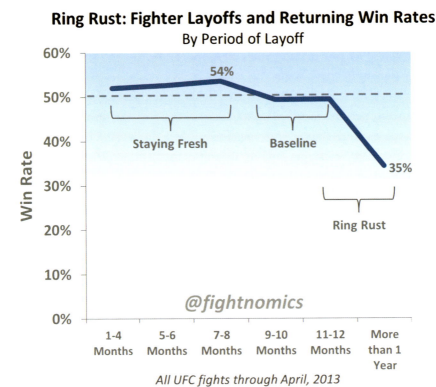

Ring Rust: Fighter Layoffs and Returning Win Rates
By Period of Layoff

All UFC fights through April, 2013

So the answer is "yes," and we have even identified a threshold when the effect kicks in. **Fighters with a layoff of eight months or less had a boost in winning performances**. The effect towards the end of that eight-month window peaked at 54% and was slightly higher than for the shortest layoffs, but all were winning more often than not. The win rate then hugged the baseline rate in the nine to 12-month range of layoffs, until finally tanking for anything more than a year. **The numbers say that severe Ring Rust is worse than a case of Octagon Jitters.**

Beyond a year, sample sizes got pretty small, so I had to lump them together. Still, the effect is pretty clear. **Returning to the Octagon after a year-long layoff results in a 35% win rate**, illustrating how difficult it is to take time away from the cage. The fighters in this rusty group either had serious injuries requiring long rehabilitations, a suspension, or other issues outside the cage that prevented competition such as movie obligations. Regardless of the reason, there appears to be evidence supporting the theory that athletes need to "stay in fighting shape" in order to remain competitive. Taking a long break from the fight game can result in a brutal wakeup call.

The Value of Streaks

I was curious about the concept of "momentum" in MMA, as media often discusses whether or not a fighter is coming off of a win or a loss going into the next fight. So I ran the numbers to check. I looked at fighter outcomes (win or loss), whether they were coming off of a win or a loss, and whether or not they were coming off of a fight night bonus. The results came back negative. Whether a fighter had won or lost his last fight did not significantly alter his next performance, as both groups won about 50% of the time. So streaks, at least in a minimal one-fight streak sense don't show any pattern. You'll have to stay tuned for more advanced research.

What's more interesting is that fighters coming off of an exemplary performance that earned a Fight of the Night bonus (regardless of whether they won or lost), also returned a negative result. But fighters who won and earned a finish bonus (Submission of the Night or Knockout of the Night) did see a change in performance in their next fight. These fighters went on to win 59% of the fights following a bonus-worthy finish. For those ready to bet on this trend, there's one last calculation. In none of these cases did the fighters outperform their implied win probability as a group.

Still, if you're looking for an edge in assessing a matchup, and one fighter was good enough in his last fight to finish his opponent in spectacular fashion, you should expect him to win almost 60% of the time in his next appearance.

Agree to Disagree: MMA Judging

MMA judges are like tax collectors, they perform a thankless but necessary job that every loves to hate. Judging in MMA incurs the wrath of fans and UFC management alike at nearly every event, and carries the specter of corruption whenever an especially egregious verdict is rendered. Even before analyzing the score cards, I expected to find some inconsistencies in scoring. Although the available data is far from comprehensive, I will share a few interesting nuggets insights gleaned from the history of judges' scores. But first, here's a quick lesson on the scoring system used for UFC fights.

According the Unified Rules of MMA, judges employ a 10-Point Must System for each round of action. Or in their own words from Section 14-B:

> *The 10-Point Must System will be the standard system of scoring a bout. Under the 10-Point Must Scoring System, 10 points must be awarded to the winner of the round and 9 points or less must be awarded to the loser, except for a rare even round, which is scored (10-10).*

And when it comes to awarding scores to each round, the judges are to follow these basic rules from Section 14-J:

The following objective scoring criteria shall be utilized by the judges when scoring a round:

i. a round is to be scored as a 10-10 round when both contestants appear to be fighting evenly and neither contestant shows clear dominance in a round;
ii. a round is to be scored as a 10-9 round when a contestant wins by a close margin, landing the greater number of effective legal strikes, grappling and other maneuvers;
iii. a round is to be scored as a 10-8 round when a contestant overwhelmingly dominates by striking or grappling in a round;
iv. a round is to be scored as a 10-7 round when a contestant totally dominates by striking or grappling in a round.

For every round of every fight, judges will award ten points to the winner, and some number less than ten to the loser, which is most commonly nine points. Given that all UFC fights are either three or five rounds, the 10-Point Must System is very similar to simply a "best two-out-of-three" contest, or for title fights, "best three-out-of-five." Fights can be close, but if a winner is recorded after each round, there's always a winner of the fight at the end, even if both fighters had competitive moments.

The problem is that there seems to be a lot of disagreement as to who is really winning each round. It is logical to assume that scores of 29-28 (totals for three judges scoring three rounds) will happen frequently, because the UFC is the most competitive MMA promotion around and fighters are generally evenly matched. So fights in which each fighter is able to win at least one round should be common. But the judges hired to watch these rounds still disagree frequently enough that split decisions occur at nearly at every event.

When it comes to disagreement, **split decisions mean that two judges agree on the winner, and one does not**. A majority decision means two judges agree on a winner, while the third scores a draw. This is rare, although I do count this scenario as disagreeing over the winner. Usually in a split decision the scores come back 29-28, indicating the rounds were competitive and the winning fighter won two out of the three rounds. When this occurs, scores are read off usually with one judge scoring the fight 29-28 for the losing fighter as a dissenting opinion. Overall, disagreement over the winner happens regularly. **Judges watching the same two fighters in the same**

fight have disagreed on who won in 23% of all UFC fights that ever went the distance. Given that there's an average of six decisions per event, you can expect at least one split decision at every single event. But picking different winners and losers is the most extreme level of disagreement, so it gets worse.

Split rounds are when the judges disagree on who won a single round, regardless of whether they end up agreeing on who won the fight. An example of this occurrence is when you hear Bruce Buffer at the end of the fight say "the judges score this contest 30-27, 30-27, and 29-28, all in favor of the winner…." I've tracked this as a milder form of disagreement since it's still important to understanding how judging works. Here's the rate and recent trend on judging disagreement at the fight-level, and also at the round-level.

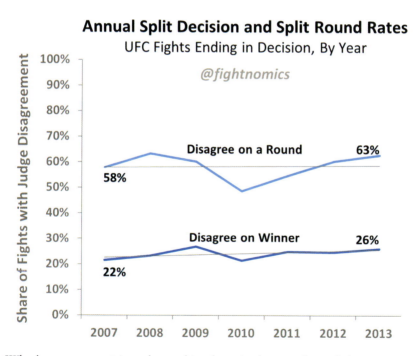

Annual Split Decision and Split Round Rates
UFC Fights Ending in Decision, By Year

What's most surprising about this chart is the number of decisions in which there is disagreement over at least one round. Already occurring in a majority of all decisions, split rounds have been trending upward since 2010 and are approaching two-thirds of all fights. **That means three judges watching the same two fighters in the same fight will disagree on who won a round in the majority of all fights.** And if anything, this number is an underestimate of the true total due to data visibility limitations on round-by-round scores. While the current level of split rounds only leads to disagreement over a winner in about one in four decisions, the amount of disagreement on both levels is on the rise. This could be due to fighter parity and closer fights, or simply a greater diversity of judges being used for the increasing number of UFC events. More judges mean more unique individuals who view the sport with their own perspective and biases.

In some cases you'll see a split decision with at least one score of 30-27 awarded to different fighters. Consider that for a moment. In this case there wasn't just a little disagreement in the fight, there was consistent disagreement over the winner of each and every round. It's these scores that get observers most fired up, and yet we rarely ever hear about any review of judges or explanations about how they reached their scores.

Since we have the data, it might be interesting to see which judges disagree the most. When it comes to split or majority decisions, which judges have the dissenting opinion most often? Do you see your favorite judge on the list?

Most Dissenting Judges

Judge	UFC Split Decisions	Dissenting Opinions	Dissention Rate
Kelvin Caldwell	4	3	75%
Barry Foley	4	2	50%
Dalby Shirley	4	2	50%
Howard Hughes	12	6	50%
Jeff Collins	4	2	50%
Susan Thomas-Gitlin	4	2	50%
Tim Vannatta	4	2	50%
Tony Weeks	22	11	50%
Patricia Morse-Jarman	15	7	47%
Mark Smith	7	3	43%

UFC 3-round split or majority three-round decisions.

Judge Kelvin Caldwell wins the prize for the fight-for-fight most dissenting judge, having disagreed with his peers in three out four split decisions to date. Tony Weeks has much more judging experience, and has been the dissenting judge for half of the split decisions he's been involved in. Or perhaps I should say that he's caused half of the split decisions he's been involved in. The most career UFC dissentions actually goes to Cecil Peoples at 14, but given the higher volume of fights he has judged, his dissention rate is in line with the average.

It's possible that the style of fights can impact the level of disagreement. Do you think fights are easier to score when they mostly take place standing, or when they're mostly on the ground? By tagging fights where Time in Position was greater than 70% standing or on the ground, we can test to see how judges are influenced by the position of the fighters, and whether or not it leads to more or less disagreement.

Rate of Split/Majority Decisions

Fights	Split Decision Rate
All Fights Regardless of Position	23%
Fights >70% on their Feet	26%
Fights >70% on the Ground	13%

Share of three-round fights going to decision since 2007 resulting in a split or majority decision.

Perhaps surprising to some, when fights spend a large majority of the time on the ground in the sometimes hard-to-understand grappling positions, there is actually much less disagreement on who won those fights. **The reason is that whichever fighter is in top control is generally awarded the round**. This generalization overlooks numerous examples of fighters who were more active fighting from the bottom than their opponents were on the top. Regardless, judges seem to find it easier to determine who won a fight when it takes place on the mat than when it's mostly a standing and striking contest. Right or wrong, that's just the reality of it. That means fighters hoping to win a round by fighting off their backs are taking a risky strategy, because either few MMA judges can appreciate how to fight off your back or they overvalue the top position.

How Rare Is a Rare Score?

When it comes to judges awarding 10-8 rounds for a clearly dominant performance by one fighter, there is again clear disagreement. In half of the fights where a 10-8 round occurred, only one judge actually scored a 10-8 round, with the others using only 10-9 scores in the fight. In only 12% of these fights did all three judges award at least one 10-8 round. So even in the case of a dominant performance, judges don't agree on when to use a 10-8 score. My theory is that everyone has a different opinion of the definition of "dominant." Without examples and benchmarks to learn from, judges are left to guess based on their own preferences, which just invites disagreement.

Take the 2013 example of the UFC women's bantamweight fight between Rosi Sexton and Jessica Andrade. The unanimous decision victory for Andrade was not in question, but the judges who scored the fight didn't agree with each other entirely. It wasn't just a victory for Andrade, it was one of the most lopsided victories in the history of the UFC. Over three rounds, Andrade landed 206 Significant Strikes, which was the second highest total all-time. In the second round alone, Andrade out-landed Sexton 91-24. It was the second most Significant Strikes landed in a single round in UFC history. Only Tim Sylvia pummeled Wesley "Cabbage" Correira worse (barely, by three strikes) at UFC 39 in 2002. Andrade literally delivered a once-in-a-decade type of round, one that had social media erupting and even UFC commentator Joe Rogan urging the fight to be stopped during live commentary. So according to the Unified Rules, this could have been a 10-7 round for "total domination," or a 10-8 for "overwhelming domination," but certainly not a 10-9 round for winning "by a close margin." How did the judges score Round Two?

Two judges awarded a 10-9 round for Andrade, while only one scored it 10-8 for her. The reluctance of judges to score anything other than a 10-9 has never been so clear. So I dug into the historical scores and calculated exactly how often a 10-8 round is awarded in UFC fights that go to decision. For that matter, how often do judges score a round anything other than 10-9? The answer is: not often.

How Judges Score UFC Rounds

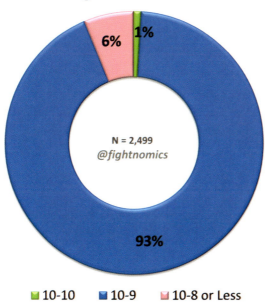

N = 2,499
@fightnomics

6% 1%

93%

■ 10-10   ■ 10-9   ■ 10-8 or Less

All UFC fights since 2001

Judges really don't like scoring rounds anything other than 10-9, and good or bad, they really don't like scoring a 10-10 even round. Perhaps this is because they know it could easily lead to a draw if the fighters split the other two rounds. Like referees committing "non-call" errors in other sports, judges may be avoiding 10-10 scores to prevent the likelihood of a draw. No one likes draws, and they also attract more attention to the cards. But don't plenty of fights have fairly even rounds?

By my calculations, about 10% of all UFC rounds see two fighters land a total number of significant strikes that is either equal to each other or off by just one. Over the course of three rounds, about 30% of fights going the distance had at least one extremely close round where the fighters landed similar strike totals. That isn't to say that strike totals are the only indicator of how evenly matched a round was, but it illustrates the frequency with which fighters match up evenly over the course of five minutes. When fighters are standing and engaging back and forth and neither lands a truly damaging blow, the ambiguity of the round leads to greater disagreement over who won, which contributes to split decisions. The alternative is to score these rounds 10-10 if the fighters are truly evenly matched, but then fighters, management, and fans would all have to live with frequent draws . . . and probably a lot of rematches. The last thing we want to see is Rocky 9.

The question of how to improve scoring and judging remains open for the sport of MMA. Whatever options we explore, we would be wise to use historical data to help understand the underlying drivers and trends in scoring. An investment into additional training for judges may be worthwhile for top promotions. Scandalous decisions may not be under the control of the UFC, as judges are appointed by independent athletic commissions. However, these decisions can and do adversely affect the UFC's core product, fan base, and business.

Consider this small experiment. I identified judges who had judged a total of at least 50 fights (11 judges in all), then found fights where all three judges were from this "experienced" sub-group. When analyzing this subset of 105 UFC fights that went to a decision, the experienced judges disagreed on the winner only 18% of the time. The improvement over the baseline split decision rate of 23% isn't huge, but it's something. When it comes to disagreement on at least one round of a fight, the experienced group of judges only disagreed 37% of the time, much lower than the 58% baseline for split rounds. **This suggests that more experienced judges are more reliably identifying round winners, and disagreeing less overall**. It could also mean that less experienced judges are "hedging" rounds, meaning they are alternating winners of close rounds to allow the final round to decide the fight. This would explain why there are much more frequent split rounds but only slightly more frequent split decisions. One would hope that the athletic commissions are analyzing data like this to understand how and why disagreement occurs, and, of course, how to minimize it. But hope is not a method. MMA needs action or else disagreements in judging will continue, which ultimately degrades from an otherwise magnificent sport.

The Money Chart: Advantages & Disadvantages in MMA

No two fighters walk into the cage truly equal, and we've covered a lot of ground assessing what matters in fights, and how much. It's time we stack some of these advantages up against each other to better see the bigger picture. This graphic represents years of research and data crunching, all boiled down to a single, simple chart. It's the chart I always wished I had in my pocket when viewing MMA and is the one every fan should carry on fight night. Consider this the Tale of the Tape Decoder Ring. It allows you to better evaluate and understand the context of the various differences between fighters, and even some more subtle factors that we've just covered. It also reminds us that two fighters rarely enter the cage without some significant differentials. The human eye may see two evenly matched competitors, but the numbers see two vastly different beings.

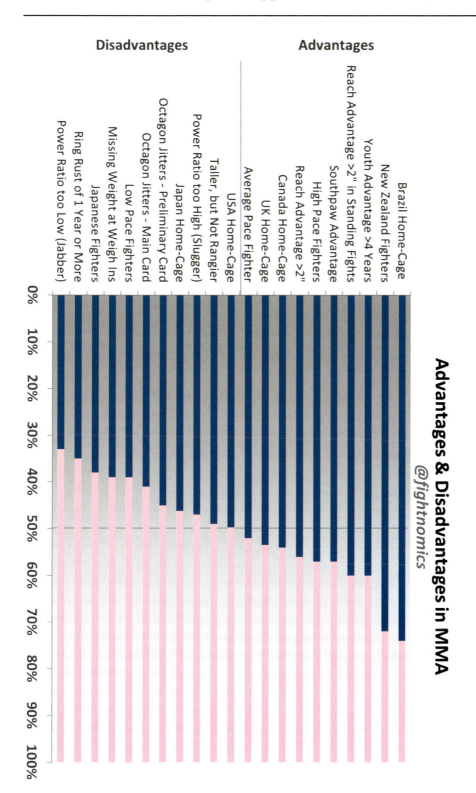

Advantages & Disadvantages in MMA
@fightnomics

13 The Fringe: Strange Forces That Matter in Fights, and Some That Don't

For the first time ever this book has put hard numbers behind some of the most common underlying drivers of outcomes in the fight game. We've confirmed some battle-worn theories about MMA, and busted a few more, but there's a lot more at work in the cage than just the Tale of the Tape, or even the basic skills and training that a fighter takes into competition. There are a few more subtle, often invisible factors at work. Some will have powerful effects on how fights go down, while others, no matter how much you think they matter, just won't. It's time we explore the fringe of these hidden forces. We're on the homestretch now, so let's get weird.

Small Fish in a Bigger Pond: The Dirty Secret of the WEC Merger

In December, 2010, Anthony "Showtime" Pettis leapt off the wall of a cage and landed a kick to Benson Henderson's face. The spectacular "wall-walk kick" highlighted the waning moments of the final fight of the World Extreme Cagefighting (WEC) organization. The consolidation of the bantam, feather and lightweight fighters into the UFC came with a bang, but while Zuffa had owned the WEC for years, and its management had already implemented operational practices from the UFC, most fans didn't know about one key difference between the two organizations.

The biggest questions surrounding the merger focused on whether smaller fighters would be enough of a draw to warrant airtime on MMA's biggest stage. Stars from the WEC like Urijah Faber and Jose Aldo certainly could put on a show and had developed strong followings but it was still an experiment into MMA's unknown. The WEC's highlight reel boasted amazing fight-ending knockouts and submissions all taking place in the vivid, electric blue WEC cage. However, the UFC's Octagon was different. It was bigger. A lot bigger. The WEC had used a 25-foot diameter cage. At 30-feet across, the full-size UFC Octagon may not seem quite so huge at only a 20% bigger diameter, but that translates into a cavernous 44% increase in fighting area. Modern military strategy dictates that warfighters must know three things: the enemy, themselves, and the ground on which they fight. In this case, the ground suddenly got much larger. So let's settle this once and for all. Could cage size possibly affect how fights go down?

Finish rates in the UFC are closely scrutinized. People want to see fights finished and the UFC wants exciting endings that feed highlight reels for future

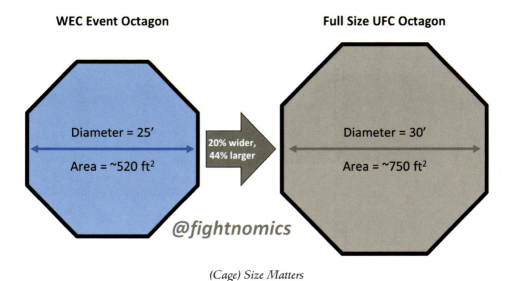

(Cage) Size Matters

promos. We already know that the most important variable affecting finish rates is the size of the fighters, but here's another factor that could influence finish rates that is usually missed by the naked eye. Accounting for the fact that smaller fighters finish less often, did moving into a larger cage have any effect on how these fighters perform? Wouldn't smaller cages force competitors to press the action – resulting in more finishes – with bigger cages allowing more room to roam?

Fortunately, we have a great way to test this hypothesis. Before the WEC-UFC merger, several weight classes operated in parallel in the two promotions. They also kept Sean Shelby as the matchmaker for the lighter weight classes after the merger, so this too was consistent going forward. Furthermore, the UFC still used a smaller cage for The Ultimate Fighter (TUF) show and Finale events that is closer to the WEC cage in size (i.e., smaller than the regular UFC full-sized Octagon). This is due to the tighter quarters of the Palms Casino where Finale events used to be held. So let's look at finish rates in those three scenarios, all while controlling for fighter size.

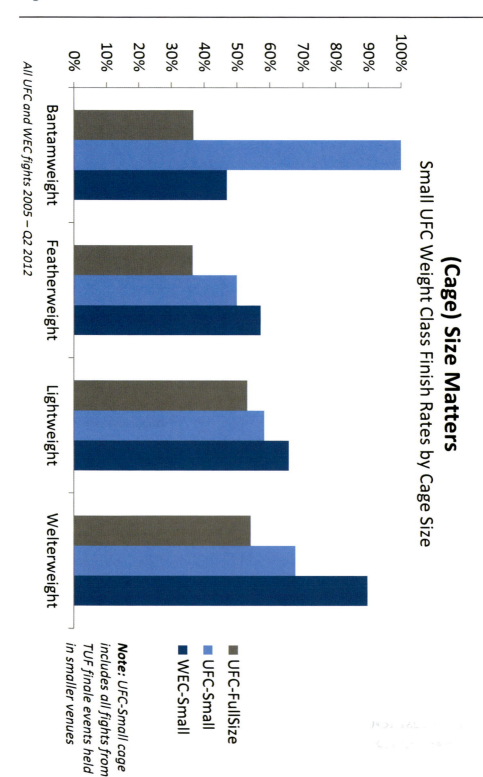

(Cage) Size Matters

Small UFC Weight Class Finish Rates by Cage Size

All UFC and WEC fights 2005 – Q2 2012

Legend:
- UFC-FullSize
- UFC-Small
- WEC-Small

Note: *UFC-Small cage includes all fights from TUF finale events held in smaller venues*

The results show that **finish rates are higher in smaller cages, and this is true for all the weight classes where we have good data**. The spike for the Bantamweights is due to the small sample size of bantamweight fighters competing in TUF Finale events, because there have only been five such shows since the merger, with seven Bantamweights fights (all finishes). But even more conclusively, we see higher finish rates in all weight classes in the smaller cages of the WEC and TUF events, including the lightweights and welterweights, who have been around longer and have more total fights to examine.

When put into a smaller cage, even larger UFC weight classes (welterweight and above) finish more fights. They also throw over 20% more strikes per minute than when they are in the full size Octagon. Same rules, same division, same matchmaker…just more action. **The idea is confirmed: smaller cages result in more action and therefore, more finishes.**

Unfortunately for fans of the WEC (this guy, right here) the days of fights in the small electric blue cage are over. The question remains if the UFC will ever redeploy a smaller cage for select events, especially when no larger divisions (above middleweight) are competing, which does occasionally happen. In fact, it's happened five times in 2013 alone, including several FOX cards. Just imagine, fight fans, a FOX card stacked with talent competing in the smaller WEC-sized cage – highlights galore.

Below the Belt: Do Low Blows Affect Fight Outcomes?

Rounds in the UFC are always five minutes long, right? No, actually that's not true. Sometimes they're a little longer, and when they are you can be sure one of the fighters is having a bad night.

Low blows are an unfortunate reality in MMA. While an illegal strike to the groin may not be intentional, it must be accounted for during competition. According the Unified Rules of MMA (Section 15, Subsection G), a fighter hit with a low blow strike (considered a "foul") has up to five minutes to rest and recuperate before deciding whether or not to continue. Fouls are the only time other than a potential equipment malfunction when a round may be stopped in the middle of action, which poses a few interesting hypotheses.

The first question is: who really pays the price here? The striker who committed the foul is very rarely penalized for the first or even second infraction. If the fight is stopped, the athletes are moved to neutral corners and coaches are told not to yell any instruction. The striker is usually told to "keep those knees up" or to "be careful with those low kicks." Meanwhile the recipient goes through varied levels of discomfort and nausea until he chooses to restart, or the five minutes have elapsed and he is forced to continue or risk ending the fight. But a penalty was committed. So who paid for it? The striker was verbally warned and the recipient received a painful, potentially dangerous strike, but both fighters received the same rest period.

The idea that low blows would carry a cost was explored by the creators of the FightMetric system. Their methodology for quantifying MMA fights does more than just count when action occurs, it also counts every second of fighter position. So when they went back through the film archives for UFC fights, occasionally they had to stop the clocks when a low blow happened. This got them thinking. Why not keep track of low blow recipients to see if it affects fight outcomes? Being curious types, FightMetric logged the duration of every low blow stoppage and calculated the win rate for the fighters who received them. The hypothesis for an effect has some merit. The penalized fighter bore no cost for his foul while the injured fighter had only minutes to recover. All other factors were ignored. So perhaps there might be an advantage to committing a low blow foul in that you get a free chance to hurt your opponent in a way that could also adversely affect him for the rest of the fight.

The numbers were crunched, and the results were interesting: there was no effect. Fighters who received a low blow severe enough to have the round stopped went on to win about 50% of their fights. **This suggests that the effect of a low blow foul was negligible**, but that's little solace to several fighters who have been unable to continue after a severe groin strike. In several MMA promotions an illegal groin strike led to a no contest due to injury, the most famous of which was Alistair Overeem's brutal knee strikes against Mirko "Cro Cop" Filipović at DREAM 6 in Japan. Cro Cop's corners were overheard reporting that his left testicle had been knocked back into his body via the inguinal canal, a condition that no doubt led doctors to stop the match against Cro Cop's wishes, forcing him to limp back to the dressing room to contemplate a rematch that sadly would never occur.

The only time a UFC fight ended prematurely due to a groin strike was at UFC 55, when in the first fight of the night Alessio Sakara suffered an illegal low blow from Ron Faircloth resulting in a No Contest. No other fights ended due to a low blow, perhaps a testament to improved protection from steel athletic "cups" over the years to protect fighters and their baby makers. But low blows have still drawn penalties from referees that include point deductions, including one fight that ended up as a draw due to the foul. The most recent (and extreme case) was when Alex Caceres committed repeated fouls against Edwin Figueroa at UFC 143 resulting in a two-point deduction by referee Herb Dean. Having won at least two rounds of the fight, Caceres ended up losing the fight by split decision due to the penalty deduction. It was the only time in history two points were taken in the same penalty, and in MMA that's all it takes to win or lose a fight in the 10-Point Must System.

These examples are extremes, so I'll only make one last point on a squeamish topic. FightMetric also timed the average stoppage when a low blow resulted in referee intervention. The average time fighters take to recuperate (assuming they stop at all) is 42 seconds. So the next time you see a low blow stoppage, don't worry. Chances are the outcome of the fight hasn't been changed. And you probably won't have to wait more than a minute before the action starts again – just long enough to have Joe Rogan take you through at least three slow-motion replays of the wince-worthy foul.

The Loser's Smile

There's another subtle hint about MMA matchups that occurs the day before the fighters even step into the cage. Before you look at the Tale of the Tape, first watch the staredown between the two fighters at weigh-ins. There's a theory that if one of the fighters smiles more when facing his opponent, then he is more likely to lose. Sound like bunk? Well, let's think back to Chapter 1 and the discussion of agonistic fighting. Human males (and many other animals for that matter) don't always really want to fight, but they sure are good at pretending they do. Posturing is critical during the decision-making process of whether to move forward with aggression or back down. Much like poker where every little body movement can give away a player's hand, determining status between rivals is often done based on body language and assessment of physical dominance. Big mean dudes who look tough mostly have to do just that: *look tough*. Potential combatants will subconsciously assess themselves against each other, and whether they like it or not, they may tip their hands through facial expressions if their brains realize they are outmatched. That means showing submissive behavior, which means smiling.

It's not every day that scientific research uses MMA fighters as subjects, but such was the case in a study published by the American Psychological Association in January, 2013. A study called *"A Winning Smile? Smile Intensity, Physical Dominance, and Fighter Performance"* by Michael W. Kraus and Teh-Way David Chen tested the hypothesis that submissive fighters will smile more, and thus facial expressions could be predictive of who wins, and by how much. The assumptions of the researchers were that **smiles are a "nonverbal sign of reduced hostility and aggression, and thereby unintentionally communicate reduced physical dominance."**

Analysis of 157 UFC weigh-in photos during a period from 2008 to 2009 was the testing ground. Each fighter had his weigh-in staredown expression scored to indicate how much he was smiling, and then fighter performance was tracked. The results suggest a subtle example of social behavior becoming a predictive variable for MMA fights. Animals are complicated and our brains work in ways we don't consciously appreciate. The savvy observer will now know that a guy who can't maintain a tough-guy pose in the face of his opponent might be a guy too smart for his own good. Everyone claims they can win a fight, but they can't all be right.

The same week the study was published, Donald Cerrone faced off against Anthony Pettis at UFC on FOX 6. Primed and biased by reading the study, I was very aware of the expressions on both fighters. Pettis stood cold and confident, while the taller Cerrone in his signature cowboy hat broke into a wide and somewhat forced smile as they went toe-to-toe for the formal staredown. Pettis went on to TKO Cerrone the next night just two-and-a-half minutes into the first round of the fight. It was a sample size of one, which is meaningless except that it caused me to research the mechanisms at work, which influenced the first chapter of this book. In actuality, Cerrone tends to smile during most of his staredowns, even against fighters he went on to defeat soundly. But more than the smile, I was mostly struck by the amount of confidence that is conveyed through body language, and how opponents interact with those signals. As fighters enter the cage, experienced observers have been known to suddenly "change their pick," sensitive to cues in the body language of fighters who are either confident, or aware of their poor chances of success. Perhaps a fighter is hiding an injury, and his demeanor reveals the ultimate conclusion that he will lose.

Men with higher testosterone have different body language, and tend to smile less. Women have been found to rate stoic looking men as more attractive than men who smile, correlating with attraction to men with high testosterone or physical status. More research could look at confidence measures of fighters or their teams prior to fights as a predictive variable. We already know that the market is fairly accurate in predicting fight outcomes. The market is right about as often as it should be, and wrong as often as it should be based on the amount of confidence (i.e., the betting odds) in any given fighter. And if success in MMA is affected by basic physical gifts and innate aggression, these characteristics may shine through in unusual ways, especially at close range, toe-to-toe. It may sound ridiculous, but when a corner man gets shaky with doubt, or your girlfriend says "that guy looks tougher," you may want to listen.

The Astrology of MMA: Pitting Zodiac Signs in a Cage Fight

In the words of John Cleese from the classic Monty Python skits: "and now for something completely different." I've talked a lot of about things that influence fights, some obvious, and some not so much. Now I'd like to talk a bit about things that might not matter at all. Why? Why spend time explaining why something is not important? Because even today in our modern and enlightened world, we still fall for the same old scams, cons, and traps. So here are a couple of items that many believe affect athletic performance or professional outcomes and what a little research does to either support or destroy them.

A 2009 Harris Poll determined that 26% of Americans believe in Astrology (with comparable numbers in Canada and the UK). More broadly, the astrology lexicon is pervasive. The majority of people today at least know their astrological sign based on their birthday, and probably a few vague attributes that the sign supposedly bestows on them. The Age of Aquarius (the 1960's and 70's in the US) may be over, but ask pretty much any person "what's your sign?" and you'll probably hear a zodiac symbol as a response.

Astrology is the notion that the location of the stars and planets at the time of a person's birth will define personality characteristics, long-term social and career paths, and even day-to-day events, personal interactions, and emotions. Astrology originates from ancient Babylon in the 2nd millennium BC, where people believed a pantheon of gods in the sky controlled different and specific aspects of life. The stars symbolized these heavenly beings and were a living connection to the mortals on earth. Understanding the cultural context in which this belief system formed is critical to understanding why it formed in the first placed. People have been looking at the sky for a really long time, and were already seasoned sky watchers during the early days of human civilization. The gods back then probably seemed pretty cruel, because it was such a high failure-rate environment. Child mortality around the globe was likely very high and surviving to puberty was a triumph. Death by disease, famine, and violence culled the weak, but also many of the strong. The randomness of one's demise intimidated the pattern-seeking brains that survived, daring them to crack the code of life and death. But without knowledge of genetics and germs, medicine and health were mostly superstition-based ceremonies with little positive effect on the patients, and frequent negative outcomes. The same mindset that developed elaborate yet meaningless rituals full of ineffectual "medicines" and barbaric procedures like bloodletting (a process of emptying someone's blood to get the sick out) also birthed everyday superstitions that prompted the need to *do something* about one's prospects in life, rather than to just let life and death *happen to you.*

Bud Light commercials keep insisting that "we'll never know if somehow, in some way, we can affect the outcome of a game," and that superstition is "only weird if it doesn't work." I disagree. You can't prove a negative (that rubbing a bald head isn't helping the field goal go in), but you sure can ignore the ridiculously implausible. Otherwise our lives would be overrun by expensive and futile attempts to give every superstition and charm a chance to work. That time, effort, wasted money, and mental bandwidth are among the burdens of irrationality. We're all smart enough to overcome superstition, but we're not all strong enough.

But since we're here and I have the data, let's give astrology a chance to work. Surely the characteristics anointed to you at birth by your zodiac symbols must include some for various physical attributes or aggressiveness that make some people better fighters than others. We could figure out which signs are the true-born fighters by grouping all UFC fighters by zodiac sign and checking their aggregate win rates for fights that had a winner and loser. Put your horoscope down, I did the math already and here are the results.

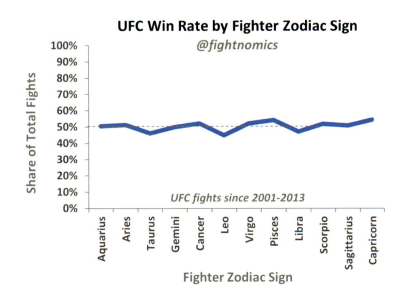

That's a pretty flat line, but there are a few rises and dips. The total mean of course is precisely 50%, but there's a peak of 54%, and a low of 45%. Those signs could be the winners and losers of the astrological lottery. The losers on the graph are fighters born under the Leo sign. The winners are, wait for it, Pisces. There it is. People born under the sign of the Fish are most likely to succeed in MMA, while those with the Lion sign are the biggest losers, which is weird, because we all know who would win between a lion and a fish. But wait! Sharks are technically fish, so maybe Renzo Gracie was right when he observed "a boxer is like a lion, the greatest predator on land. But you throw him in the shark tank and he's just another meal." BOOM! #mindblown. Another win for Gracie wisdom.

Can we call it then? Is the "Pisces Effect" in MMA the sneakiest way yet to hack the Tale of the Tape and predict who will win? No, of course not. First, those rises and dips are pretty small, and much smaller than numerous other reliable effects that we've discussed in this book already. The trend is even less meaningful when we remember our sample size gets cuts into twelfths. Not only do we have no reason to believe that astrology has any impact on human lives, let alone their specific performance in very specific athletic endeavors, **the analysis shows us exactly what we would expect if there was no relationship whatsoever**: a randomly bumpy line that is hugging the 50/50 threshold. There's also the problem that the experiment was set up to fail from the beginning. I'll explain.

Fishing for Pisces

A critical explanation of what we might call the "Pisces Effect" is that it's an example of statistical "fishing." Oh wow, see what I did there . . . I didn't even plan that. If we run an analysis of a random variable like birthdays and then look at win rates, there will always be some noise or volatility due to randomness. "Fishing" means we run a whole bunch of numbers and simply see which one we can catch, in this case looking for the biggest win rate. That Pisces fighters scored the highest win rate of 56% doesn't support the idea that this is a meaningful finding from a scientific standpoint. Rather, we threw our line in, pulled something and said "Aha! A Pisces! Check out the size of *this* fish!"

This happens all the time, and you've certainly seen the headlines for statistical fishing. One day a newspaper reports that caffeine causes cancer, and the next it reports that caffeine prevents cancer. Research results are reported all the time, but the media and their consumers are terrible at understanding the context of scientific findings. If a study is run where 1,000 people with a certain cancer are asked about their dietary habits, and lo and behold a majority of them are frequent consumers of coffee, we cannot properly conclude that coffee is the cause of that cancer. This was data fishing, not *hypothesis testing*, which is the truest and most brutal intellectual Octagon of them all. Scientists who really believed that coffee (or any other particular item) is the cause of a certain outcome must isolate for a variety of other influential factors, and then run a new test to pit their hypothesis in a cage fight with the null hypothesis (that the substance doesn't cause cancer). If the hypothesis survives, it advances to another round of larger and more elaborately controlled testing before we declare it a champion. If it fails, the initial study that fished for clues was probably suffering from the granddaddy of all logical fallacies, *post hoc ergo propter hoc.*

The *post hoc* logical fallacy literally translates into "after this, therefore because of this." You may have heard the rule that "correlation doesn't imply causation." It's the most frequently quoted phrase I hear in arguments where someone is harnessing their inner debate team. Actually, correlation *does* imply causation, it just doesn't *require* it. Two things that tend to happen together may be connected, or may not be. Humans are excellent at identifying these relationships, a driver of our evolution as a species to understand cause and effect on an intellectual level which spurred us to survive, adapt, learn, communicate, and advance. However, when the pattern we recognize is false, we have a hard time accepting that there is no real causation at work. Fishing for potential causes of wins falls into this trap. The only way to fight our way out is by sound, scientific hypothesis testing, which will determine if the pattern is real or just in our heads. In this case, we have no evidence that the location of distant constellations at birth can possibly affect anything going on here on earth, so it's hardly worth testing the idea to begin with. The gravitational pull of the doctor who delivered you is more powerful than the distant planets or stars. And weren't you born inside a hospital, shielded from the sky anyway?

When we run the analysis for fun, we lump all people all over the globe (billions!) into 12 very large buckets with a lot of randomness involved. The fact that there is some bounciness to the UFC win percentage line as it zooms across the list of zodiac symbols is expected. If we had alphabetized middle names of fighters, for example, and examined win percentages alphabetically we would have seen something similar. Some more frequently used letters in the alphabet might have led to large sample sizes, with more stable regression to the mean. On the other hand, a less common letter, randomly rare in MMA or otherwise, might have a smaller sample size and a lucky representative might skew the win rate. In fact, Pisces has a below-average sample size for the zodiac population, meaning the wins of Renan Barao, Jon Fitch, and Michael Bisping, who happen to be some of the most successful members of that birthday group, have a larger effect on the Pisces win rate. If we really wanted to test this idea, we'd first need a plausible mechanism for a certain zodiac sign to generate better fighters. We'd need a prediction based on this, and then new and independently verified data that confirms that this particular sign leads to a higher winning rate at a statistically significant level in order to even begin to conclude that astrology belongs on the Tale of the Tape. Suffice it to say, we don't have that, and it gets worse.

For a more focused test that could tease out a meaningful effect, I identified "stronger" and "weaker" signs based on popular interpretations of the zodiac. At the top of the strong list we got Ares and Taurus. The wimpiest sign was far and away Pisces. The second most cited "weak" sign was Capricorn. In the 91 instances where a strong sign fought a weak one, the result was a win rate of 50.5% for the astrological kickass group, and 49.5% for the zodiac weaklings. Not much difference, and actually a much closer statistical tie than many other factors we've looked at. It's exactly what we would expect if there was no relationship at all between the zodiac and real life. Your birthday may be important to predicting your performance in a fight, but that stops at the year of your birth (see: the "Youth Advantage"), with the particular day and its association with constellations not being of any importance. Cat's out of the bag now.

Whether or not you succeed in love, life, or the cage, does not depend on the time of your birth or the stars in the sky, but rather on more immediate inherent physical and mental attributes, as well as training, coaching, nutrition, and all the other things athletes require throughout their careers. Instead of thanking their lucky stars, fighters should give credit where credit is due: their own hard work and perseverance, their parents and genetics, their teams, coaches, and nutritionists, and maybe even their statistical consultants...ok, no one has thanked me yet, but it's coming. It's in my stars. If in the end you still disagree, just put your money where your horoscope is and I'll gladly take your bets.

Snake Oil in the Cage

All right, fine. I'll give you some credit. You're smart, and you haven't fallen for the old astrology scam since you were twelve years old. You're rational, skeptical even. You don't visit psychics, don't pay for palm readings, and almost never buy from late night infomercials selling the first device ever proven to quickly and painlessly spot-reduce belly fat! Not so fast. Not every scam artist shows up selling the same old shtick. Some of them bear the fruits of technology, which when combined with ancient superstitions turn into the kind of awesome secret power only ninjas and Jedi know about.

Let's consider some modern day snake oil that you may not have identified as such. The term "performance enhancement" can take many forms. Maybe it's as generic as referring to practice or weight training as performance enhancement. Exercising your technical skills or your muscle tissue will generally have the same effect: they get stronger. It's the beauty of the living system; we adapt. If you take a non-living object and bang on it, flex it repeatedly, stretch it out, it will get weaker and eventually break. Not so for the mostly hairless apes who inhabit fitness centers in every town. The more they flex their muscles, the stronger they get.

This is an oversimplification obviously, because it's a lot harder than it sounds. Due to the lofty ideals and standards for beauty that we set for ourselves thanks to modern marketing, humans are still constantly looking for an edge. Few activities exemplify the competitive drive that pushes people to do things they don't understand, or even to take dangerous risks they do understand, than sports. The sports world is rife with unethical pursuits of advantage, mostly of the biological and pharmaceutical variety, and it doesn't stop there. There are dubious ways to employ just about any science in sports, from simple equipment tricks, to biological enhancement, and even to psychological manipulation. Yet not all advantages are illegal. Many nutritional supplements and exercise technologies simply offer better-controlled and optimized routes to basic fitness and diet. Access to modern athletic facilities would amaze the athletes of a century ago, who despite dominance of their contemporaries, might not even be remotely competitive on today's courts, fields, and mats. The fruits of technology keep pushing the human form closer to its ideals, rewriting the record books every shot, sprint, and swing along the way.

Now there's a new, powerful performance enhancer that is currently legal for athletes. It costs less than a dollar to make; it's a small rubber bracelet with a hologram sticker that can enhance your performance in the gym, in life, and in competition. It boosts power and agility, making it a critical training asset for every athlete. Or so say the marketers of "Power Balance Performance Technology," who promise a broad range of performance-improving characteristics through their product line of $29.99 wristbands.

NBA all-stars and NFL Super Bowl MVPs have publicly endorsed these bracelets, and CNBC honored Power Balance as the "sports product of the year" in 2010. Carl Sagan popularized the rule that "extraordinary claims require extraordinary evidence," so let's dig deeper into Power Balance's magic.

Part of the sales pitch is that Power Balance taps into invisible energy fields flowing through all living things. If that sounds familiar, it's because Obi Wan Kenobi offered the exact same explanation for "the Force" to Luke Skywalker. This should make this pitch ridiculous to everyone except aspiring Jedi Knights, but it gets worse. The company's explanation for how an invisible, undetectable, and immeasurable force can possibly be real and affect human athletic performance is that the technology is based on the same principles as those behind acupuncture and Feng Shui. This particular lapse in logic is called the "Argument from Antiquity." Just because a practice or idea is old, doesn't mean there's evidence to support it. Ancient superstitions come in all flavors, but only a sucker assumes that tradition equates to efficacy [see also: human sacrifice].

Image used with permission of the James Randi Educational Foundation

Those examples of corroboration should sound fishy for another reason. The claims of acupuncture and Feng Shui are both modern residuals of superstitious attempts to explain how the world and the human body work. The existence of "Qi" sounded like a reasonable explanation before modern physics, chemistry, and biology, but it never holds up under close inspection. While rearranging your furniture to be in balance with the universe may sound like harmless fun, acupuncture has been proven to be an expensive and occasionally dangerous placebo effect, which is the real Power Balance conduit.

Magic jewelry aficionados may believe that they feel different just because they think they're supposed to, but our human tendency to conform to expectations and even self-delude are not evidence for technological claims. The placebo effect is strong, and also predictably limited. "Ionic" bracelets don't have a power source or any other design characteristics that would enable them to impact human physiology in any meaningful way. It literally can't *do* anything other than sit there. Any perceived effect is just in our heads.

Snake oil cure-alls of the 19th century have been pushed aside by modern science and improving pharmacology, but when it comes to unquantifiable "performance enhancement," the 21st century has resurrected the smooth-talking salesmen of yesteryear. They've replaced exotic herbs and animal products with technical jargon that fraudulently insinuates cutting edge innovations. The marketing bells, whistles, and even parlor tricks are all the same. In the case of Power Balance, an in-person demonstration at sports expositions can be quite a production, but in the end it's just a trick.

Despite all the hype and awards, several real research studies were done on the bracelets in what was the scientific researcher's equivalent of a parent looking under the bed to make sure there are no monsters. There was probably a long sigh, some rolling of the eyes, then they tested the claim and said "See? What did I tell you? There's nothing there! Now stop being ridiculous…." The two published studies both reached the same, very simple conclusion: **holographic bracelets do not improve strength, flexibility, or balance**. A deluge of more casual experiments reached the same conclusion, often resulting is a stumped salesmen searching for excuses as to why it stopped working. The trick in those experiments (or the anti-trick) was simply to blind the salesman from knowing if it was a real bracelet or a placebo. Voila, the effect vanished.

This story isn't new. I've seen highly educated friends explain to me how their new magnetic bracelet is going to improve their golf swing. Here's how to spot sports scams before they steal your dollars. If a company can't answer "Yes" to all these questions, it doesn't deserve your time or money.

- Is there a plausible cause and effect for the product and its claims?
- Are the claims reasonable, clearly defined, and easily measured?
- Do they use accepted performance measurements, avoiding scam jargon like "ionic, quantum, and energy fields?"
- Does the product emphasize research published in *established* scientific literature with numerous, corroborating studies, rather than rely on celebrity endorsements?

At the 2010 UFC Fan Expo, Power Balance made a concerted effort to capture the MMA market demographic with UFC-branded products. But executives within Zuffa pushed back, suggesting their products were bunk. After a commanding presence at prior UFC expos, Power Balance was notably absent at the summer gathering of 2013, and one way or another UFC-branded bracelets never made it to market. Unfortunately, the same cannot be said for the more influential NBA or MLB although I will credit Mark Cuban for making the Dallas Mavericks one of the few teams not to buy into the hype and vocally denying the claims of bracelet salesman.

Just because Power Balance is no longer an official sponsor of UFC fighters, that hasn't stopped other new-age scam artists from pursuing the MMA audience. This year's UFC Fan Expo featured a booth selling $60 "quantum necklaces" that make similar claims. Their necklaces allegedly vibrate at special frequencies (not true) that instantly interact with your blood (not even possible) to align your aura (which doesn't exist) to "enhance strength and balance" (sound familiar?). Like energy bracelets, the phrase "a sucker born every minute" is painted in invisible homeopathic ink on the lining. It's true, I swear. Try to prove me wrong.

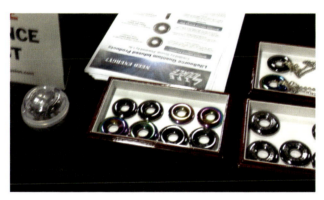

2013 UFC Fan Expo booth selling "Quantum Necklaces." What? Quantum? You keep using that word. I do not think it means what you think it means....

Because jewelry can't be worn during MMA competition, the quantum necklace salesmen created oil that can be applied to the skin to replicate the benefits. Just a drop of oil is all it takes to go from Average Joe to MMA Champ in seconds, and the salesmen confided that many UFC fighters and trainers were interested in their product. Modern day scam artists have brought us full circle back to the days of magical snake oil.

As for Power Balance, despite lawsuits and admission of their false claims, they're still allowed to sell their product in the United States. It's harder down in Australia where proactive citizens applied pressure and Power Balance has been forced to admit to fraud and issue a public apology for lying. The statement on their Australian website read: "We admit that there is no credible scientific evidence that supports our claims and therefore we engaged in misleading conduct in breach of s52 of the Trade Practices Act 1974." They offered full refunds. Internet searches from other countries, however, would not see that admission of guilt thanks to lax laws that actually allow "harmless" claims that are misleading. That includes the US, which no doubt was (and still is) a primary market.

That's not the justice-served ending we'd get from a movie version of this myth-busting investigation, and Power Balance is still laughing all the way to the bank. In all it has grossed nearly $100 million in sales just by selling toy stickers that do absolutely nothing at all. Not a bad haul. We can chalk up the fortunes made by scam product creators as an "idiot tax" on society, or we can educate ourselves to not fall prey to them in the future. Then at least we've gained some value from this whole fiasco. Remember, there's a large marketplace out there after your hard-earned dollar, far more than you could ever afford. It's okay to be skeptical. Critical thinking and little bit of science is all you need to avoid getting ripped off and colorfully showcasing your gullibility with an expensive, not-so-magical bracelet.

The days of bombarding the MMA world with a bad-ass, t-shirt brand-of-the-week are over. The new wave of products is crashing ashore, and they are claiming to bear the fruits of science and technology. From mouth guards that will make you impervious to knockouts, to masks that promise altitude training simulation at ground level, to a maelstrom of flash-in-the-pan dietary supplements, there are tons of claims being thrown around that are likely strong on marketing promises, but weak on science. Do the diligence, isolate their claims, and think objectively and rationally about them, looking for direct tests of the claims whenever possible. Of the many products out on the market that do NOT deserve your money, which ones will you be able to spot? You'll pay the price for each one you can't.

In short, there will always be people with "more dollars than sense." And there will always be someone there to sell them a "secret" and take their money. Unfortunately, the secret is always the same: "you're a sucker." The next time you find yourself considering new athletic equipment, do your research first!

14 Deciphering the Fightnomics "Uber Tale of the Tape"

"Showdown" Joe Ferraro is quite a character. A TV and radio personality and host of Canada's "UFC Central" show, Joe was the very first MMA media interview I ever did. During our conversation about the basics of the Tale of the Tape we talked a little about why it's unfortunate that we continue to use the same metrics that MMA inherited from boxing. The sport has its own identity yet still languishes under the yoke of boxing's ox collar in many ways. Aside from being on the vanguard of recognizing the value of MMA analytics, Joe is also a licensed MMA referee, judge, and promoter, which collectively influences his uniquely informed opinion about the sport and how it's presented to audiences. During that fateful interview he challenged me on what variables I would suggest including on some sort of "new and improved Tale of the Tape." So I set out to assemble something that would harness the great deal of information we have on fighters based on their prior performance and try to package it in (nearly) as small a Tale of the Tape.

The tool I have created to help me understand UFC matchups more succinctly, yet also more informatively, is what I call my "Uber Tale of the Tape." While we've already seen that the traditional Tale of the Tape can offer some clues into the context of a certain matchup, the Uber tape was a happy middle ground of additional performance metrics boiled down from a much larger list of variables that I crunch prior to every UFC event. Über is a German prefix meaning a superlative example of something. We can attach this prefix to a word or phrase to mean a version that is better, the best, or above and beyond the norm. Those of you following @fightnomics on Twitter or read my matchup analysis articles online will recognize this graphic immediately, but you may still have questions about some of the variables that I show. Here's an example that I will walk through in detail that will help clarify a common tool that offers additional insight into each fight that you can see on the TV screen.

Fightnomics: Uber Tale of the Tape		Michael McDonald	Brad Pickett
BIO	Last Fight Weight Class	BW	BW
	Age at Fight Date	✔ 22.6	✘ 34.9
	Height	69	66
	Reach	✔ 70	✘ 68
	Stance	Orthodox	Orthodox
	Analyzed Minutes	56 Mins	102 Mins
Standup Striking Offense	Knockdown Ratio (Total Scored : Received)	4 : 0	2 : 2
	Distance Knockdown Rate	✔ 10.0%	✘ 1.8%
	Head Jab Accuracy	✔ 43%	✘ 22%
	Head Power Accuracy	✔ 23%	✔ 23%
	Total Standup Strike Ratio	✔ 1.05	✘ 0.95
Striking Defense	Total Head Strike Defense	✔ 71%	✘ 67%
	Distance Knockdown Defense ("Chin")	✔ 100%	✘ 99%
Significant Striking	Significant Strikes Attempted per Minute	✘ 6.5	✔ 11.0
	Significant Strike Accuracy	✔ 40%	✘ 32%
The Ground Game	Takedown Attempts per 5 Minute Round	✘ 0.7	✔ 1.8
	Takedown Accuracy	✔ 75%	✘ 57%
	Opponent Takedown Atts	✘ 16	✔ 27
	Takedown Defense	✔ 63%	✔ 63%
	Share of Total Ground Time in Control	✘ 39%	✔ 73%
	Sub Attempts per Trip to Ground	✔ 0.33	✘ 0.16

Analysis revealed lots of performance advantages for Michael McDonald over Brad Pickett when they fought at the debut of the UFC on FOX Sports 1 in August of 2013. McDonald won by submission after dominating the standup striking and knocking Pickett down twice.

The "Bio" portion of the Uber Tape supplements some of the traditional information with the addition of the fighting stance. Since the Southpaw Advantage is real, it's important to note in a matchup especially if an orthodox stance fighter is inexperienced. The bottom of the Bio section shows how many minutes of analysis went into these metrics. Data usually includes all UFC, WEC and Strikeforce fighters. Although FightMetric quantified some additional fights from other promotions in their database, I exclude these due to less consistent matchmaking, lesser competition, occasionally differing rules, and usually the fact that they took place a long time ago. The Analyzed Minutes therefore demonstrate two important things. First, it shows how much experience the fighter has competing at a high level, and second, it shows how big the sample size is for the rest of the Uber Tape. The more minutes of data we have, the more confidently we can draw conclusions about the relative strengths and weaknesses of each fighter. Small sample sizes mean the data can be skewed heavily by a single fight, which may have been against a much tougher or easier opponent, causing the metrics to sway accordingly. Usually, a few recent fights are all we need to understand the tendencies and relative skills of a fighter.

Fightnomics: Uber Tale of the Tape		Michael McDonald	Brad Pickett
BIO	Last Fight Weight Class	BW	BW
	Age at Fight Date	✓ 22.6	✗ 34.9
	Height	69	66
	Reach	✓ 70	✗ 68
	Stance	Orthodox	Orthodox
	Analyzed Minutes	56 Mins	102 Mins

In the Bio section, I only marked two variables to demonstrate advantages: age and reach. We've already seen that height alone does not carry much of an advantage, unless it also comes with reach. And we've also seen how critical age is for MMA. So these two metrics have been scored with a check mark or "X" to indicate which fighter has an inherent advantage or disadvantage, respectively. If one fighter was a Southpaw it would be listed, but not scored because it's not a quantitative value. Such are the limitations of my off-the-shelf charting tools. We're also limited to just the data that the UFC reports, although it's certainly possible that new metrics like "leg reach" could come to market soon.

The next level on the Uber Tape is Standup Striking Offense, and these five metrics summarize the key performance variables that allow you to assess a fighter's striking abilities. The first value is a ratio of the total number of knockdowns scored to the number of knockdowns received (a glass jaw disposition). Great strikers have a much higher first number, and a minimal second number. This is also a hint to identifying fighters who have suffered some knockdowns, and who are therefore at increased risk of going down early. The next value is the Distance Knockdown Rate, which normalizes the punch-for-punch power for each fighter. As we covered in Chapter 3, Knockdown Rate measures how many distance knockdowns were scored divided by how many landed power head strikes it took to score them. It tracks who does more damage per strike. This value can be compared directly to other fighters or to their weight class to get a relative indication of how powerful a striker is, or just how good he is at finding the vulnerabilities of his opponents in causing knockdowns. It's even more telling when one fighter shows up as well above average while the other is below, as is the case in this matchup example.

Further down we assess the accuracy of each fighter in terms of distance head striking. I've broken out jabs and power strikes separately because many fighters will perform differently depending on the strike's strength. This allows us to differentiate fighters with a great jab but poor power striking from others who use a lazy jab only to set up their precise power hand. The overall averages for these metrics are 28% for jabs and 24% for power head strikes, but remember they do vary slightly by weight class.

Last in the category is the Standup Strike Ratio. Regardless of what type of strike is thrown at whatever target, I'm interested in knowing the total volume of standup strikes a fighter throws compared to his opponents on average. A number of 1.0 indicates a completely even ratio and represents a fighter who exactly matches the pace of his opponent. Ratios higher than 1.0 identify fighters who tend to outwork their opponents and likely have more effective cage control. Fighters with a ratio of less than 1.0 tend to get outworked by their opponents, and are on the receiving end of more strikes than they are able to throw themselves. This is a supporting metric for the "Pace Advantage."

The Striking Defense metrics combine all distance head strikes to show what percentage is avoided by the fighter. A higher number means fewer strikes get through. Defense is calculated as one minus the accuracy of opponent head strikes. The same goes for the "Chin" calculation, which is one minus the Knockdown Rate of opponents for a certain fighter. Generally, you should see good fighters showing better accuracy and power than their opponents while fighters with poor accuracy and low defense probably won't last long in the UFC.

The last striking metrics show Significant Strikes Attempted per Minute and the overall Significant Strike Accuracy. This metric was detailed in Chapter 3 and is an aggregated metric for strikes that are potentially important in a fight, rather than just superficial. While it's true that great strikers will tend to have a good Significant Strike Accuracy, that number can be heavily influenced by how much time the fighter spends in positions with higher success rates for strikes, or for fighters who mix in a lot of body and leg strikes, which have higher accuracy than head strikes alone. The average for the UFC is 6.8 attempts per minute with a success rate of 41%. Generally, I look at pace more than accuracy to find high output fighters, but because accuracy is often quoted in UFC broadcasts I keep it on the Uber Tape for reference.

Fightnomics: Uber Tale of the Tape		Michael McDonald	Brad Pickett
Standup Striking Offense	Knockdown Ratio (Total Scored : Received)	4 : 0	2 : 2
	Distance Knockdown Rate	✔ 10.0%	✘ 1.8%
	Head Jab Accuracy	✔ 43%	✘ 22%
	Head Power Accuracy	✔ 23%	✔ 23%
	Total Standup Strike Ratio	✔ 1.05	✘ 0.95
Striking Defense	Total Head Strike Defense	✔ 71%	✘ 67%
	Distance Knockdown Defense ("Chin")	✔ 100%	✘ 99%
Significant Striking	Significant Strikes Attempted per Minute	✘ 6.5	✔ 11.0
	Significant Strike Accuracy	✔ 40%	✘ 32%

It was clear when looking at this matchup that McDonald (on the left) has some advantages in the standup game over Pickett (on the right). Most importantly, McDonald's Knockdown Rate is over three times the Bantamweight average. Combined with Pickett's suspect chin, McDonald went on to score two different knockdowns in the first round of this fight. The one metric that favored Pickett was still revealing in this instance. His high average rate of Significant Strikes Attempted per minute indicated he is a fighter who likes to press the action. And despite being on the losing end of most exchanges, Pickett fought with admirable bravery and a frenetic pace, which helped earn both fighters the Fight of the Night Bonus. Remember the rule about the Pace Advantage: having high pace is good, but having low pace is terrible. In this matchup Pickett did have the higher pace, but McDonald was safely in the middle group in terms of his own pace, and so was not at too much risk.

The last category on the Uber Tape encompasses a lot of variables that are key parts of the Ground Game. The first area is takedowns. The Takedown Attempt rate shows how often a fighter attempts takedowns, while the success rate indicates how often they achieve them. That's fairly straightforward. In the UFC the average number of takedowns attempted by a fighter per five-minute round is 1.5, with an overall success rate of 40%. Looking at the Uber Tape can tell us which fighter is more likely to try to get the fight to the ground, and also who is more likely to succeed.

Below that, Takedown Defense is calculated as one minus the success rate for opponent takedowns, or the percentage that a fighter has successfully defended when facing takedowns. Great wrestlers don't always have high offensive takedown success rates due to the frequency with which they make attempts and the fact that their opponents are expecting them. But the best wrestlers in MMA often show very high Takedown Success values. Because the average success rate for takedowns is 40%, that means 60% is the UFC benchmark for takedown defense. The other metric shows how many actual takedowns a fighter has faced inside the Octagon to give some level of fidelity to their takedown metric. Seeing a Defense metric of 100% is less meaningful if they've only faced two takedowns. That's like saying a pitcher is undefeated after only one win. Similarly, seasoned veterans may learn from experience and improve their defense over time.

Second from the bottom is a critical metric for understanding the grappling tendencies of a fighter: the Share of Ground Time in Control. Using the Time In Position (TIP) data from FightMetric, I rolled up aggregated data for every UFC fighter and calculated what percentage of time spent on the ground was in a position of dominance. The UFC average must be 50%, so any fighter above that threshold has been more likely than not to be in ground control. That leads to the final metric, Submission Attempts per Trip to Ground. I know, I know, fighters can attempt submissions while standing too, but most either occur on the ground, or lead to a grounded position eventually. The alternative metric was submission attempts per minute of fight time, but the value would be skewed by how much time was spent in various positions. Many fights don't see any submission attempts because the two fighters stand and trade for the entire three rounds. Generally, active submission artists will show up either way and so I've included the metric regardless of its imperfection, and in this particular matchup, the metric still proved to be prophetic.

Fightnomics: Uber Tale of the Tape		Michael McDonald	Brad Pickett
The Ground Game	Takedown Attempts per 5 Minute Round	✖ 0.7	✔ 1.8
	Takedown Accuracy	✔ 75%	✖ 57%
	Opponent Takedown Atts	✖ 16	✔ 27
	Takedown Defense	✔ 63%	✔ 63%
	Share of Total Ground Time in Control	✖ 39%	✔ 73%
	Sub Attempts per Trip to Ground	✔ 0.33	✖ 0.16

Despite Pickett's higher pace of takedown attempts, McDonald was evenly matched with slightly better than average takedown defense, and good offense of his own. One differentiator was the ground control stat, which suggested Pickett was much more likely to end up in top control and work from the top. On the flipside, it was McDonald who was more than twice as likely to attempt a submission if they ended up on the ground. After dominating the standup game McDonald did end up on his back, but then used the position to sink in a triangle choke that ended the fight in the second round and earned him a Submission of the Night bonus.

The betting lines at 5Dimes.com opened at -215 for McDonald, making him a clear, but not huge favorite in the matchup. By the time the fight began the market had pushed the moneyline odds to -320, boosting his implied win probability from 68% to 76%. The market had the right hunch in this case, but understanding the big advantages that McDonald had in the fight would have presented a lot of value for bettors when the moneyline was released, and in my opinion even on fight night.

And that's the Uber Tale of the Tape. In this case, my Uber Tape revealed overall anthropometric and performance metric advantages in the McDonald-Pickett matchup, enough to prompt me to write a short matchup analysis and prediction of McDonald winning inside the distance, all the way down to foreseeing a Fight of the Night bonus (cha-ching). The "Tale" isn't always so compelling a story. Often fighters are very evenly matched, or advantages for one are offset by advantages of the other. Such is the nature of a competitive environment. Even in this case, despite the seemingly lopsided nature of the matchup, Pickett was by no means out of the fight. Any fighter worth a roster spot in the UFC is a highly trained athlete capable of hurting his or her opponent in a flash. That's why we watch – anything can happen on any given fight night.

There's No Such thing as a Fair Fight

Contrary to popular belief, stars don't align, but the stats sometimes do. Watch out for Uber Tape on high profile matchups when they are announced and again leading up to the fight. From these numbers, we can usually glean a few hints as to who might have the advantage, and how the fight might play out. There's no such thing as a fair fight, because no two fighters are identical in their genetic and experiential profiles. Understanding the particulars of how each fighter is different makes the contest more interesting by spotlighting likely battlegrounds within the fight itself. They can also be used to understand the context of who should be favored, and therefore also better appreciate surprising performances.

As technology and time progress, the metrics we analyze will evolve much like the sport itself, and we can look deeper into each matchup to better understand fighters and the sport. As with many other places in this book, I expect that this section too will become outdated. I won't be sad; progress is a good thing. Soon enough pre-fight analysis for blockbuster MMA matchups will include information that fight fans of yesteryear never dreamed of. Analysis of MMA statistics will provide increasingly valuable insight into how fights go down and what fans should be watching for as they do. Understanding any given subject matter only makes the appreciation of it more fulfilling. With each landed jab, arm bar attempt, or slam on a shooting takedown, spectators should appreciate the subtle and skillful demonstrations that occur each second in the cage, because during any of those seconds anyone can win.

 The Future of MMA: The Last & Greatest Combat Sport

MMA Killed the Kung Fu Star

Martial Arts have frequently been caricatured on movie screens and mass manufactured in McDojos across every town, both by the purists who wish to preserve them and the profiteers who know a good cash cow when they see one. As recently as 20 years ago martial arts still carried the mystique of harboring a magical Secret, the kind you might find in a book recommended by Oprah Winfrey. Practitioners of every combat art discipline were confident that their traditions and skills were the best and everyone else's was inferior. There were "five-fingered death punches," no-touch knockouts, Chi-anchoring, Tiger paw backflips, cobra strikes, crane kicks, and the belief that one fast-moving striker could defeat an army of combat-trained fighters. It wasn't just the stuff of legend, it fueled the dreams of every 10-year old kid bursting with energy and aspirations of heroism. As one of those kids in the late-1980's I probably rented every VHS tape available with the word "ninja" in it, succumbing to the allure of martial arts legends portrayed by Sonny Chiba and Bruce Lee. It didn't take long for fans like me to yearn to see martial arts masters leap from the movie screen to the sports arena, any arena, for a chance to see their lightning-fast strikes and acrobatic feats of violence destroy evil doers "for real."

But a funny thing happened on the way to the pay-per-view market: a science experiment. The promoters and participants of the first Ultimate Fighting Championships conducted an experiment so simple I would call it "elegant" if I didn't worry it might cause John McCain to risk a myocardial infarction. The science that occurred on November 12th, 1993 in front of 2,800 live guests and approximately 86,000 pay-per-view households was not lost on many. A lanky, awkward Brazilian guy worked his way through a field of highly trained (and far more intimidating) fighters, forcing his will on all three and manipulating them into excruciating submissions in a grand total of five minutes and one second of fight time. It should have taken even less time, honestly, as referee Joao Alberto Barreto failed to save several of Gracie's opponents in a timely manner. Strikes landed with dull thuds instead of theatrical slaps. Contests were bloody, sweaty, body-on-body confrontations that contained none of the crisp and decisive striking combinations of movie kung fu artists. It was gritty, it was in your face, and it was the realest fighting most people had ever seen.

The stunned audience, dressed in Saturday night's best instead of white lab coats, was able to observe science in action and reach a collective conclusion. Brazilian Jiu Jitsu made a claim about being the best hand-to-hand combat system on Earth and on that night, under those circumstances, the hypothesis could not be rejected. Don't let the sciency subtlety of that statement misrepresent the awesomeness of what transpired. It was a historic chapter in the world of sports and competition. There were probably high fives among all the BJJ and grappling aficionados while the fans of the other martial arts and plenty of casual observers were stunned into disbelief. The cage proved to be a brutally honest test-tube for fighting, unforgiving of hype or arrogance, "Qi" or tradition. Effectiveness ruled and there could be only one winner. With one painful surrender after another, the Gracies killed the mystique of the kung fu star.

The Science of the Circus: Why UFC Shows Are So Thrilling

One cannot argue with the meteoric success of the UFC as a business, and any two-million dollar investment that turns into a multi-billion dollar global juggernaut is worth a closer look for any lessons that could be replicated. The UFC is an entertainment business and the primary product that it sells is fights. But long before Zuffa rolled out a diverse product line of UFC-related programming, it first had to put on one hell of a show on fight night.

The early years of fighting in an Octagon were primitive by today's standards. The original design plans by its founders included a moat around the cage filled with alligators to maximize the level of extremeness of the spectacle. Today, a live UFC show is slick, polished, and efficient, while the televised broadcast represents the cutting edge of modern sports programming. Underneath all these bright lights and fancy on-screen graphics there is some basic science at work that ensures the UFC audience is entertained on fight night. The principles have been tested by time (as well as by researchers and the market) and are employed by leading entertainment entities. The UFC actually has just as much in common with a circus, an amusement park, or a cruise ship as it does with mainstream team sports leagues.

The science behind putting on an exciting show is simple when we consider the underlying psychology of human excitement. Given the logistical complexity of an

MMA event, getting fans as invested as possible into each event, then maximizing stimulation while minimizing boredom is paramount to success. Here are a few hidden forces at work to be on the watch for the next time you attend or watch a UFC event.

- **Excitement:** people love watching sports and movies because it gives them a chance to dream in public. Vicariously experiencing something that is high-stakes, thrilling, and above and beyond the normal ingredients of everyday life (especially if it's taboo), while not taking those risks ourselves, stimulates our brains and bodies. The proverbial adrenaline junkie is simply someone who is especially sensitive to these swings. With well-organized and well-timed manipulations of this effect, any savvy entertainer can create a thrilling and memorable experience for the audience. Especially fighters.

- **The Pre-Fight Montage:** attending live UFC events means being treated to the ultimate highlight reel set to "Baba O'Riley" by The Who just before the main card goes live. The video is so dramatic and inspiring, the crowd always responds with exuberant applause. The montage transitions right into the opening credits for the main card, another musical compilation of highlights that is synchronized with the sweeping crowd shots of the broadcast's introduction.

- **Context:** it's important to provide fans with context in order for them to get the most out of what they see. Recently the UFC introduced rankings, and much more recently, the betting odds. The average fan may not know many fighter names beyond the top matchups at an event, but giving a hint that a fighter is highly ranked or that he is an underdog allows fans to better appreciate what they're watching. They think, "well that makes sense, he's a highly ranked favorite who won, I'd better keep an eye on him." Or possibly "hey, that underdog just beat a ranked contender; I just witnessed something rare."

- **Personal Connection:** immediately prior to each UFC matchup, the audience sees interview footage of the fighters, building a connection to the people about to step in the cage. Humans can decide whether they like or dislike someone in just seconds (just ask anyone who has ever been on a blind date), and thus short video clips of people talking are all that's needed to pick a side, even between two people who were completely unknown to you.

- **Vested Interest:** the more fans know and care about the fighter about to compete, the more intense the experience will be of watching him fight. As much as possible, pre-fight marketing will try to give you a storyline to follow, like an underdog with a puncher's chance, a battle between bitter rivals, or a changing of the guard matchup. If you don't care about the fight before it starts, chances are high that you won't remember it after it's over. A basic truth of any form of entertainment is that people are interested in people who overcome obstacles, so this is a surefire way to get you invested in the fighters.

- **Rivalry:** few things accentuate sports like rivalry. Leading up to every fight, every taunting tweet, brash press conference prediction, and especially face-to-face aggression gets replayed constantly. Although MMA is an athletic competition, just like in any other sport a little direct antagonism goes a long way towards making a contest compelling. The fighters used to date the same girl and they hate each other now? Hell yeah, I'm watching.

- **Saturday Night Fight Night:** the vast majority of UFC events take place on Saturday night, a time when most people are already primed to enjoy themselves. As much as possible, the UFC wants you to feel as though it's a special evening. You'll be more psychologically primed to have fun and get excited for anything on a Saturday night, which is another reason you should never schedule a first date on a Monday.

- **Ring Card Girls:** sexual cues arouse the senses of a predominantly male audience (no. . . really), and that's where Ring Girls come in. A man's mind and body often cannot distinguish between the various forms of arousal stimuli, occasionally being sexually excited simply through thrilling (but non-sexual) experiences. The opposite is also true; "eye candy" can add to the physiological excitement of the moment, and even prime the male brain for more risk-seeking behavior. Men are essentially more open to extreme physical acts in the presence of attractive women. No fight night would be complete without manipulating this trusty old trick.

- **Lights:** the atmosphere at a live UFC event can feel like a dance club, or even a rock concert. The fun and excitement of fight night is accentuated by an environment that feels like other places where you've had a great time. A dim ambient arena with lots of colorful and flashing lights will immediately make you feel like you just arrived at a huge party.

- **Music:** the in-house DJ at UFC shows let no moment between fights go unfilled. While our eyes have plenty to occupy them, our ears also get a heavy dose of the party spirit on fight night. The official UFC DJ is Albert Lineses, III, a VIP and award-winning DJ who once set a world record by mixing a live show for 66-consecutive hours. His always unique and up-beat mash ups frequently have people dancing in the aisles between fights and make sure that even after lulls in the cage, the party keeps going.

- **The Voice of the Octagon:** whipping you into a state of excitement is Bruce Buffer, the cage announcer famous for his intense and inspiring fighter introductions. The crowd loves Bruce and his catch phrases are now a chorus line for the arena of loyal fans who get an added rush of excitement with the announcement of each name, the declaration of main card, and finally the main event. Even when you are excited already, you can always go higher – and Bruce tells you exactly when "it's time!"

- **The Psychology of Waits:** minimizing the down-time during events is a multi-faceted risk management process. When fights end quickly, empty space opens in the time schedule for the event, requiring the UFC to ensure that fans don't get too bored or restless as to remember these "lows" more than the "highs" of the evening. Fortunately, they have a variety of tools at their disposal to keep viewers occupied and entertained, like video previews of upcoming events, Ring Card Girls, loud music, and a roving camera to show celebrities in the audience. Disney has this down to a science to minimize the perceived wait time in lines for rides. The UFC should employ a few more tricks, but they've made good progress.

- **Peak-End Theory:** when recalling experiential memories, we tend to focus on the most memorable moments (peaks) and the final moments (end), judging the overall experience primarily by these limited factors. The most important fights are always last in the evening, and the UFC hopes at least one fight earlier on the main card will be an on-your-feet memorable slobber knocker or spectacular finish that will give you more than one thing to tell your friends about.

There's a lot going on in the fight night environment, a symphony of elements tweaked and perfected over time in order to maximize the objectives of the entertainment system. It's come a long way to get here, but just imagine where it will be in another 20 years.

The Future of MMA

Now that MMA has worldwide recognition, it will likely grow to outshine all other combat sports. It's only a matter of time. The powerful combination of universal rules and the widespread cultural appreciation of competitive fighting equates to a truly global combat sport. It doesn't take a lot of theatrics either. If a fight is on TV and it's being broadcast in Mongolese, it doesn't matter. It's a fight and you want to watch it no matter what language it's in. You can mute the TV and still enjoy it. Soccer is perhaps the world's most popular sport, with no signs of losing ground. Many other major sports, however, see a great deal of localized variance in popularity. Individual sports like golf, tennis, track and field, or even race car driving allow for athletes from any country to enter the global stage, but the audience for these sports is still dispersed. Even more fragmented are national sports of small countries like lacrosse or volleyball. The regional aspect of combat sports before the dawn of MMA created a commercialization nightmare. There was demand for combat sports in underserved markets, but having a single product to market globally was impossible. Not anymore.

What the UFC has accomplished in modernizing and popularizing a universal combat sport has raised the bar immeasurably for the business of fighting and we haven't yet approached the maximum potential. Not until the UFC has fully penetrated the large markets of China, India, Russia, Indonesia, Mexico and the Philippines (to name a few) will we begin to understand how big MMA can be. Despite signs of saturation in core markets like the US, the UFC now has a mature and robust product line to take to new geographies inclined to combat sports tradition and loaded with fresh talent. While we're on the subject of speculating about the future of the sport, let's consider a few last scientific and analytical potentialities for MMA.

Octagon Genetics

As part of the perpetual arms race of athletic competition, natural selection and technology will both intervene to improve the athletic suitability of fighters entering the Octagon. Fighters will continue to "grow" within their weight classes for the foreseeable future to the point where anyone the size of Kenny Florian wouldn't even think of competing at welterweight, let alone middleweight. The wingspan to height ratio will drift ever upward as less rangy fighters get filtered out by larger fighters of equivalent skill. All along the way athletes will learn to optimize every ounce of body mass they take with them to the scales on weigh-in day.

Knockout resiliency will also improve, which may slightly reduce the knockdown rates over the long term. Punch-for-punch and pound-for-pound, knockdown rates have already declined significantly in the UFC since the slugger's heyday of 2005. Athletes newer to the sport are spending less time competing in the unregulated no-holds-barred fights of yesteryear. The next generation of athletes will be cross-trained, with no long history of underground fights or even legitimate boxing records to contribute to their cumulative brain damage score. Fighters will also be better informed about the implications of inadequate recovery time for head injuries and rules and regulations will continue to trend towards greater safety for all athletes. Don't be surprised if genetic testing is utilized by the MMA promotions of the future to identify fighters at increased risk of brain trauma due to concussions, if for no other reason than to allow them to make more informed choices in their own lives.

Consider the conundrum documented in David Epstein's "The Sports Gene." NBA player Eddie Curry was discovered to have an irregular heartbeat while playing for the Bulls in 2005, one that could be caused by the same genetic condition that contributed to the on-court deaths of Hank Gathers in 1990 and Celtics small-forward Reggie Lewis in 1993. In contract negotiations, the Bulls included a contract clause for genetic testing, whereby if Curry was identified to have a feared genetic heart disease, he would not be allowed to play ball but would receive $400,000 annually for fifty years. That's $20 million not to play basketball. Some might consider an offer like that as having hit the lottery, but Curry rejected the contract and was promptly traded. Eight years later after an up and then down NBA career that included financial troubles, he now plays for a Chinese Basketball Association team at the age of 30, but hasn't suffered any notable heart problems.

The ApoE4 variant gene1 appears to be a driver of some athlete's more severe symptoms, longer recovery periods, and greater long-term impairment from concussions. It's also a key factor in the development of Alzheimer's disease. As the cost of genetic testing plummets and the actionability of tests soar thanks to new scientific research, young athletes being informed of major risk factors may never play certain sports to begin with. A more durable breed of fighter that is more genetically predisposed to full contact competition may be worse for highlight reels (because the likelihood of a KO is lessened), but better for everyone involved in the sport, especially themselves. Although no death has ever resulted from a UFC fight, the possibility of such a catastrophe remains a real threat to athletes and the sport as a whole. Risk is often quantified as the product of impact and likelihood. It certainly appears that the UFC has excellent controls in place to prevent fighters from competing with any health complications that would increase the likelihood of a head trauma resulting in death, but the impact of such an event is so high that the risk is material.

Similarly, other genes have been identified as leading to increased risk of ligament damage. For an aspiring NFL running back, an increased risk of tearing an anterior cruciate ligament could spell career disaster. Certain mutations of the COL1A1 gene adversely affect the collagen fibrils that make up connective tissue like ligaments and tendons, making them more fragile and susceptible to injury. If this is the Grappler's Kryptonite Gene, then mutations of COL5A1 or COL3A1 could lead to a Grappler's Savior Gene. Mutations in this family of gene can cause Ehlers-Danlos syndrome, a disorder resulting in super-stretchy tissue that allows for hyper-mobility, and extreme contortionism. If Gumby were a real person, he probably suffered from Ehlers-Danlos. Unfortunately, the syndrome comes along with a variety of severe downsides that precludes high-level athleticism and probably fame as a submission-defying escape artist. It's certainly within reason, however, to believe that some individuals have genes making their ligaments and muscle tissue more resilient to extreme stress, thus enabling an athlete to be more durable in MMA competition. Genetic screens might identify these individuals at a young age.

Either way, the increasing awareness and mapping of genetic factors to physical characteristics as they pertain to athletic performance certainly boosts the potential that diagnostics may identify future participants who may be more or less accurately matched to certain sports. All of these forces will likely increase the specialization of athletes within their best-suited pursuits such that the overall bar of competition will continuously rise.

When Good Genes Aren't Good Enough

The harder issue looming for future athletes is how to handle individuals who wish to overcome their genetics. Consider a fighter born with pronounced brow ridges on the bones of the face. If the ridges are too prominent they will get cut. A lot. Fighters may have a surgery on this area to reduce the likelihood of suffering cuts during fights. Nick Diaz's own prominent brow line led to a career of cuts that were likely not closed properly, so he mitigated the risk of future problems with surgical intervention.

It was a procedure that other fighters would never need, thanks to their own genetic predisposition. Soft-faced boxer Oscar de la Hoya famously did not wear the damage of his fights the same way sharper-featured opponents did. In MMA, there are clear haves and have-nots in the visible damage factor. Fighters like Junior dos Santos will finish a fight looking like Dr. Frankenstein's monster, while others like Anderson Silva can absorb round after round of ground and pound without a visible scratch on them.

Diaz's procedure included cadaver tissue integrated into the brow line, essentially replacing the normal (and in Diaz's case shredded) padding underneath the skin to make it more resilient to cuts. The intended result of the surgery was to allow Diaz to withstand strikes without cutting as easily, which ultimately would allow him to fight longer and limit visible damage that might influence judges or referees. Was this performance enhancement? Or was it just repairing damage from an injury? If there's a line between the two, should athletes be allowed to cross it?

Had he been surgically reinforcing some offensive part of his body, he probably would have drawn criticism. But no one has a problem with athletes repairing broken parts, even if they use something external like a bone screw or borrow a ligament from a cadaver. Most of these procedures are reactive and seek to hold the athlete together longer, but all that changes when a procedure is proactive. Diaz's surgery was the first to open the question of what is an acceptable threshold for medical intervention in an athlete going into competition, rather than recovering from it. Can fighters who have broken their hands during fights get reinforced plates to ensure future punching stability?

Jake Rossen speculated about the possibilities for performance enhancing surgeries in MMA in his article about the Diaz surgery in "Wired" from March, 2011: The speculation involves muscle transfers, which could see a surgeon taking a quadriceps muscle and inserting it into the biceps. Adding stiffness – incidentally, that could be scar tissue – to a joint like an ankle or elbow could make an MMA fighter less susceptible to submissions. Cartilage around the trachea could be reinforced to make someone less likely to tap from a rear-naked choke. And why not insert some silicone around the jawline to make a knockout blow harder to inflict?[3]

Sound overboard? Just wait. In a short period of time we've gone from only the toughest athletes enduring and accumulating injuries to an era of $100 million-dollar superstar athletes willing to gain any edge in their performance. The well-documented trait of excellent eyesight for elite baseball players has led some players to seek out Lasik surgery despite already having better than 20/20 vision. At what point does eye correction cross the line from surgical correction to performance enhancement? It's a question we'll have to deal with soon. Just as sure as the science of medicine will continuously innovate new ways to repair and even improve the human body, athletes in ultra-competitive markets will seek out the most pioneering methods to gain an edge.

Next Generation MMA Analytics

As I write this, the UFC is about to celebrate its 20th anniversary, and I'm sure we'll see another 20 more. A lot of what's presented in this book just covered the basics of historical trends in high-level metrics, understanding performance between weight classes and benchmarking skill metrics, and exploring and testing a few more advanced theories about MMA. However, data mining isn't always science. The Statistical Fishing I mentioned in chapter 14 could be a trap for some of my analysis on the Southpaw advantage, for example. To truly do "science" I'll be using more tightly controlled data and different forms of analysis to test key hypotheses with an eye on true significance. That analysis is less appropriate for a book like this, and more suited to a science journal. Regardless, the science of statistics (even for MMA) will march steadily forward and you all got in on the ground floor. With your new understanding of the data available and the examples of analysis, we've drawn back the curtain to look at competitions mischaracterized as a chaotic blood sport through the lens of an analytical microscope capable of elucidating even the most subtle trends, and it's only going to get better.

The future of MMA statistics will eventually layer in all kinds of mind-blowing details currently unavailable. For those familiar with basketball shot selection heat maps, think of a similar map of strikes thrown each round to illustrate the position of each fighter. That type of data will enable deep analytics of "cage control," more detailed exploration of fighter tendencies in standup movement, as well as testing ideas about how stance or size differences translate to cage dynamics. That would all be cool, but we can go even further.

One rule of technology is that processing speed gets faster at a predictable pace (Moore's Law), and that generally the size and weight of the same technology gets smaller and smaller while able to do more and more. These trends could even affect the world of MMA. Imagine placing accelerometers (currently worn inside the jerseys of all top-level rugby players) in the gloves of fighters, each measuring all aspects of the movement of a fighter's hands. These small gadgets could be embedded in MMA gloves underneath the wrist where they are generally out of harm's way. Sending detailed real-time signals to nearby computers that interpret the action, we could instantaneously determine the frequency, strength, and accuracy of all arm strikes. The detail of the signal would be differentiated for strikes that land clean versus those that are blocked, miss, or glance off target. Even the type of the strike (uppercut versus hook) could be identified. Imagine all of this in real time scoring.

Like being able to see that a fastball exceeded 100 miles per hour an instant after it hits the catcher's glove, or being able to see speed, or lap time of racing athletes, the future of MMA will enable real-time statistics that will not only enhance the viewer experience during a fight, but enable vast analysis after the fact to understand what really happened in excruciating detail. Doctors will know exactly how often a fighter might have been struck in the head, and more importantly, how hard. A glancing blow that causes a cut might be less of a factor in swaying judges' decisions when they can check to see the maximum punch that was landed in a round. Data documenting a stiff and repetitive jab might build a strong case for a fighter mounting an effective attack using simpler, less spectacular strikes.

Perhaps this is fantasy, or maybe these technological changes will be adopted rapidly by the UFC, which has already shepherded a fledgling contest into a mainstream, highly competitive sport. Surely, the fight game will continue to evolve, just as it has over the last two decades.

Optimizing the Ultimate

As a loyal fan and someone who has invested countless hours and enough money into pay-per-views to have paid off a practical car of choice, I can easily conclude that the UFC has honed a valuable and marketable product. Some would speculate that with such success, the UFC would be crazy to make any changes. But in my career as a consultant, I repeatedly found that the most successful companies are the most forward-thinking, open to new ideas, new markets, and new processes. The landscape can change at any time. The market is fickle and people change their minds as often as their pants. Dominant companies succeed in the long-run by assuming that they will change, and endeavoring to determine how with great vigilance. As we look forward, we have to consider the possibility that some changes could improve the system of MMA as a whole, and even the UFC specifically. Determining which changes are best is the billion-dollar question, but it's one management consultants ponder, research, test, calculate, and deduce in every other industry on the planet. So let's consider a few potential areas of change.

Before fighters enter the Octagon, several important factors affect how they will perform. The UFC has recently offered health care coverage to all fighters on its roster, a critical step in helping them be at their best on fight night and providing them with the peace of mind that they will be taken care of should anything bad happen in the Octagon. Economic growth of the sport (especially a rise in fight purses) will improve fighter condition as those who can afford to train full time and have access to adequate facilities, partners and technology can dedicate a greater share of their time to mastering their craft. In the meantime, maximizing the endorsements fighters receive is a good way to overcome any gap in compensation the least-paid fighters have. The UFC controls which brands are allowed to sponsor fighters on fight night, which in some ways limits the size of the marketing budget pie that is accessible to fighters, but also protects the brand and image of the promotion. Soon there will be a way for technology to help increase the size of the pie that gets split.

Developments in video technology have enabled uniforms to be digitally overlaid with logos during broadcast. Imagine someone wearing a shirt made of the same fabric as a "green screen." Digitally, any coloring or image can be substituted for the green, meaning once the person is put in video, they can be made to wear anything that is in the shape of that shirt. In European soccer leagues where audiences frequently comprise citizens of different nations and who speak different languages, this technology provides great value. If a cellular brand pays big bucks to put their logo on a team's jerseys, but half of the time that team is playing teams from other countries where the service is unavailable, there's lost efficiency in the marketing. However, if the team wears dynamic jerseys that enable all domestic audiences to see the logo, while foreign audiences see different logos specific to their language and regional brands, then everyone wins. The UFC has a very international fan base, one that is increasingly diversified with every year of global growth. Utilizing this technology makes perfect sense to allow fighters to display different logos on their fight shorts specific to each market that may be watching the fight. American audiences could see a logo for MetroPCS, Brazilians would see one for Guaraná, while Russians would see Baltika.

As fighters take the cage, we should consider the variables that impact the viewer's experience. The UFC already utilizes a number of tried and true techniques to maximize the wow-factor, but what else is out there? How about the Octagon itself? In Chapter 13 I demonstrated that finish rates are higher in smaller cages, which was a contributing reason for the excitement and success of the now-integrated "World Extreme Cagefighting" promotion. The smaller cage of the WEC saw higher finish rates for all weight classes, and since the merger with the WEC, the same smaller fighters are now finishing fewer fights. So the question gets asked repeatedly: why doesn't the UFC shrink their cage size to drive more action-packed fights?

In Zuffa's defense, when something doesn't make sense under a certain lens (in this case, maximizing viewer entertainment), the truth may be discovered by changing the lens. In the slow but deliberate process of turning mixed martial arts into a mainstream US sport, and hopefully the primary global combat sport, there are a variety of tradeoffs that have been, and will be, made. Chief among these is sponsor relationships. Big-time US leagues like the NFL and NBA rely heavily on TV contracts, but also on blue-chip sponsors. Ensuring sponsor placement within a sport's venue is a job served by small armies of sports management majors in all professional leagues and team franchises. These dollars are critical to the survival of a sports entertainment business, and any fan who has attended small regional MMA promotion events will have surely noticed the difference in sponsors. Even the different UFC products have noticeably different quality of advertisements. It's the difference between Montel Williams pushing dubious financial loans on FuelTV and Super Bowl quality beer commercials on FOX. And it's a big, big difference. It's also a reality of business and sports.

The UFC is no different from any other entertainment business in their quest for viewers and sponsor dollars. And therein lies the answer to the UFC cage-size conundrum. In order to place legible sponsor logos on the Octagon mat, they need plenty of space and a neutral (in this case gray) background to ensure maximum viewer visibility. In the "minor league" of the WEC, fewer sponsors meant more flexibility with the cage. Not only was the cage smaller, but it had a vivid, and highly recognizable blue mat with few sponsor logos or ads. One more casualty in the WEC-UFC merger was the ability to have a small, cool looking cage. Business boils down to tradeoffs. If the UFC is going to achieve its lofty goals of global domination in the combat sports market, this appears to be one of the small tradeoffs they had to concede.

We have to wonder about the value of these logos relative to the product itself, now that we know that a smaller and/or more brilliantly colored cage would be better for excitement and for viewing appeal. If the amount of revenue from mat logos was a large contributor relative to the bottom line, then altering the cage may not be possible. If over time, however, the importance of this revenue stream changes, it's possible the Octagon could be optimized for the viewer with a more visually sexy cage that makes highlights on Sports Center pop off the screen. The smaller cage would also mean more highlights worthy of replay, and more excitement for fans on fight night.

During fights, there are other ways to improve the fan experience by offering more layers to the fight itself. The UFC has begun to offer real-time statistics online, mirroring what has been available in many other sports for years. Streaming viewers of a UFC event can even select camera angles and microphone locations to customize their experience. By adding more features and more available data, fans will have more reason to more fully engage with each fight broadcast. Interactive features will allow fans to score each round and see real-time information about the fight. I fully expect richer features to be brought to market soon.

Once the fight concludes there are a few more ways to optimize the system. The first is ensuring fair and accurate judging. While some controversy is inevitable in a highly competitive environment, taking action to prevent and limit the damage poor decisions can have on the sport is a worthwhile investment. That may mean education and training, access to replays and statistics in between rounds, and greater transparency in judges' scores. Of course these steps need buy-in and cooperation from the state athletic commissions and that's not always easy to come by.

Once the fights are over, the UFC wants every fan to already be invested in the next event. This is perhaps the most significant challenge facing the UFC today. Currently, it's a promotion model, which is unlike any team-based sport and even many individual sports. The UFC must promote every event, practically from scratch. In 2014, the rapid growth of the organization will have doubled the number of annual events held over the 2006 total. Some observers say the frequent events have oversaturated the market, or diluted each fight card (pick your chemistry analogy). More MMA isn't bad for the fans, especially since most of the growth in events have been on free channels, but the perception remains that fan-fatigue is growing.

Compared to fans of baseball, basketball or hockey, this claim seems ridiculous. Being a loyal fan of a single baseball team means following 162 games per season, each lasting ~2.75 hours. That's 445 hours of baseball if your team does not make the playoffs. Following a league champion could require 500 hours of game time, to say nothing of news and related media outside of games. And that's just one team. Watching every single UFC broadcast in a year with 36 events would take 234 hours – but much, much less for actual fight time. That total means seeing every fight that gets competed in the organization, not just one "team." The totals for watching an NBA or NHL team are closer to the UFC total, but again only represent following a single team with no playoffs. So why then is there such a disparity among fans and media that there's actually too much UFC content?

It's not fan-fatigue, and it's not MMA-fatigue – it's hype-fatigue. Numerically, a large portion of fans need to see quite a bit of hype to commit to watching a UFC event. The small core of diehard fans will likely watch regardless, but this group makes up a small portion of the maximum audience. Reaching the wider audience requires a unique and heavy multi-media marketing campaign for weeks on end leading up to an event, which gets almost immediately scrapped as soon as a pay-per-view broadcast begins. At the end of the night, commercials have already begun for the next major event, and in the weeks in between, promotion of fight cards of less importance will trickle primarily through online streams feeding the fans.

What mainstream sports have that the UFC doesn't is continuity. Seasons and set schedules, reliable reset points, and the slow annual build of increasing relevance ensures that major league fans don't need to know what's coming next, they already care about it regardless. They don't even need to know the opponent. In the case of football, many fans are barely even aware of the schedule, simply making a quick confirmation of what day their team will play each week. As the season progresses, their own team may fade from contention, while the pool of potential champions shrinks, but that's when the single most important thing in all of sports happens: playoffs.

Playoffs, and not championships, are the greatest ratings bonanza for all team sports. Fans love tournaments. Whether it's the first few rounds of the NCAA basketball tournament known as "March Madness," NFL Wild Card Weekends, or even the round robin groups of the World Cup in soccer, playoffs are the ideal combination of relevance now and relevance soon. Fans watch playoffs of teams they don't even follow because no matter who wins the game, the outcome will impact the rest of the mini-tournament. The shortcoming of the UFC system is not a lack of championships. Unlike team sports, "championship" contests can occur dozens of time per year in the UFC. And each fight, no matter where it's it placed on a card, still has very real meaning for the fighters involved. Any single performance can catapult a fighter up the ranks or lead to an open roster spot courtesy of a departing loser. So it's not the lack of meaningful "regular season" play or the lack of championships. The challenge facing the UFC is the lack of playoffs in between.

Sports fans savor the fleeting nature of the all-important waning moments of a contest, but they also rely on the anticipation of the next one. Playoffs and tournaments are when fans get to have their cake and eat it too. Each game is a finale, but the fun doesn't end, it just escalates. By the time a championship occurs in many team sports, aggregate viewership may actually have declined because only two teams remain. But each round of the playoffs offers a synergy that is unmatched by games that precede or follow.

The tournament concept was actually how the UFC was founded, though the brackets took place in a single night. It didn't last long. The UFC held its last same-night tournament in 1998 at UFC 17, the same night the term "mixed martial arts" was brought to the public. Since then, the only tournaments in the UFC system have been held in the Ultimate Fighter reality show and a one-time four-man flyweight tournament to determine the new division's first champion. However, almost immediately after the UFC bought Strikeforce in early 2011, Strikeforce put on a heavyweight "Grand Prix" tournament that generated a lot of media buzz and eventually turned out a dark horse winner in Daniel Cormier. The tournament took place in rounds over the course of several events instead of all in one night (as they had previously), and gave fans a reason to care about each and every fight, even if they only followed one fighter.

The fact that the UFC has previously flirted with mini-tournaments keeps hope alive that the Grand Prix format might find its way back to the largest stage. Just imagine the excitement a 16- or 8-man tournament featuring the top fighters of a single UFC division would generate. Each fight would be important as it would affect the next round of matchups. The Bellator promotion currently employs this system, but lacks the star power to fill each slot with high-profile fighters. Brackets also present logistical challenges, but these can be overcome. The UFC could have the best of both worlds.

I've made a case here for a pretty drastic change. I believe that there are powerful forces at work in the marketplace connecting entertainment media to fans that can be accentuated with a system like this. The sport has evolved quickly in a short period of time, but as any successful business knows, constant reevaluation and optimization is needed to ensure continued success.

The Final Word

If you've made it this far, I thank you. We've covered a lot of ground and I've thrown a lot of material (and over 100 graphs!) at you. If you're like me, you enjoy the sport of MMA and want to see it continue its inevitable path towards global domination. Or you just appreciate analytics applied to a competitive environment like fighting, or sport in general.

We love watching sports, because our imaginations powerfully connect us to the competitors and the competition. We can immediately vest ourselves emotionally in what we watch. The thrill and glory that athletes feel in triumph, just as their suffering and potential redemption in defeat, all trickle down to those who support them. Because we are emotional and competitive creatures who thrive on challenge and success, sports will always run through our cultural backbone. Mixed martial arts is as thrilling and addictive as any other sport. The purity of MMA cuts through and transcends the diverse dialects of combat sports. Our species has layered on rules and gimmicks to all manner of sporting contests, resulting in some absurd games. Yet fighting remains the purest of them all. Without a stopwatch, a scale, or a French judge to watch for point deductions, a person can only really test himself against another in the truest of challenges. The sport of MMA has coalesced the concepts of physical competition, and intellectual and emotional strategy into a single contest. It is primal, yet simultaneously it is highly evolved. There's no reason this sport shouldn't spread through global culture like blue jeans and rock n' roll, because it connects with us on a fundamental, and visceral level.

The original master plan of the Gracie-influenced sport was successful. Today young movie watchers are less satisfied with the artificial and choreographed strikes that defined much of our glamourized image of conflict. If a fight doesn't involve close-quarters limb manipulation or wrestling then it doesn't live up to modern standards. A fight today is a highly developed human chess match that is the ultimate expression of force.

The UFC has popularized new syllables in the universal language of aggression. They have set a new standard of fighting that requires fluency in both striking and grappling arts, such that the fundamental and primal essence of combat sport has evolved even for the widest of audiences. You don't have to step into harm's way to appreciate this evolution; just watch it. There's a lot of science behind why this sport is compelling, but when it comes to fight night, just let the wave of excitement take over, and connect with the thrill of competition and victory. Just don't forget that there are invisible factors at work that will influence the outcomes along the way. You can accept and understand these underlying laws, or you can surrender to the thrill of the moment. Either way, I think you win.

Dan Hardy experiences the thrill of victory after knocking out Rory Markham. Photo by Martin McNeil.

Chapter Notes:

1. For more on genetic links to athleticism, check out "The Sports Gene" by David Epstein, Penguin Group, New York, New York, 2013.

2. Visit the FightMetric website to explore stats on your favorite fighters, including their box scores from UFC fights and current UFC record holders at: www.fightmetric.com.

3. "How MMA Fighters Use Plastic Surgery to Bleed Less," by Jake Rossen, "Wired Magazine" March, 2011 via Gizmodo.com.

16 Always Read the Credits

This book has covered a lot of basics for MMA analytics, and even a few advanced subjects. Yet I've really only just scratched the surface. As with any field of knowledge, advancement happens very quickly, and I fully expect the level of understanding in this sport to push forward at a rapid pace, all while statistics and analytics become an increasing integral part of the fan experience. With the addition of new types of data, far more advanced and nuanced analysis will follow. For anyone who fears it will detract from the sport, just consider how baseball, football, basketball, and hockey have fared through their own analytical evolutions. These sports are thriving, and the excitement that their athletes offer is no less mysterious after we have gazed upon them with greater clarity. It will be no different for MMA. If anything, the numbers will allow the casual observer to understand the sport more efficiently, possibly counteracting some of the negative bias MMA experiences from outside pseudo-observers. Whether I continue to explore new data and solve new riddles, or new analysts or even entire companies come to market and replace me, the net effect should be advancement of the sport as a whole, and a greater appreciation from ever-growing audiences.

Deciding to leave my career in consulting to write a book on MMA analytics certainly raised a lot of eyebrows. I wasn't the only one who recognized the great risk of this endeavor. But thanks to the support of friends and family I pushed forward to scratch both an intellectual itch and one more item from my bucket list by writing this book. I've logged a lot of hours watching MMA and keeping up with related media, and I've often forced reluctant conversation upon people who probably had no interest in it. I've been thoroughly distracted and have worked long and odd hours, all while my wife had to be ready for 4 AM wakeup calls and hospital shifts. My parents edited this entire work, and did so at a professional level book (any mistakes that slipped through are definitely my fault for after-the-fact edits). My mother – who can't even sit through a boxing match – went through every word and punctuation. The patience of those closest to me is very much appreciated.

So here's a sincere thank you to the people who took me behind the velvet rope of the professional MMA world. Nick Palmisciano, founder and president of Ranger Up, took me to that first UFC Fight Night in Nashville. That might have been the end of my sojourn into the world of professional fighting if it weren't for his continued support and active participation in pushing this idea forward.

The same goes to Eric Talent, who got me my first MMA related gig offering analytical advice, and continually challenged my hypotheses forcing me to put numbers behind my answers. And to my first "clients" Jorge Rivera, Tim Burrill, Matt Phinney and Scott Rehm, thanks for listening to my insane idea that charts and graphs might tell us something about how fights go down, and where fighters might excel or be vulnerable.

Thank you to the wise minds at FIGHT! Magazine, Sherdog, CagePotato and MMA Oddsbreaker who considered my work worthy of sharing with their audiences.

I've been a stranger in a strange land. I've worked with many fighters, trainers, managers, and media members over my short career in MMA, and I sincerely appreciate each of you and your time, wisdom, and willingness to help.

And thank you Kelly Crigger, without you this book would not be possible. I wasn't a trained writer, nor did I know a thing about how to write a book and take it to market. There's a thousand little To Do's for a project like this, each one an opportunity to make the whole better, or simply to make my dream of publishing a book more achievable. You saw a unique opportunity where others saw a distraction, saw value where others saw confusion, and didn't miss a beat in offering your support of this book. Thanks for making this a reality, and your continued support and motivation in my research.

And a final dedication to Lorenzo, Dana, Joe, and the rest of the Zuffa team: thank you for pioneering and shepherding the last and greatest global combat sport. Consider this the world's longest cover letter. I hope you enjoyed it, and I look forward to meeting you.

Get the latest Fightnomics research, stats, and Uber Tales of the Tape:
www.fightnomics.com
www.twitter.com/fightnomics
www.facebook.com/fightnomics

Get other books by New York Times bestselling author Kelly Crigger:
www.kellycrigger.com

Check out Ranger Up for military and MMA themed apparel, or just some crazy stories and funny videos:

www.rangerup.com

Book cover art and logo design by:
www.vangeffen.com

Book design and formatting by Lance Freimuth.

Reed Kuhn is a Washington D.C.-based strategy consultant with over a decade of professional experience. Reed's foray into sports statistics began during his graduate studies when he mined data of National Football League team performance. In 2009 he began analyzing professional mixed martial arts through a research fellowship with FightMetric, the sport's leading statistics system, and the official statistics provider to the Ultimate Fighting Championship. Reed holds a bachelor's degree in Physics from Washington and Lee University, a master's degree in Systems Engineering from the University of Virginia, and an MBA from the Fuqua School of Business at Duke University, where he specialized in strategy and decision sciences.

Kelly Crigger is a retired US Army Lieutenant Colonel with a bunch of degrees that he never used. Crigger began writing about MMA in 2006 and has published three other books about the sport including Title Shot, Into the Shark Tank of Mixed Martial Arts. A twelfth-level cleric of the Ranger Up order, Crigger lives in Northern Virginia where he writes, plays rugby, critiques bourbon, and prepares for doomsday. Crigger considers himself privileged to be a Jayhawk, honored to be a Ranger, and blessed by God to be American.